THE INDIAN OCEAN:
REGION OF CONFLICT OR 'ZONE OF PEACE'?

THE INDIAN OCEAN

*REGION OF CONFLICT OR
'PEACE ZONE'?*

by

DIETER BRAUN

translated from the German by
CAROL GELDART *and* KATHLEEN LLANWARNE

ST. MARTIN'S PRESS, NEW YORK

All rights reserved. For information, write:
St. Martin's Press, Inc., 175 Fifth Avenue, New York, NY 10010
Printed in Great Britain
First published in the United States of America in 1983
ISBN 0-312-41396-3

Library of Congress Cataloging in Publication Data

Braun, Dieter.
    The Indian Ocean.

    Translation of: Der Indische Ozean.
    Bibliography: p.
    Includes indexes.
    1. Indian Ocean Region--Politics and government.
2. Indian Ocean Region--Strategic aspects. I. Title.
DS341.B7313 1983   327'.09182'4   83-9680
ISBN 0-312-41396-3

PREFACE

It is only since the beginning of the 1970s that the Indian Ocean and its littoral states, which belong predominantly to the Third World, have begun to take on the characteristics of a major political region. The main factor contributing to this development was the assertive global strategy of the two super-powers, referred to by the code-names 'Diego Garcia' (United States) and 'regular naval presence' (Soviet Union). Some of the littoral states attempted to counter this trend with a policy of refusal: their demand for an 'Indian Ocean Peace Zone', first voiced in 1971, has become yet another element in the North-South confrontation. Conflicts with their origins outside the area (East-West and Sino-Soviet), which gained in intensity in the course of the 1970s, spread to the Indian Ocean area. These outside influences, together with a growing number of conflicts between states within the region, point clearly to a need to seek and implement guidelines for limiting conflict and encouraging regional co-operation. This perception has so far been only partially translated into practical policies, most effectively by the setting-up of the Association of South-East Asian Nations (ASEAN).

In the second half of the decade, policies and strategy in the Indian Ocean were largely determined by the dependence of the West — and also of the majority of Indian Ocean states — on oil from the Persian Gulf. Meanwhile, the Socialist camp openly supported individual states in the area with ideologically inspired military assistance. The web of interaction between outside and regional interests thickened. At the end of the 1970s, primarily as a consequence of events in Iran and Afghanistan, the whole framework affecting developments in the area underwent significant change: in the United States the concept of the 'arc of crisis' was forged. From the point of view not only of the super-powers but also of the Indian Ocean states themselves, security policy moved clearly into the forefront, at the expense of development policy. The chances of establishing a unified 'peace zone' dwindled accordingly, while paradoxically this cause received more official support than ever before at the United Nations in 1980. Developments in the 1980s will determine whether the Indian Ocean littoral states come to form a region of pervasive conflict or whether they will succeed in building up patterns of limited co-operation — partial 'peace zones'.

The present study was the first comprehensive monograph to deal in German with the themes connected with this question. Since the beginning of the 1970s the topic has been receiving increasingly extensive treatment, particularly in English-language publications but also in French, Soviet and Indian journals and books. In West Germany too, since the energy crisis of 1973–4, there has been a developing awareness of the debates and as yet unresolved conflicts which have been accumulating in the Indian Ocean region with repercussions reaching as far afield as Europe. It is true that there have been analysis and detailed study of the most significant developments, but only rarely has reference been made to the wider geographical and functional context. This context is synonymous with the new reference term 'Indian Ocean'.

The geographical and historical framework, outlined at the beginning of this study, provides important clues for an understanding and evaluation of present trends. The following section describes the super-powers' policies, their characteristic modes of behaviour — which are in part related to each other ('rivalry') and in part derive from different priorities — and the most important interests of other outside powers as well as the reasons for and consequences of their involvement. Specific developments in the individual sub-regions viewed from a local perspective are then placed in the context of these outside interests and influences. This regional view is combined with an assessment of respective power balances and foreign policy determinants. Lastly there is a discussion of regional and multilateral security concepts and initiatives, dealt with mostly in a United Nations framework.

The bibliography is restricted to works referred to in the text; nonetheless, it includes numerous important publications on a range of questions related to the Indian Ocean.

It is always a pleasure for an author to see his work translated into another language. In this connection I have to thank the translators for doing their work with great ability and intelligence. In the Fall of 1982, at the request of the British publisher, I carried out a number of minor revisions in order to make the work as up-to-date as possible. However, in every essential respect, the present edition is the same as the original German one. I should add that the responsibility for all opinions expressed in the book is mine alone, not that of my Institute, the Stiftung Wissenschaft und Politik (Research Institute for International Politics), Ebenhausen.

Finally, I should like to acknowledge with gratitude the assistance and advice given me in preparing the book by Karlernst Ziem and Michael Strauss at the Stiftung.

Ebenhausen, January 1983   D.B.

CONTENTS

Part I
CHARACTERISTICS AND GENERAL TRENDS

Part II
THE REGION VIEWED WITHIN THE GLOBAL POWER BALANCE

Part III
INTERACTION BETWEEN EXTERNAL AND REGIONAL POLITICAL AND STRATEGIC INTERESTS

(Chapter 5)

Part IV
REGIONAL AND MULTILATERAL SECURITY CONCEPTS AND INITIATIVES

Part V

ABBREVIATIONS

ANZUK	Australia, New Zealand, United Kingdom
ANZUS	Australia, New Zealand, United States
ASEAN	Association of South East Asian Nations
ASPAC	Asian and Pacific Council
AWACS	Advance Warning Aircraft System
BIOT	British Indian Ocean Territory
BMWi	Bundesministerium für Wirtschaft (Federal Economics Ministry), Bonn
BPA	Bundespresseamt (Federal Press Office), Bonn
CCD	Conference of the Committee for Disarmament
CENTO	Central Treaty Organisation
CIA	Central Intelligence Agency
EA	*Europa-Archiv*, Bonn
EPLF	Eritrean People's Liberation Front
FAO	Food and Agricultural Organization of the United Nations
FAZ	*Frankfurter Allgemeine Zeitung*
FEER	*Far Eastern Economic Review*
IOPZ	Indian Ocean Peace Zone
IHT	*International Herald Tribune*
IISS	International Institute for Strategic Studies
IUCN	International Union for Conservation of Nature
CPSU	Communist Party of the Soviet Union
CSSA	Collective Security System for Asia
CSCE	Conference on Security and Co-operation in Europe
NWFZ	Nuclear Weapon-Free Zone
MD	*Monitor Dienst*, Radio Deutsche Welle, Cologne
MMM	*Mouvement Militant Mauricien*
NPT	Non Proliferation Treaty (nuclear weapons)
NYT	*New York Times*
NZZ	*Neue Zürcher Zeitung*
OAU	Organization of African Unity

OAPEC	Organization of Arabian Petroleum Exporting Countries
OPEC	Organization of Petroleum Exporting Countries
PDRY	People's Democratic Republic of Yemen
PFLOAG	People's Front for the Liberation of Oman and the Arabian Gulf
RDF	Rapid Deployment Force
CMEA	Council for Mutual Economic Assistance (Comecon)
RSA	Republic of South Africa
SALT	Strategic Arms Limitation Talks
SEATO	South East Asia Treaty Organization
SSBN	Ballistic Missile Submarine, Nuclear (strategic submarine)
SWAPO	South West Africa People's Organization
SWB-FE/ME	(BBC) *Summary of World Broadcasts,* Far East/Middle East
SWP	Stiftung Wissenschaft und Politik (Research Institute for International Affairs), Ebenhausen
SZ	*Süddeutsche Zeitung*
TOI	*Times of India*
USWB	*United States Wireless Bulletin*
UAE	United Arab Emirates
VWD	*Vereinigte Wirtschaftsdienste* (economic press agency), Bonn

Satellite photograph:
the Indian Ocean region

Source: L. Griswold,
'From Simonstown to
Singapore', *US Naval
Institute Proceedings*,
vol. 97, no. 11 (November
1971), pp. 52–3.

Part I
CHARACTERISTICS AND GENERAL TRENDS

Chapter 1
THE INDIAN OCEAN AS THE THIRD OCEAN

(a) *The maritime infrastructure*

Ranking after the Pacific and the Atlantic, the Indian Ocean[1] is the third largest ocean in the world. If the generally accepted definition of its boundaries (see Appendix B) is adhered to, it extends over more than 75 million km². It is about half the size of the Pacific and only slightly smaller than the Atlantic. The Mediterranean would fit into it thirty-five times. There is, however, one fundamental characteristic which sets the Indian Ocean apart from the two larger ones: its northern part is surrounded by Africa, Asia and Australia to the extent that it tends to resemble a huge bay — and this is one of the factors contributing to its geopolitical and geostrategic significance. It is to this part of the Indian Ocean — situated between the Tropic of Cancer and the Tropic of Capricorn — that the present study will be almost exclusively restricted, while the southern and — in terms of area — predominant part of the Ocean, reaching as far as Antarctica, will be considered only marginally.

Before the discovery of America, the Indian Ocean was — after the Mediterranean — the sea with the greatest volume of maritime traffic. Since earliest times there has been oceangoing as well as coastal shipping, and for the latter the monsoon winds and the currents were decisive. Today the volume of maritime traffic in the Indian Ocean is the third largest in the world.

It was the predictability of the winds in the area around the Equator which, for example, in the seventeenth century enabled the Dutch to set up a regular link between the South African Cape

---

1. In West Germany the Indian Ocean is increasingly referred to as the *Indik*, by analogy with the *Atlantik* and *Pazifik* and in accordance with current military usage in the Federal Republic. The Soviet Union also uses this term in its German-language publications, and it has been adopted in East Germany too.

and — turning north 90° off the west coast of Australia — the Spice Islands or Indies. The winds and currents were also an essential factor in determining the migratory trends of peoples and races as, for example, the Malay settlement of Madagascar, the Arab settlements in East Africa and in South-East Asia and the early Christian settlement on the Malabar coast of India. In this way many historical developments in the states surrounding the Indian Ocean can be explained in terms of the geographical and physical characteristics of the Ocean itself.

Until recently the Indian Ocean had been subject to little systematic scientific exploration. Then, between 1960 and 1975, the International Indian Ocean expedition made possible the collection of a wealth of data which is still being analysed.

Modern historical developments created a situation (see page 8) in which the vast majority of trade with the littoral states was conducted by outside powers (as a result of colonisation) while, to this day, intra- and inter-regional traffic has remained minimal. The significance of the Indian Ocean was further enhanced in that it offered a line of communication between the Atlantic and — after the opening of the Suez Canal — between the Mediterranean and the Pacific. This increased the importance of the various gateways to the Ocean: in the west via the Cape of Good Hope, in the north-west through the Suez Canal, the Red Sea and the Bab-el-Mandeb Strait, in the east via the Malacca Strait and further south-east via the Indonesian islands as well as past Australia to both the north and the south. On top of all these approaches to the Indian Ocean, it was in the relatively recent past that the entrance to the Persian Gulf dramatically increased in importance.

Negative consequences were bound to develop from the Indian Ocean's incorporation into the global ecosystem. Marine pollution is already widespread, and the population growth in important coastal areas (especially in the Indian sub-continent and in Indonesia) is taking its toll, as is the oil tanker traffic from the Persian Gulf: oil leaks are destroying the fish reserves and lowering the oxygen content of the water.[2]

The tropical waters of the Indian Ocean are not especially rich in edible fish supplies. The total stock is believed to be of the order of 15 million tons, 2.5 million tons of which (according to an estimate

2. In 1980, in response to these dangers, representatives of 15 coastal states drew up a proposal for the creation of an 'Indian Ocean Alliance for Conservation': it was forwarded to all coastal state governments; see IUCN (International Union for Conservation of Nature), Gland, Switzerland, June 1980, pp. 1f.

made in 1976) are caught each year.[3] The greater proportion of this catch is taken by the traditional coastal fisheries and is destined for immediate consumption. (In the continental shelf waters, the main catches are sardines, anchovies and mackerel.) However, the share taken by modern industrial fishing fleets from outside states (mainly from the Soviet Union, Japan, Taiwan and South Korea) is fast increasing and they systematically plunder the tuna and related fish stock. If the present trend continues, certain species of fish could be threatened with extinction. The introduction of 200-mile zones (fishing zones and exclusive economic zones) will therefore be an important political issue. In this connection some hard bargaining can be expected both between local and more distant fishing states and also between littoral states with the advantage of long coastlines and those with less favourable coastal positions and hinterland states.[4]

Nor can the possibility be excluded of conflict breaking out between local states and outside states, or even between littoral states themselves, in connection with offshore oil deposits and deep-sea mining. Up to the present around 40 per cent of world offshore oil production comes from Indian Ocean coastal states (their share of natural gas production is, however, very small). Apart from those in the Persian Gulf, promising areas for further offshore oil supplies are, at present, the continental shelves around the Indian sub-continent, off North-West Australia, near Mauritius and around South Africa. Treaties to fix the sea boundaries between most of the coastal states still remain to be agreed.

Developing countries are not, for the most part, in a position to carry out, unaided, exploration and exploitation of ocean resources. In cases where deep-sea mining is required, this is undoubtedly even more true.[5] Reasonably large deposits of manganese, which also

3. Central Intelligence Agency (CIA publication), *Indian Ocean Atlas*, Washington DC 1976, p. 15.

4. Under the aegis of the Food and Agriculture Organisation (FAO) of the United Nations, two committees have been set up which include representatives of local and more distant fishing states. Their task is to keep up with fishing problems in the Indian Ocean and, where possible, to introduce counter-measures to reverse undesirable trends: they are the Indo-Pacific Fisheries Council, set up in 1948, and the Indian Ocean Fishery Commission, set up in 1967.

5. So far, India is the only Third World country with the capacity for exploration — with the aid of German technology — if not for commercial exploitation. At the beginning of 1981 an exploration vessel brought up manganese nodules from a depth of 4,500 metres in India's south-west economic zone; *Economic and Political Weekly* (Bombay), 11.4.1981, pp. 640 f.

contain nickel, cobalt, copper and iron, have been detected in the Indian Ocean, especially in the Eastern part, both within and outside 200-mile zones. Deposits were also discovered recently in the Western Indian Ocean, off Mauritius and Madagascar. They are found at depths of between 3,500 and 5,000 metres. Other commercially useful deposits on the sea-bed, such as zinc, copper, lead, silver, vanadium and molybdenum, are to be found in the Red Sea at depths of about 2,000 metres. A Saudi-Sudanese-West German consortium is planning to exploit these resources: in typical fashion, a West German company, Preussag, is providing the technology and Saudi Arabia the finance, while Sudan is placing its waters at their disposal.

(b) *Historical outline*

The history of seafaring in the Indian Ocean — unlike in the Atlantic and the Pacific — dates back to very early times.[6] This is especially true of the north-western area between Egypt, the Horn of Africa, Persia and the West coast of India — the very area in which international interest is particularly concentrated today. Very early in recorded history, trading links, colonisation and conquests all began to conform to a geographical pattern which still forms the basic structure underlying the situation there today. The western and eastern parts of the Indian Ocean underwent separate developments and the Indian sub-continent thus faces in two directions and at the same time separates the two parts. In the west the Egyptian and Persian empires, in the two thousand years BC, also extended their influence seawards, later giving way to the Romans and Muslim Arabs, while in the east, from about the beginning of the Christian era, it was the Indians (extending seawards towards South-East Asia), the Malayans and the Chinese who travelled the seas. In this part the Chinese junks proved the most seaworthy vessels, yet even before the arrival of Vasco da Gama around 1500 — the most significant turning-point in the history of the whole Indian Ocean region — the Chinese had already retreated.

In sailing around the Cape of Good Hope, the Portuguese formed

6. See especially A. Toussaint, 'Shifting Power Balances in the Indian Ocean' in R.M. Burrell and A.J. Cottrell (eds), *The Indian Ocean: Its Political, Economic and Military Importance*, New York, 1972, pp. 3–13; F.A. Váli, *Politics of the Indian Ocean Region — The Balances of Power*, New York, 1976, pp. 1 f.; *Hemisphere*, vol. 23, no. 3, special issue on the Indian Ocean, published by Australian Government Publishing Service (Melbourne), May/June 1979.

the vanguard of the European penetration of the Indian Ocean, its coastal states and islands, which was to last for centuries. Yet the Portuguese were still too weak actually to rule the Ocean (in the sense of driving out rival influences); they occupied only a handful of strategically important sites and trading points and all the while traditional traffic continued to ply between the various coastal zones. They encountered decisive opposition, especially from Muslim Arabs on and off the east coast of Africa, and their control of the Malacca Strait was threatened by the Sultan of Sumatra, also a Muslim. Then in 1641, they were driven out of Malacca by the Dutch who were interested predominantly in the Malay archipelago (Spice Islands).

The Dutch also established themselves firmly at the Cape of Good Hope, in Mauritius, on the coast of India and in Ceylon. Unlike Portuguese interests, those of the Dutch were scarcely dictated by political and ideological (missionary) considerations but almost exclusively by commercial ones. They discovered Australia but found it unsuited to their purposes — yet the continent was henceforth referred to on sea charts as Hollandia Nova. Overall the Dutch were not in a position to gain strategic control of the Indian Ocean, nor evidently were they at all interested in doing so.

In the course of the seventeenth century, the Portuguese retreated considerably while France and England, competing with one another, were advancing, and until the middle of the eighteenth century the focus of their clashes gradually shifted towards Southern India. England (the East India Company) quickly succeeded in penetrating important areas of the Indian sub-continent, and protected its position mostly by treaties with native rulers. The French, on the other hand, subsequently directed their interest to the western Indian Ocean and began by taking over Mauritius from the Dutch who had voluntarily abandoned it. Historians doubt that England actually had a 'master-plan' for the conquest of the Indian Ocean region. What most likely happened was that a series of coincidences fell into shape and, above all, that the trading interests of the East India Company gradually formed a pattern on the basis of the motto 'the flag follows trade'. The Company acquired territories and had to defend and administer them, thereby creating the nucleus of future dominion by the British state. The turning-point came with the Treaty of Paris (1815) at which England was awarded the Cape Province, Mauritius and Ceylon while the Dutch secured a hold on their Indonesian possessions and France on Réunion.

In the following decades England, now with a sense of mission, forged its Indian 'empire', founded its Singapore colony to safeguard the Malacca Strait (1824), conquered Burma — albeit not without difficulty — and towards the end of the nineteenth century took over the protectorate of the Malay Peninsula. Australia had been British since the beginning of the century. Aden, in the western Indian Ocean near the southern entrance to the Red Sea, became a British possession in 1839 and the significance of this foothold increased greatly with the opening of the Suez Canal in 1869. Britain then occupied Egypt and thus secured for itself the new sea-route to India. It was not long before the same fate befell the Sudan. With regard to the Cape route, Britain behaved in an equally determined manner, first cutting the Boers off from Natal and, after the Boer War, finally annexing the Orange Free State and the Transvaal. Likewise, at the end of the nineteenth century, Britain completed its domination over the whole of the Indian Ocean region by creating a protectorate in Zanzibar and by colonising Kenya. In 1885 France — with British consent — took over Madagascar and, in addition, the Comoro Islands and Djibouti. The colonial possessions of other countries are of little relevance in this context, but a significant factor was the discovery in 1890 of oil in the Persian Gulf. Both Britain and Russia showed an interest in this, in view of its potential as a fuel to drive machines and ships. An armed conflict seemed inevitable. But Russia's defeat at the hands of the Japanese in 1905 had the effect of enabling Britain to consolidate its position in the Gulf, and the Russo-British treaty of 1907 divided Persia up into spheres of interest.

Thus by 1900 Britain had turned the Indian Ocean into a British lake and had military control over all the important approaches and exits. Of the littoral states at that time, only Ethiopia and Siam (later Thailand) remained formally independent, while all the others found themselves in varying degrees of (mostly direct) dependence on one or other of the European powers.

In the period between the two World Wars, Britian was able, in spite of her imperial drive now being markedly weaker, to make further gains, above all as a result of the German and Turkish defeats in 1918. Yet at the same time in the heart of the colonial empire, in India, the political movement that was ultimately to bring the whole colonial age to an end was already taking root. The Second World War then altered the whole balance of power throughout the region although the full outcome of this process was not obvious at the end of the war and continued to unfold in stages into the 1960s.

Since the Second World War, new outside forces had begun to make an impact alongside the autochthonous aspirations to independence in the colonised regions. By its dramatic activity in the War, Japan had shown Europeans and Americans the hurricane-like destructive potential of an Asian power. Without this development the process of decolonisation in Asia would doubtless have taken a very different course. In the post-war period the United States also appeared in the Indian Ocean in a political as well as an economic and military capacity. By 1960 it was in a position to present itself to the littoral states as — at least potentially — the strongest power, whereas Britain's power was rapidly declining. From the middle 1950s, the Soviet Union showed its interest in the newly-independent Afro-Asian states, at first in a selective and bilateral way, later also on the basis of more sophisticated concepts[7] and, after 1968, by the appearance of the Soviet fleet in the Indian Ocean.

In the course of the decolonisation process there was no lack of accompanying circumstances that were both dramatic and generative of further conflict. The partition of India in 1947 was a particularly traumatic event which had a sequel in the secession of East Pakistan (Bangladesh) in 1971. It should also be stressed, however, that the central state, the Indian Union, has so far managed to retain its political integrity — something that could in no way have been taken for granted in 1947 and in the years that followed. On giving up its empire, Britain secured a continuing influence for itself in the Commonwealth, to which a large proportion of the now independent coastal states and islands of the Indian Ocean belong. The exact degree of this influence is, however, hard to gauge; in some cases it is still strong (as revealed in the Zimbabwe settlement of 1979) but overall it is declining. France was very keen to achieve similar special status in the Western Indian Ocean but encountered success for a limited time only. The increased desire to keep its distance from France manifested by *'La Grande Isle'* — Madagascar — in the 1970s was symptomatic of this.

Today the region is again fragmented just as it was before the Europeans arrived on the scene. The way in which regional interests interact with those of outside powers, together with the complex intra-regional relations around the Indian Ocean region itself, are the subject of the following study. First however an outline will be given of the network — determined predominantly by economic factors — of international connections and entanglements in and around the Indian Ocean. For these factors largely contribute to its contemporary significance for the super-powers, for seafaring nations and, above all, for transcontinental communications. In this area future conflicts seem to be on the agenda: widely differing concepts of an ideologically preconceived world order confront each other, such as Communism and Islam, or state-planned versus

7. For example by the proposal for an Asian Collective Security System in 1969 (see p. 54 below).

free-enterprise economies. But conflicts could be reduced if opportunities are sought for compromise wherever possible.

(c) *Main trading and transport connections*

Every year something like 30,000 ships, some 1,500 of them tankers, travel the sea routes which are so important for the economy of the West — through the Indian Ocean, through the Suez Canal and the Bab-el- Mandeb Strait, around the Cape of Good Hope and through the Malacca Strait.[8] On average, two tankers an hour pass through the Strait of Hormuz, forty ships a day through the channel between Mozambique and Madagascar, and almost as many through the Malacca Strait.[9] Although oil is today the most valuable commodity to be transported by way of the Indian Ocean (about one-third of world supply), there are other products of the area which are also important for world trade. Foremost among these are minerals, the greatest proportion of which comes from Southern Africa. These are shipped principally to the United States, Europe and Japan. (Among them are certain 'strategic' minerals which are essential for military purposes.) Overall, the dependence of the West on these raw materials is considerable, and the consequences of a cut-off in supplies would be serious. Claims and estimates on this score diverge greatly depending both on whether they are made from the point of view of the producers or the importers of raw materials; also on the way in which the data, obtained from various sources, is processed statistically.[10] Outside Southern Africa, certain of the minerals are to be found only in the Soviet Union. In the mid-1970s, by far the greatest proportion of the Indian Ocean states' total trade was with Western Europe (33 per cent), ahead of Japan (19 per cent) and the United States (13 per cent). In comparison, the share of the Eastern bloc countries was very small (5 per cent).[11] The industrialised states in the region (Australia, South Africa) tend to trade predominantly outside the area.[12] Oil exports by Indian Ocean producers (including Indonesia) make up 26 per cent of the region's total exports.

8. To a lesser extent also through the Lombok or Sunda Straits in the Indonesian archipelago.

9. See *Le Monde Diplomatique*, Feb. 1980, p. 15. One-third of all international air routes also cross the Indian Ocean.

10. For this reason no figures are given here.

11. See CIA, op. cit., p. 20.

12. One particularly frequented trading route is that between South Africa and Japan. Japan is South Africa's third foreign customer and its fourth supplier. This trade mainly consists of an exchange of minerals in return for manufactured goods, especially motor-cars and electrical goods.

Regional trade in 1976 was only 18 per cent, a figure which indicates the low level of industrialisation of these states. However, it has been growing slowly since then, for example as a result of close co-operation among the states belonging to ASEAN and of the increase in volume of Indian trade, mainly with the states of the Persian Gulf but also with those in ASEAN. East Africa has, on the other hand, so far taken only a small share of trade within the region. One obstacle to such trade is the fact that very few of the Third World states in the region have their own merchant fleets. Here again India is an exception (in 1976 it ranked sixteenth in the world, measured in gross registered tonnage and in Asia second only after Japan); yet even India until recently exported only a quarter to a third of its goods in its own vessels.[13] The developing countries of the Indian Ocean region consider themselves discriminated against by the 'shipping conferences' which have so far been dominated by the traditional seafaring nations and in which most of the freight rates and insurance provisions are laid down; however, they have recently been entitled to more of a say in such matters as a result of changes in the composition of the majority.

Overcrowded ports are a special problem throughout the region. They are a consequence of the rapid expansion of maritime trade with which the building of port facilities has not been able to keep pace. Poor organisation, dockers' strikes[14] and other 'human' obstacles frequently serve to increase the objective problems.

The closure of the Suez Canal between 1967 and 1975 created problems and expense for most of the countries involved, while benefitting only a few (principally South Africa). One outcome of this situation was the construction of more super-tankers which could ply the route around the Cape more economically. These tankers then increasingly encountered difficulties in passing through the Malacca Strait, and the largest among them, when loaded, have to travel via the Lombok Strait which adds an extra 1,500 nautical miles (or three days) to the journey. The Suez Canal is now itself being widened as a result of the political crisis in the Middle East in 1979–80 (Iran and Afghanistan), mostly at the insistence of the United States, so as to enable it to take aircraft-carriers — and larger tankers.[15]

13. In 1980 a quarter of large capacity container freight and a third of general freight but two-thirds in oil tankers; *Far Eastern Economic Review* (FEER), 6.2.1981, p. 62.

14. The same is even more true of 'developed' Australia.

15. In May 1981, the first aircraft-carrier, the *America*, sailed through from the Mediterranean into the Indian Ocean.

The main points of access to the Indian Ocean (see p. 12 above) are international straits more than 6 nautical miles wide, which means that the ships and aircraft of all nations are entitled to free passage through or over these straits.[16] Since the late 1960s, new arrangements have been drawn up by the Third United Nations Conference on the Law of the Sea or its preparatory sessions. These arrangements should continue to guarantee such entitlement provided the strait countries adhere to the Convention — which is by no means certain. The use of important channels for passage into and out of the Indian Ocean must thus be regarded as potentially threatened. This applies particularly to maritime traffic to and from Israel but also to the trade routes (particularly for tanker traffic) to the Western industrialised countries. International law could be disregarded if the littoral states in question were to choose this means of exerting economic pressure. An example of such behaviour was provided by the coastal states of the Malacca Strait, Malaysia and Indonesia, which in 1971 and in subsequent years wanted to make the right of passage subject to their sovereign control. They placed strong pressure on Japan, which was induced as a result to make significantly increased contributions in development aid to these two countries. One response by Japan was the construction of supertankers which, as already mentioned, no longer use the Malacca Strait which is too shallow in places, but sail round through the Indonesian archipelago.

Another curtailment of the freedom of the seas could arise out of armed conflict between individual littoral states in the region around a strait. An example of this was provided by the situation immediately following the outbreak of hostilities between Iran and Iraq in the autumn of 1980. In the event the Iranian revolutionary government chose to abide by international law (in this case concerning countries at war) and refrained from any obstruction affecting third countries. Iraq did not carry out its threat to invade three of the islands in the lower Gulf which Iran had occupied, in 1971, but had it done so this would have led to an escalation of the conflict. (In 1982 Iraq bombed the Iranian oil terminal on Kharg island, damaging and even sinking third-party ships, but Iran decided to play down this episode in order not to deter foreign tanker traffic.) The rapid build-up of Western naval forces at the entrance to the Gulf in 1980 at least served to make it quite clear to the two warring states that access to and from the Gulf (via the Strait of Hormuz) would, if necessary, be preserved by force.

16. An exception is the narrow Tiran Strait between Saudi Arabia and Sinai. The Camp David Agreement ((1979) secured rights of passage and overhead flights for Israel. This settlement will always remain dependent on the continuation of friendly relations between Israel and Egypt.

Chapter 2

COASTAL STATES, HINTERLAND STATES AND ISLANDS

(a) *The political characteristics of the region*

Almost one-third of all independent states and almost one-third of the population of the earth belong to the geographical system of the Indian Ocean. Problems of definition with regard to the hinterland states have been largely overcome by means of consensus within the United Nations. According to UN classification, the countries which belong in this category are those which have access to the Indian Ocean only via the coastal states and whose security is affected by developments in these states.[17] In 1980 the Indian Ocean states numbered forty-five in all (see Appendix A). The region thus defined exhibits, in the nature of things, irreconcilable political and demographic differences. Yet there remain a series of factors which are distributed in broadly similar fashion throughout the region and which have given rise to the situation whereby almost all these states form a loose community of interests in the United Nations (see pp. 172 f.).

The most important of these factors is the experience, common to almost all, of a colonial past. The predominant fruit of this is, admittedly, a traumatic memory of foreign domination and exploitation; yet there are some positive aspects that are also significant. Some of the features now common to independent states date back to the colonial past when they were part of the same empire — such as, for example, the language of administration and education, institutions, transport and other economic infrastructure, and the formation of élites. Historically, the most important influence up to the present has been that of the British, and this has been institutionally preserved in the form of the Commonwealth. Comparable links exist in the former French territories. On top of this is the fact that we are dealing here with a developing region *par excellence*. Less than 2 per cent of the inhabitants are of European extraction and a considerable part of the region (predominantly the Indian sub-continent) was already relatively densely populated before the Europeans extended their influence. In 1975 less than a quarter of the population lived in cities, and the overwhelming majority were engaged in agriculture. Industrial infrastructure is

17. See K.P. Misra, *Quest for an International Order in the Indian Ocean*, New Delhi, 1977, pp. 4 f.

11

extremely limited. For this reason, as well as for reasons associated with the colonial mode of economic development, the region is the poorest in the world. Only one-twelfth of its population live in states with a *per capita* annual income of over $1,000. Thus the efforts of industrialised countries in the sphere of development are espe ially important for this region.[18] It forms a substantial part of the 'South' which, since the early 1970s, has been locked in combat with the industrialised 'North' (this is known as the 'North-South Dialogue' or the 'North-South Conflict' depending on the standpoint of the person concerned and the side on which his interests lie), with the aim of seeking an improvement in its conditions of trade. In this connection the oil-producing states on the Persian Gulf today have a specific role to play, because the rise in oil prices since 1973 has heaped burdens on the oil-importing developing countries which are reaching a clearly recognisable limit. At the beginning of the 1980s, highest priority should be given to the question of how a new system of distribution and payments could be set up between industrialised countries, the oil-producing states and those developing countries which lack energy, technology and capital (the 'Fourth World').[19]

Development problems of this type (elaborated in the Brandt Report in 1980) come up against other trends which, in the 1970s, had the effect of dragging the Indian Ocean region more deeply into the confrontation between East and West. In this context the states involved play for the most part the role of pawns; they find themselves involved against their will in the political and strategic calculations of foreign powers. Their protests are expressed in the emphasis they place on non-alignment, in their endeavours to reach agreement at the sub-regional level, and in collective statements ('peace zone') to the effect that they want to be left alone, without interference, because they know best how to manage their own affairs.

Several factors make a logical follow-up to this quite plausible fundamental stand more difficult. The importance of the area's resources — first and foremost oil — to outside powers is too great

18. See J.C. Caldwell, 'Population and Development in the Indian Ocean Region', in A. Kerr (ed.), *The Indian Ocean Region: Resources and Development*, University of Western Australia Press, 1981, pp. 1–17.

19. Mr Shihata, the OPEC Director General for International Development, warned the developing countries, at a conference held in Colombo in early 1981, against placing too high expectations on the potential of his organisation. He claimed that because of their high birth-rates and their expenditure on arms and prestige projects, the developing countries' shortages were partly self-induced. See *Times of India*, 16.1.1981, p. 15.

for it to be reasonable to expect those outside powers not to secure their influence wherever possible in the region. Moreover, already today the Indian Ocean, on account of its topographical characteristics, is involved in the super-powers' endeavours to secure, in their global confrontation, strategically favourable positions. Water, airspace (including satellite orbits) and land are all reduced to the level of grid calculations against which protests from the countries involved could achieve nothing. A final factor is that it is an aspect of the actual (as distinct from the verbal) policy of many of the littoral states to seek outside protection and help with defence against potential threats from within or outside the region; the result of this is that the international entanglement of interests is further increased.

It is thus important to bear in mind that, at the beginning of the 1980s, the Indian Ocean area consists of a highly heterogeneous assembly of states, most of them young, which nonetheless have a considerable fund of experience in common (colonisation), from which in the process of 'nation-building' they are able to derive benefits. The Indian Ocean area is a typical developing region in which structurally determined poverty is prevalent. It is thus in the forefront of the debate concerning a New International Economic Order. The fact that the oil-exporting countries of the Persian Gulf belong to the Indian Ocean region opens up possibilities for finding new ways of overcoming the multiple handicaps suffered by the oil-importing developing countries of the 'Fourth World', and the task becomes one to be tackled in the region itself. Against the primacy of an appropriate development policy stands the fact that the area is being rapidly drawn into the East-West confrontation. Protests and demonstrations of independence on the part of littoral states could at best slow down this process — on the one hand because these states themselves often enough contribute to the establishment of links with outside powers, and on the other because the global-strategic significance of the region has increased so far that no special status given to local states could alter this state of affairs. Power politics now reigns supreme. In this situation the super-powers form only the top of the pyramid; the same motives and methods, namely securing of influence and intimidation, apply to relations between the Indian Ocean states themselves.[20] In the foreseeable future the oil-producers will retain a strong position in the

20. In 1976 Andrew Peacock, then Australian Foreign Minister, commented: 'It is well to remember that in power terms we are still living in an old-fashioned world of nation states', Foreign Affairs News Release, Canberra, 13.9.1976.

equation. The 'oil glut' notwithstanding, both the West and the developing world depend on secure supply under calculable conditions. The war between Iran and Iraq has brought a further dimension of danger into focus, that of substantial obstacles to oil supplies resulting from violence attributable to regional instabilities and contrary to the interests of all external powers.

(b) *Demographic survey*

The population in the Indian Ocean region is extremely unevenly distributed.[21] In 1978, out of a total of 1,150 million inhabitants in the region, almost three-quarters (71 per cent) lived in the Indian sub-continent, and of these almost three-fifths in India alone. Of the remaining population more than half (16 per cent) is in South-East Asia, just under half of this total in Indonesia alone. In population terms it is thus India, followed — a long way behind — by Indonesia, which 'dominates' the Indian Ocean region.

Life expectancy in the Indian Ocean littoral states of Africa is between forty and forty-five years (comparable with the level in England between 1860 and 1870), and the country on the lowest rung of the ladder is Somalia. In the states on the Arabian Peninsula and Persian Gulf, life expectancy is between forty-five and fifty, which is comparable with England at the beginning of the twentieth century; North Yemen, followed by South Yemen and Saudi Arabia, are at the bottom of the scale, while Iran and the United Arab Emirates are at the upper end. In South Asia, Bangladesh has the lowest life expectancy (forty-five years) while in India, according to the 1981 census, it is fifty-four years (in 1971 the figure was forty-seven years),[22] in Pakistan it is fifty and for Sri Lanka the suprisingly high figure of sixty-five years is given, despite its very low *per capita* income. In South-East Asia the figures for Burma and Indonesia are between forty-five and fifty years whereas in Malaysia — as in Sri Lanka — life expectancy is a good sixty-five years. Singapore is comparable with Western industrialised countries, as is Australia. On the islands in the Indian Ocean life expectancy is also relatively

21. See Caldwell, op. cit. Caldwell's investigation is based only on the coastal states and islands and not on the hinterland states. Nor does it include the states of North-East Africa (Ethiopia, Sudan, Egypt) or Iraq.

22. See *Times of India*, 19.3.1981, p. 1. Recent investigations in India have shown that there is a clear line separating the west from the east (especially the north-east). In the western part indicators show a considerably higher standard of living.

high, with the exception of the Maldives and the Comoros. It emerges from these figures that high life-expectancy in a country cannot be equated exclusively with high *per capita* income. More decisive factors are the general situation with regard to health, the educational system and other socio-economic indicators. One particularly significant factor in this respect is the level of education and training available to women. The greater the degree of equality in this field, the better the effect on all other areas which determine living standards. For this reason, those societies in which the role of women is by tradition severely restricted (especially Muslim societies) are subject to distinct handicaps.

A more important figure than life expectancy for assessing future development is that of population growth (the birth rate minus the death rate). In the African coastal states the average yearly growth rate is 2.5 per cent, in the Arabian peninsula and Persian Gulf area it is 3 per cent, in South Asia over 2 per cent (in India according to the 1981 census it is 2.47 per cent), and in South-East Asia 2.5 per cent with the notable exception of Singapore where there is a strict policy of birth control; on the islands the average is 2.5 per cent. With an annual growth rate of 3 per cent the population of a country doubles in twenty-three years and with an annual rate of 2.5 per cent it doubles in twenty-eight years.[23] Yet these figures must be seen in the light of increased life expectancy and the result would seem to indicate that overall conditions of existence in this typical Third World region cannot have deteriorated in the course of the last generation.

Meanwhile the largest cities are growing. Within the foreseeable future Calcutta, Bombay and Djakarta, including their suburbs, will each have 15–20 million inhabitants. The general proportion of town and city dwellers in the Indian Ocean region taken as a whole is expected to rise steeply from 24 per cent in 1975 to 35 per cent in the year 2000 and 47 per cent in the year 2025. It is thus most likely that within thirty years the total population will approximately double while the growth rate will continue to gather speed before the various effects of social change offer an opportunity to halt this trend. Demographers also assume in relation to this distant future time that population distribution in the Indian Ocean will remain much as it is

23. An extreme example is Pakistan: between 1951 and 1979 — a period of twenty-eight years — the population rose by 130. 8 per cent from 33.7 to 77.9 million (figures relating to the area within the present state boundaries); *Dawn* (Karachi), 5.8.1980, p. 7. In contrast the population of India 'merely' doubled in the space of thirty-four years (1947–81); See *Times of India*, 19.3.81, p. 1.

today; around two-thirds in South Asia, one-sixth in South-East Asia and the remainder distributed among the other sub-regions.

With such population density, together with migration towards the cities, the agricultural sector will be forced to raise production substantially if it is to provide enough food for the people. Measured against the European experience, this is not an impossibility — provided that enough new sources of energy are found — but it would have to be accompanied by a radical change in attitude on the part of the rural population, and in this respect there have so far been few indications that this is happening. In attempting to forecast beyond the year 2000, one of the greatest unknown factors is precisely this question of the interaction (and not just in the material sphere) between country and city — or megalopolis. What does appear certain is that between 1980 and 2000 there will be an extra 2,000 million people in the world, 90 per cent of them in developing countries. Of this growth 60 per cent will be in Asia as against 30 per cent in Africa and Latin America.[24] The Indian Ocean region will thus take a very large share.

(c) *The sub-regions: an attempt at classification*

Because of their ethnic, socio-economic and cultural diversity, the coastal, hinterland and island states of the Indian Ocean region permit only a very rough division into sub-regions. Yet an attempt at such sub-division is necessary if a study of the Indian Ocean region is to be undertaken at all. In the literature to date — predominantly Anglo-Saxon, French and Indian[25] — the criteria used for classification have been extremely varied. The 'classic' division comprises four sub-regions: Southern and Eastern Africa and their offshore islands; the Horn of Africa, the Red Sea and the Persian Gulf including Iran; South Asia; and South-East Asia and Australia. The political developments of the 1970s in the north-western quarter of the Indian Ocean have, in particular, meant that a further sub-division is now required in that area between the Horn of Africa and the Red Sea and the Persian Gulf.[26]

24. See UN Fund for Population Activities, *State of World Population*, 1980, quoted in *The Statesman Weekly*, (Calcutta), 21.6.1980; see also *Global 2000, Report to the President*, Council on Environmental Quality and the US Department of State, July 1980.

25. The most comprehensive bibliography to date has been compiled by the National Library of Australia and is entitled *The Indian Ocean: a Select Bibliography of Resources for Study*, Canberra 1979, 190 pp. It is restricted to historical, social and scientific studies and includes over 6,000 titles.

26. See Váli, op. cit., p. 28.

Since the twofold political crisis in Iran and Afghanistan in 1979 and 1980, with its repercussions on the Persian Gulf and the Arabian peninsula, the term 'South-West Asia' has come into widespread use in political circles (especially in the United States) and in literature on the subject, whereas it was previously scarcely used at all. Pakistan is now frequently included in this area[27]. Other writers, mostly French, treat the islands of the western Indian Ocean as yet another sub-region.

All these sub-divisions are to a great extent arbitrary, i.e. subjective and conditioned by the priorities of the moment. Yet there are two sub-regions which can be so clearly defined and delimited that it is unlikely that their classification will be subject to rapid change. These two regions are South Asia and South-East Asia. The identity of both as sub-regions is amply based on cultural factors stemming from historical developments and ethnic composition. The two are neighbours, and yet the line separating them is quite distinct and there are trends in progress which will lead to increasing divergence between them.[28] Viewed thus, South Asia consists of India, Pakistan, Bangladesh, Nepal, Bhutan, Sri Lanka and the Maldive Islands, while the states belonging to South-East Asia are Burma and four of the five ASEAN states which have coastlines on the Indian Ocean, namely Thailand, Malaysia, Indonesia and the city-state of Singapore. However, in terms of their political, economic and cultural features, all four of these states are more strongly inclined towards the Pacific than towards the Indian Ocean.

With regard to Australia, this Pacific orientation is even more evident since it is only fairly recently that the Australian West coast has been able to assert its own relative importance as against the dominant eastern (and above all, south-eastern) part of the continent.[29] Today it must be asked whether one is still justified, when discussing the Indian Ocean region, in 'tacking Australia on' to South-East Asia. Australia has become an entity in its own right and its very distinctive ethnic and socio-economic characteristics scarcely allow comparison with the ASEAN states. And yet it does

27. In India this is seen as an American attempt to detach Pakistan from the Indian sub-continent. See *Times of India*, 19.3.1981. p. 1.

28. 'There is an increasing relationship between the politics of the Middle East and those of the subcontinent; there is a diminishing relationship between those of the subcontinent and South East and Pacific Asia but a close relationship between those of the two latter groups' (Alastair Buchan, *The End of the Postwar Era*, London 1975, p. 281).

29. One indication of this is furnished by the Indian Ocean Festival, held in the summer of 1979 in the Western Australian capital of Perth and upon which considerable expenditure was lavished.

seem quite reasonable to group them together in cases where some degree of simplification is required, for there are other characteristics, in addition to their common leanings towards the Pacific, which appear, despite the very fundamental differences in many respects, to be leading to growing interrelatedness between Australia and South-East Asia.

Moving west from the Indian sub-continent, to which Pakistan must undoubtedly be held to belong in spite of its affinities with the Islamic Middle East (affinities which became stronger after the secession of East Pakistan), regional sub-divisions become harder to make. This applies already to Afghanistan, which combines characteristics of Central Asia with others more akin to the Indian sub-continent and still others which cause it to resemble Iran. Whereas hitherto there were good reasons[30] for including Afghanistan within the political orbit of South Asia, a fundamental change has come about since the Soviet intervention at the end of 1979, and its effects on the future development of Afghanistan are not yet discernable. It would, however, seem likely that, as a result of this act of violence, the Central Asian features of the country will in future tend to predominate.

The states bordering on the Persian Gulf have developed in the course of the 1970s, whether by co-operation or by conflict, an increased level of mutual involvement exhibiting sub-regional features. The question of oil production has created parallel problems and interests for these states and, as a result of the high level of outside involvement, these are quickly escalated further. 'Gulf Politics' has thus become a specialised discipline which has already given rise to a considerable number of scholarly publications in the field of international politics and economics. The states to be classified as belonging to the Gulf region are Iran, Iraq, Saudi Arabia, the United Arab Emirates, Qatar, Bahrain, Kuwait and — on the fringes — Oman.

The division between the Gulf region and the Red Sea and Horn of Africa is fluid. Saudi Arabia, in particular, with its Red Sea coastline, faces in both directions. In 1976–7, efforts were made towards greater co-operation among the Red Sea states, and South Yemen too was involved. As a result of the Ogaden war between Ethiopia and Somalia at the beginning of 1978 and its consequences, all such co-operation plans have lost their meaning, at least for the time being. South Yemen today forms one pillar of the bridge which — supported by the Soviet Union and its allies — links the

30. See, for example, R.S. Newell, *The Politics of Afghanistan*, Ithaca, NY, 1972.

Arabian peninsula to Ethiopia. On the other hand, the effect of the 'Camp David Process' has been to some extent to loosen Egyptian ties with regional Arab politics. Nonetheless, it does still seem justifiable, mainly on account of their traditional neighbourly ties, to regard the countries around the Red Sea and the Horn of Africa as a single sub-region. The states belonging to it are the People's Republic of Yemen (South Yemen), the Arab Republic of Yemen (North Yemen), Saudi Arabia, Egypt, Sudan, Djibouti, Ethiopia and Somalia. On the southern confines, Kenya is also to be included, as are, in the north, Jordan and Israel on the Gulf of Akaba.

The main focus of Kenyan identity is, however, in the sub-region comprised of the coastal and hinterland states of Eastern and Southern Africa which are linked together by reason of common interests as well as on historical and ethnic grounds. This sub-region extends from Kenya in the north across mainland Tanzania and Mozambique to the Republic of South Africa and includes the hinterland states of Uganda, Zambia, Malawi, Zimbabwe and Botswana.

The allocation to this sub-region of the islands and groups of islands lying off the coast of Africa would create more problems of identification than it would solve. It is true that these islands are becoming increasingly involved in various political processes, especially within the context of the Organisation of African Unity. In some cases there are also close bilateral links, for example between Tanzania and the Seychelles. Nonetheless, the features that set these islands apart from Africa are the predominant ones. The mixture of races, which varies from one island to another but is everywhere strong; their ocean-directedness, and their similar economic bases. With the exception of Madagascar, all the islands are small and yet densely populated. There is very little industry. Political systems are centralised and, in most cases, dominated by personalities. Culturally the French element predominates and this situation is deliberately nurtured by France. Contacts between islands and groups of islands — Madagascar, Mauritius, Réunion, the Comoros and the Seychelles — are increasing, and this too serves to stimulate the trend towards political rapprochement.[31]

31. A trend with a time-fuse was set in motion by Mauritius when, in 1980, it caused the Organisation of African Unity fully to support it in its claim for the restoration of the Chagos archipelago, i.e. principally Diego Garcia, which the United States had built into a base. Britain had separated the group of islands — situated far out in the middle of the Ocean, southwest from Sri Lanka — before granting independence to Mauritius, and had given Mauritius financial compensation. These islands, together with

For the purposes of this study, it seems appropriate to divide the major Indian Ocean region into seven sub-regions:
— Southern and Eastern Africa;
— islands and groups of islands in the Western Indian Ocean;
— the Horn of Africa and the Red Sea;
— the Persian Gulf;
— South Asia;
— South-East Asia;
— Australia.

---

some others, became the British Indian Ocean Territory (BIOT). This act was never recognised by Mauritius. *Realpolitik*, as well as geographical factors, certainly militate against the success of Mauritian endeavours, but even so this claim will probably give rise to diplomatic difficulties for Britain which owns the island and for the United States which uses it for military purposes.

Part II
THE REGION VIEWED WITHIN THE GLOBAL POWER BALANCE

Chapter 3
THE INTERESTS AND INSTRUMENTS OF THE SUPER-POWERS

(a) *Reciprocal and asymmetrical modes of behaviour*

In most of the declarations made by the littoral states regarding the presence — and above all the military presence — of the United States and the Soviet Union in the Indian Ocean region, the concept of 'super-power rivalry' is used. This same concept pervades the resolutions adopted by the United Nations in connection with the demand for a peace zone. The expression has also been adopted, to an astonishing extent, by Americans in discussing the activities of the United States. The Soviet Union ritually opposes both being labelled as a super-power and being equated with the 'supreme imperialist power' in terms of its intentions and actions. And yet from Soviet statements it can easily be shown that Moscow in fact sets great store by its super-power status[1] and, by virtue of its ideology, is strongly attached to the notion of rivalry, i.e. of constant and competitive comparison with the opposing power. It thus stands to reason that the motives and actions of both powers in relation to the Indian Ocean should be largely decipherable — reciprocally — in terms of their interaction.

As a matter of fact, the notion of rivalry corresponds only partly to the real situation. Numerous activities of both super-powers in this major region, at sea and on land, in both the past and the present, are not based on reciprocity. A more important conditioning factor is a distinct asymmetry of interests and potential which has its roots in geography: the Indian Ocean is the United States' most distant ocean while, for the Soviet Union, it is the second nearest (after the Pacific), even though its maritime access is both distant

1. See V.V. Aspaturian, 'Soviet Global Power and the Correlation of Forces', *Problems of Communism*, vol. 29, no. 3, May/June 1980.

and fraught with complications. If the significance of this factor had not previously been fully realized, the Soviet invasion of Afghanistan in December 1979 forced general awareness of it and served to correct many previous strategic appraisals in both the West and in the Indian Ocean states themselves. With its strong military potential along the frontiers of the coastal states of the north-western Indian Ocean and only a few flying hours away from Karachi harbour, the Persian Gulf, the Bab-el-Mandeb Strait and the Horn of Africa, the Soviet Union moved suddenly into the field of vision as the most powerful Indian Ocean hinterland state. Since the middle of the 1970s it has shown that under a variety of circumstances it is both able and prepared to mobilise this potential. In such an event there is little that the United States could at present do — even if it were to exhaust its available military and strategic resources — to counter such a move, simply by reason of its geographical disadvantage.

In many ways, asymmetry has been a feature of the situation since the time when the two powers respectively turned their attention increasingly to the Indian Ocean region.[2] In the case of the United States this change took place at the end of the Second World War (construction of the Dharan air base in Saudi Arabia) and in the years that followed (in the context of the Truman Doctrine). In the 1950s, John Foster Dulles' policy of securing multilateral agreements stood in the forefront of American policy (see p. 73). In the following decade it became clear that Britain would no longer be able to continue its traditional policing role in the Indian Ocean. The joint investigation by the British and Americans, begun in 1963, of the possibilities of putting various Indian Ocean islands to strategic use marked the beginning of a period of transition which was completed with the *de facto* takeover of Diego Garcia by the United States. At the same time, because of the demands of the Vietnam war, the Americans were compelled to reduce their political involvement in the littoral states. Also instrumental in this was the assumption that the United States shared certain interests with the Soviet Union, not least *vis-à-vis* China. Still implicit in the Nixon Doctrine of 1969, which paved the way for overtures towards China, was some degree of US trust in the Soviet Union's role in maintaining stability in Asia. On top of this, both super-powers reacted in a similarly defensive manner to initiatives by littoral states which sought to restrict freedom of movement and action in the Indian Ocean through special arrangements. But here too the United States

2. Particular reference is made to this in K.C. Beazley and I. Clark, *Politics of Intrusion: the Super Powers and the Indian Ocean*, Sydney 1979.

must have overestimated the extent to which its interests ran parallel to those of the Soviet Union, for it soon proved more advantageous to the Soviets to give diplomatic support to the wishes of local states, thereby setting up an additional front against the United States.

The Nixon-Kissinger policy was founded mainly on the assumption that the Soviet Union would play the traditional balance-of-power game. But in assuming this it took insufficient account of the ideological roots of Soviet actions. This meant in turn that the policy of détente was conducted under a cloud of illusion. That policy was based — particularly on the US side but on the Soviet side as well — on the assumption that the other side shared, at least as a starting-point, its own definition of the most important principles to be negotiated (beginning with the very conception of détente). This misunderstanding on both sides was clearly evident in the 'Basic Principles of Relations' between the super-powers, a document signed in Moscow in early 1972.[3] One of the points stated in the document was that neither side would attempt to seek advantages for itself at the expense of the other, but already in the following year this tenet was being disregarded; by 1975 there were increased misgivings on both sides, and at the end of the 1970s the contradictions broke out into the open. Antagonism, the result of a bipolar world system, again came to the fore.[4]

The principal reason for the Soviet Union's initial involvement in the Indian Ocean region was the need for reciprocal arrangements which would assist its attempts to break through the Western containment of its long southern flank, effected in the 1950s principally through the Baghdad Pact and to a less extent through SEATO. It was to this end that the Soviet Union began to construct for itself a network — initially quite a modest one — of bilateral relations, primarily with India, Afghanistan, Indonesia, Burma and Egypt. At the same time it used this means to rehearse its own specific Third World policy, which was sharply antagonistic towards the West, making use of diplomatic, economic and ideological channels, supplemented by military aid. The main feature distinguishing this policy from that of the Americans stems from Soviet doctrine; it is claimed that it is historically inevitable that progressive forces in

3. The text of this statement can be found in M. Willrich and J.B. Rhinelander (eds), *SALT — The Moscow Agreements and Beyond*, New York 1974, Appendix 3.

4. 'At the beginning of the '70s, the United States and the Soviet Union were talking with each other about their common interests. At the beginning of the '80s, they are talking again as they did in the '40s and '50s about their differences.' James Reston, *International Herald Tribune*, 31.12.1979, p. 4.

these Third World states will find themselves united against reactionary ones and will subsequently ally with the Socialist camp in order to help shift the global 'correlation of forces' increasingly in favour of socialism. It became evident that Moscow still had a lot to learn in this field, and the subsequent years brought forth all sorts of setbacks.

Meanwhile, the Soviet Union was also involved in a persistent struggle with the United States for recognition of its military and strategic parity. Around 1970 it met with some success in these endeavours, evidence of this being SALT I. To exercise the role of a world power and thereby gain the right to a say in all matters of major importance, a powerful and versatile navy was required, something which the United States had long possessed. So in the 1960s the Soviet Union undertook a building programme to this end and from 1968 onwards this new instrument, by giving the Soviet Union access to the southern seas, represented a new element in the balance of power in the Indian Ocean.

In many ways the Indian Ocean was a more favourable area for the Soviet Union to operate in than it was for the United States. Diplomacy and economic and military aid had created preconditions for drawing important Indian Ocean states into the Soviet sphere of interest. The Soviet Union showed more consistency in the conduct of its policy than did the United States. The decision to give support to any one state was based on an analysis of the power balance and of the trends developing in the sub-region in question. Such a decision, once taken, was seldom subject to change where Moscow was concerned. In marked contrast, however, American policy towards the Indian Ocean was mostly subordinated to the constantly changing priorities of domestic policy in Washington. Moreover it was clear for all to see that there were too many parties with a say in this policy (the White House, the State Department, the Pentagon, the CIA etc.) and they tended to stand in each another's way or even oppose each another. An analysis of the respective policies of the Soviet Union and the United States towards India and Pakistan would furnish particularly clear examples of this asymmetry of behaviour between the two super-powers. (US behaviour in this respect was, and continues to be, the outcome of factors conditioned by the American system, and its negative consequences should not thus be imputed solely to individual American Presidents.)

A comparison of super-power behaviour in Africa provides a somewhat different picture. In this continent, after the collapse of the Portuguese empire, the United States followed a policy which, among other things, paved the way for the peaceful transfer of power in Rhodesia/Zimbabwe and thus facilitated good relations between the West and important African states such as Nigeria and Kenya. Yet here too the Soviet Union made adroit use of circumstances which it turned to political advantage (the OAU condemnation of Somali action against Ethiopia and before that of South Africa's military intervention in Angola), whereas the United States appeared indecisive (Somalia) or was unable to act (Angola).

With the deployment of more powerful forces, the Soviet Union has, in the view of Third World states bordering the Indian Ocean, become very similar to the United States (readiness to intervene, 'counter-imperialism'), but even so the common conclusion that the behaviour of one super-power unleashes similar behaviour on the part of the other applies only to a limited degree. The classification of the Persian Gulf as vitally important for Western security dates from the first energy crisis of 1973, which was triggered off by the activities of local states and OPEC. The Soviet Union came into the picture only indirectly. This situation has undoubtedly been modified by the Soviet invasion of Afghanistan, yet not fundamentally so. Prevailing West European opinion holds that this invasion was not directly related to the scenario of a Soviet intervention in the Gulf.[5]

The concern in America, and in the West generally, over oil supplies has its counterpart in the Soviet Union in the form of the threat represented by the 'China syndrome'. This parallel is far-reaching. When the Soviet Union moves nearer the Gulf and spreads its military net in an ever widening circle, against a background of instability in Iran and in the Arab Gulf states, this is qualitatively equivalent to increased *rapprochement* between China and America (as well as Japan and Western Europe). Both developments raise the super-powers' perception of threat — in the United States on the basis of the formula 'Oil Dependence plus the Soviet Union' and in the Soviet Union according to that of 'Collusion between the Main Adversaries'.

Even leaving aside the increasing degree of understanding between the West and China in the field of security and foreign policy, the Soviet Union experiences a constant challenge from China in the Indian Ocean. If the Soviet Union has a geographical advantage in South and South-West Asia, the Chinese have a corresponding advantage in South-East Asia, especially in Indochina. The Soviet Union is already finding it very expensive to keep its treaty partner,

5. For a view which is broadly representative of opinion in Western Europe, see *The Soviet Invasion and its consequences for British Policy*, House of Commons Foreign Affairs Committee (5th report), London, July 1980.

Vietnam, and its 'affiliated' client-states, Cambodia and Laos, alive and fit for military action. In the medium-term, China can be expected to gain the whip-hand since it is in a position to apply pressure in measured doses and to distribute it far afield. The United States is involved in this conflict chiefly by virtue of its support to Thailand, but the heart of the conflict lies in the antagonism between China and the Soviet Union. This antagonism also affects other areas in the Indian Ocean region, especially South Asia, but it is nowhere so virulent as in Indochina, China's geographical glacis.

It is in the military-strategic field that reciprocal patterns of behaviour between the super-powers are, on the other hand, most clearly observable. In this sphere there have indeed been many signs of an 'action-reaction cycle', especially in times of crises such as in 1971 (India versus Pakistan), 1973 (the October war), 1977–8 (Ethiopia) and since 1979 (Iran, Afghanistan). Military thinking and technical requirements in the military sphere create parallels which transcend different political systems, and yet even these should not be viewed simplistically. For example, technological progress on both sides has developed satellite communications to such an extent that military reconnaissance is becoming increasingly sophisticated.[6] The construction rate is incredibly fast. At the same time, the ability to wage satellite warfare (using 'killer satellites') is advancing. Satellite reconnaissance could in many ways help to compensate the United States for its loss of access to Iran, Afghanistan, Ethiopia and Angola. The Indian Ocean is heavily involved in these developments because of its topography. This includes the equatorial belt which is vital for geo-stationary satellites. Yet even here the concept of 'rivalry', of which the Indian Ocean states make such play, is not strictly applicable since it is only a regional part of global offensive, deterrence and surveillance systems.

From a retrospective glance at the bilateral negotiations to limit military forces in the Indian Ocean (1977–8), broken off by the United States when the Soviet Union and Cuba deployed forces in Ethiopia, it would appear that this was an unsuitable test case. This is precisely because in this Third World region there was no way in which the respective military doctrines and key political and ideological concepts by the super-powers could be made to coincide. The attempt was therefore bound to fail, even though both sides — and most of the Indian Ocean states as well — had in 1977 pinned their hopes on these talks for an end to military escalation in the region. In the final analysis, however, this attempt failed less as a result of

6. See H. Feigl, 'Satellitenaufklärung als Mittel der Rüstungskontrolle', *Europa-Archiv* (EA), vol. 34, no. 18 (September 1979), pp. 555–70.

incompatibilities in the Indian Ocean region itself than because of a rapid deterioration in the general global political climate for negotiation between the super-powers from this point (the end of 1977) onwards. Reciprocal mistrust grew accordingly, and each side kept a register of the other's sins. As far as the Americans were concerned, Afghanistan was the last straw that broke the camel's back, while the Soviets, for their part, pointed to the delay over SALT II, the political restrictions on trade, their exclusion from the Middle East peace process and Sino-American *rapprochement*.

This global hardening of attitudes is likely to make it much more difficult in the foreseeable future for the super-powers to co-ordinate their respective independent interests in the Indian Ocean — which would result in a reduction of misunderstandings and conflicts. 'The behaviour of the United States and the Soviet Union in the late 1970s and 1980s suggests that they may be forfeiting the claims they had begun to build up in the 1960s and early 1970s to be regarded by others as responsible managers of the affairs of international society as a whole.'[7] In place of an understanding there is now the possibility of a direct military clash between the super-powers. Whether according to or against their own wishes, the Indian Ocean states are being drawn into this escalation.

Once again therefore events are being determined by something more than mere rivalry between the super-powers. There is a deep-rooted antagonism between the two systems, which Third World states in the 1970s had precipitately assumed could be dismantled in order to push to the fore in its place the issue of the worsening gap in development between North and South. Such ideas have not been borne out. On the contrary, in view of the renewed intensification of the East-West conflict, the Third World's structural problems risk being pushed into the background, thereby giving encouragement to the forces of disorder and anarchy.

(b) *The United States*

(i) *From the Nixon Doctrine to the Carter Doctrine.* Despite their differing experiences in the 1950s and 1960s with the newly independent states of the Third World, it was at about the same time, 1969–70, that both the United States and the Soviet Union acquired new concepts which were subsequently formulated as policy

7. Hedley Bull, 'The Great Irresponsibles? The United States, the Soviet Union, and World Order', *International Journal*, vol. XXXV, no. 3 (Summer 1980), p. 437.

guidelines. In the case of the Soviet Union, this policy centred on the proposal for a Collective Security System for Asia and the associated policy of bilateral treaties of friendship (see below) while, in the case of the United States, the Nixon Doctrine marked a retreat from previous readiness for military intervention. It was also at this time that both powers began to regard the Indian Ocean region as a single entity whereas formerly they had taken an interest in individual sub-regions, mostly without reference to the wider geopolitical framework.

At the heart of the Nixon Doctrine lay a narrower definition of national interest, on the basis of which it offered selective support to allied or friendly states which were willing to make a significant contribution to their own security. Questions of ideology moved increasingly into the background since, in Nixon's own words, 'accommodation to the diversity of the world community is the keystone of our current policy.'[8] With this concept of greater aloofness from regional conflicts, the navy and air force acquired heightened significance. Allies of the United States such as Japan and Australia were expected to contribute economic assistance to the underdeveloped states of Asia. Regional associations of states (ASPAC, ASEAN etc.) were to be fostered and given support. Asia, the Middle East and Africa were, as far as possible, to be kept away from the centre of confrontations between the great powers (including China) and were to be brought into a new equilibrium of their own that still remained to be discovered. This process was to be influenced by a peaceful contest between the two systems.[9]

The doctrine was open to a variety of interpretations. On the one hand, it testified to a considerable measure of confidence regarding future sharing of responsibility for the Third World with the Soviet Union and China. On the other hand, it meant that for a number of states in this region the nature and extent of further American support had suddenly become uncertain. The United States, moreover, was still heavily involved in Vietnam. Furthermore, Nixon's ideas of a balance with Soviet and Chinese influences were not very clear. Were certain preferred spheres of influence to be conceded to these two powers? Or was the United States rather to attempt to balance out such influence where it existed through means of its own devising? And how, in this context, was the increased significance of the US navy and of its lobby to affect the future US presence in the Indian Ocean region? To what extent could political influence on

8. Quoted in M. Bezboruah, *US Strategy in the Indian Ocean*, New York 1977, p. 51.
9. See Beazley and Clark, op. cit., pp. 9 f.

land be reinforced or replaced by the knowledge that 'over the horizon' there was a mobile naval strike force? In Washington these issues sparked off an internal political controversy that lasted throughout the 1970s and which periodically led to violent swings in policy.

The fundamental traits of the Nixon Doctrine managed to retain a certain degree of political effectiveness during the greater part of the decade. Détente between the super-powers contributed to a general balancing out of their respective influence in the Third World. In Asia in 1976 and 1977 there were encouraging signs of a desire for *rapprochement* at the sub-regional level (Persian Gulf, Indian sub-continent, South-East Asia). The military presence of the United States and of the Soviet Union in and around the Indian Ocean enabled an approximate balance of power to be maintained at a relatively low level. This 'matching balance' suffered its first blow at the end of 1977 and beginning of 1978 with the Soviet and Cuban build-up of forces in the Horn of Africa, a development which brought the bilateral negotiations on force limitation between the United States and the Soviet Union to a standstill and which coincided with the beginning of a phase of rapid general deterioration of relations between the super-powers. As a result of these activities, however, the most important assumption on which the Nixon Doctrine had been based — namely that both Washington and Moscow were prepared to show restraint in areas of conflict in the Third World in order to avoid harming the predominant central East-West balance — had been destroyed.

In South-East Asia it was the Cambodian crisis which altered the priorities of American policy in the Pacific. The Soviet-backed Vietnamese advance in December 1978 led, for the first time since the fall of Saigon, to clear American support for the ASEAN states. The decision to step up a naval presence in the Indian Ocean in early 1979 resulted in part from the conflict there. Increased military and political support was also given to Thailand.[10]

At the same time, the main pillar of US policy in the region, Iran, collapsed and Saudi Arabia too showed the limits of its reliability as a regional partner. The thesis that allies in the Third World could co-operate closely with the United States, and over a longer period take on important security tasks, proved to be untenable. (The Soviet Union has had similar experiences and doubtless has more in store.) The elements of instability in the 'arc of crisis' are too great for a

10. See M. Leifer, *Conflict and Regional Order in Southeast Asia*, International Institute for Strategic Studies (IISS), London, Winter 1980, pp. 17 f.

strategy involving this level of support to succeed.

In this connection, the Soviet invasion of Afghanistan served to demonstrate as well the weakness of the third component of the Nixon Doctrine. In the event of an attack on the source of the West's principal oil supplies, the US navy and air force operating as mobile instruments far from their home bases would be decidedly inferior when faced with Soviet ground- and air-based forces. The Carter Doctrine, an *ad hoc* formulation which took shape at the beginning of 1980 under the impact of this collective danger signal and which envisaged a substantially stronger and direct US military commitment in the Gulf region and the Indian Ocean generally,[11] made at least one point very clear: a period of American policy *vis-à-vis* détente and the Third World, which had in many ways been unrealistic and based on wishful thinking, was now at an end. A new phase had begun, which involved painful re-thinking and a search for new premises on which to build and secure global power.

(ii) *The Persian Gulf as the focus of American interests.* As already mentioned, the prevailing attitude of the American administration towards the region at the beginning of the 1970s was one of calm assessment of where its own interests lay. But there was opposition to this attitude from the naval lobby which called for a stronger commitment, principally on account of the alleged possible threat to the oil routes following the establishment of a regular Soviet naval presence. This dual approach, the contradictions of which were largely determined by differing assessments of the situation coming from the State Department and the Pentagon, continued through the following years.

In the view of the State Department, set forth in mid-1971 in a statement to a Congressional Committee,[12] the priority interests of the United States at that time concerned:

— oil from the Persian Gulf, principally with regard to its significance for America's allies;

— the political stability of a region containing one-third of the world's population;

11. The Gulf region was defined as an 'inviolable sphere of US interest'; see President Carter's State of the Union message, 23 January 1980 in *Current Policy*, no. 132, US Department of State, Bureau of Public Affairs, Washington, DC. The underlying ideas had already been widely discussed since 1978 in American publications dealing with such topics. The Pentagon had first put forward its plan for a rapid deployment force in the Persian Gulf in 1977–8.

12. See R. Spiers, 'US National Security Policy and the Indian Ocean Area' in *Department of State Bulletin*, vol. 64, no. 1678 (Aug. 1971).

— unimpeded access to and passage through the region.

In connection with the last of these three points, mention was made of the need to develop Diego Garcia (see p. 39) into a 'modest communications centre'. Furthermore it was pointed out that Soviet aims in the area required careful observation on the part of the United States particularly with regard to the 'choke points', i.e. the entrances to the Red Sea and the Persian Gulf. The view was expressed that in the foreseeable future the significance of the Indian Ocean for the United States would remain substantially inferior to that of the Pacific and the Atlantic and that it would not need to control the ocean or individual states in the region, provided that freedom of access were preserved. Recent initiatives by littoral states ('peace zone') did, however, affect the principle of free use of international waters.

Shortly after this assessment of the situation was made, the Bengal crisis in the second half of 1971 (leading to the creation of Bangladesh) caused tensions to mount sharply to the point where, in addition to its opposition to an important littoral state, namely India, the United States came into confrontation with the Soviet Union. Washington's crisis management, which in the decisive phase emanated almost exclusively from the White House, was geared to its global policy (setting up relations with Peking, a balance with Moscow) and was for this reason ill-suited to giving adequate consideration to the specific regional aspects and developments which ultimately proved decisive. The assessment of this conflict by the White House, as extensively outlined by Henry Kissinger in his memoirs,[13] once again confirms in detail the foundations and goals which determined American behaviour at that time. Hindsight has contributed nothing to their persuasiveness.

It should nonetheless be pointed out that by dealing with the Bengal crisis the Sino-Soviet controversy was for the first time manifested in the United Nations as well.

At the same time this was the first occasion on which American and Chinese interests could be seen to run parallel. Nixon's visit to Peking in 1972 consolidated the relationship which developed into a constant feature of the decade. Not least among its effects was the perception by the Soviet Union that the foundations of its understanding of détente were being progressively undermined. The

13. *The White House Years*, London 1979, ch. XXI. For an informative critical assessment of the Nixon-Kissinger policy during this crisis by a well-placed official in the State Department at that time, see C. Van Hollen, 'The Tilt Policy Revisited: Nixon-Kissinger Geopolitics and South Asia', *Asian Survey*, April 1980, pp. 339–61.

'China factor' of the early 1970s became the 'China card' during the later years of the decade, and the Indian Ocean region (including Indochina) became an important locus for conflict between Moscow and Peking.

Yet over and above this new constellation of forces in Asia, it was the world energy situation that soon made the State Department's 1971 assessment of the comparatively minor global significance of the Indian Ocean obsolete. The first energy crisis, in the wake of the Middle Eastern war of October 1973, suddenly brought the issue of oil supplies from the Persian Gulf into the forefront of Western priorities. Once more after 1971 the Indian sub-continent was accorded a very low political priority by Washington, while Africa had still scarcely been discovered. After the end of US involvement in Vietnam, the Persian Gulf sub-region thus became the centre of American interests in the Indian Ocean.

The US government had already realised the new significance of this crisis zone before the autumn of 1973. This fact emerges clearly from a comparison of the two annual foreign policy reports presented to Congress by the President in February 1972 and May 1973. In the former report there was no reference at all to the energy question, and the Gulf was mentioned only in passing. In the second report there was talk of the 'radically' altered situation concerning energy supplies, together with the increased significance of the oil states in the Persian Gulf. In retrospect it is thus evident that during 1972 the United States first became aware that the Western world and the United States itself would soon become highly dependent on Middle East oil. Naturally, at that time no one had any premonition of boycotts and price rises. During the October war in 1973 it also became clear for the first time that the Arab states of the Gulf were prepared to join the front against Israel. And yet, in the years that followed, the United States continued to underestimate the extent to which this represented a threat to its position in the Middle East. It was not until the 'Camp David Process' that the full effects of this development emerged.

The October war and its consequences did at any rate cause the United States to focus its attention on the Persian Gulf in much the same way as the British had formerly concentrated their efforts on the defence of their Indian empire.[14] From 1972 Iran had stood in the centre of American commitments to this region, and it subsequently proved even more valuable to the United States by later refusing to be a party to the oil boycott. After a slight interval, Saudi Arabia followed Iran's example, and in 1974 its momentarily disturbed

14. See Beazley and Clark, op. cit., p. 47.

relations with the United States improved once more. In the years that followed, Iran and Saudi Arabia were the chief 'forces of moderation' on which the US government based its policy. Both states were or believed themselves to be under threat from countries or rebel movements receiving support from the Soviet Union (Iraq, South Yemen, the Dhofar rebellion in Oman). This resulted in a polarisation, which also furthered the revival of the CENTO Pact (see below). With some modifications, this polarised situation still prevailed at the beginning of the 1980s.

There were other conclusions which the United States was to draw from the October war and which likewise remained valid on into the 1980s. In its capacity as protector of Israel, the United States met with the disapproval of even moderate Arab states and since 1979 has also had to face the hostility of Iran. Even more serious for the United States was the unreliability of its European allies (and Japan) in a conflict which affected Israel's security. The decision to strengthen its own military presence in the Indian Ocean region after 1974–5 — albeit only moderately — resulted from this situation. The plans for the extension of Diego Garcia (see below) are to be viewed in this context, as are the repeated references since 1974 to the possibility of military action to secure the oilfields in the event of a 'strangulation of the industrial world' (Kissinger).[15] Utterances such as this, which were understood in the Gulf region as a threat to intervene, had the effect there of fostering a willingness to co-operate on a regional basis — a tendency which has since increased significantly but which has at the same time been subject to modification on account of Iran's self-imposed isolation in 1979 and later the armed conflict between Iran and Iraq.

In 1975 the events connected with the collapse of Portugal's colonial empire in Africa also attracted a good deal of attention in the United States, but not to the point of effecting any substantial change in America's priorities, which continued to focus on the Gulf region and the Arabian Sea.[16] The Soviet presence in Somalia was to the end regarded and treated by the United States from this perspective and in the context of the Gulf and Diego Garcia rather than as a development in another regional framework — a typical American mistake and similar to that made during the 1971 crisis in East Bengal and, later, in Afghanistan.

15. *Business Week*, Dec. 1974, quoted in Beazley and Clark, op. cit., p. 34.

16. Mr Akins, the US Ambassador to Saudi Arabia who was dismissed by Kissinger, testifying before a Senate Committee in 1976, described the attitude to the Persian Gulf in the State Department at that time as 'bordering on the hysterical'. See Beazley and Clark, ibid., p. 39.

In Africa and on the islands of the Western Indian Ocean, the United States lost influence and opportunities for access as a result of various political changes in the mid-1970s, while the Soviet Union won increased freedom of movement (also at China's expense). The US Congress prevented a more substantial intervention by the United States in the Angolan civil war. But there is no conclusive evidence that greater involvement would in the long run have led to a more favourable outcome; after all, South Africa was a party to the conflict. Subsequently the United States succeeded in regaining lost ground by means of more forceful diplomacy and economic and military aid. It also tried to mediate in Zimbabwe. This made African states more favourably disposed towards Washington but at the same time had the effect of increasing rivalry with Moscow in this area. Under new auspices — after President Carter came to office — this trend seemed at first to increase still further. But new factors were soon brought to bear on the situation in connection with the Indian Ocean.

The Carter Administration initiated negotiations with the Soviet Union with a view to mutual force limitations in the Indian Ocean, and in these talks emphasis was placed on linkage with other arms limitation topics (see p. 68 below). The littoral states and their demand for a peace zone were also referred to, at least indirectly (see p. 69 below). As already mentioned, the reason for the breakdown of these negotiations was the full-scale intervention by the Soviet Union and Cuba on the side of Ethiopia at the end of 1977 and beginning of 1978. Although Washington's policy towards Ethiopia and Somalia while the conflict between these two states had been gathering steam had not been either clear or consistent in any way,[17] the United States regarded the nature of the Soviet action and the way it was conducted as an infringement of the basic rules of competition between the super-powers. Mistrust in Washington grew stronger and there were suspicions that the Soviet Union had embarked on a major attack against Western positions in Africa. The American response to the attack by 'Katanga gendarmes' in Zaire in May 1978 was symptomatic of the hardening that had set in.

The development which ensued in the 'arc of crisis' in the Indian

17. The United States vacillated between encouraging Somalia (supported by Saudi Arabia, Iran and even Iraq) and respecting OAU principles, especially as these affected its important partner Kenya which also considered itself threatened by Somalia's irredentist claims. See p. 159.

18. Brzezinski at the beginning of 1979. See D. Braun, ' "Krisenbogen" am Indischen Ozean. Regionale Einflusssicherung und die Rolle der Ideologien', *Europa-Archiv*, vol. 34, no. 17 (Sept. 1979) pp. 513–22.

Ocean[18] exhibited clear features of an action-reaction cycle. In addition to its position in Ethiopia, the United States also lost its most important regional ally, Iran, while the Soviet Union was able to consolidate its position in South Yemen still further; Saudi Arabia had also been disappointed with the United States on more than one occasion. At the same time, however, anti-Soviet tendencies were gathering strength in South-East and East Asia, as revealed by the Sino-Japanese Treaty, the *rapprochement* between China and the United States, and the tension between Vietnam and the ASEAN states following Vietnam's invasion of Cambodia. These developments again led to a distinct polarisation between pro-American and pro-Soviet forces, further reinforcing the estrangement between the two super-powers themselves, which had already been strengthened by other events since the end of 1977 (e.g. SALT and the Middle East).

Violent Soviet activities in Afghanistan from the end of 1979 were also a consequence of US neglect of that country since the mid-1960s.[19] The United States had withdrawn still further after the overthrow of President Daoud in April 1978 and the subsequent assassination of the American ambassador in Kabul, leaving the country subject to overwhelming Soviet influence. Invasion and occupation could then be interpreted as the exercising of a regulatory function (in conjunction with a distinctly anti-Chinese component) which had become necessary in the Soviet sphere of influence. An interpretation of this kind undoubtedly corresponded to the Soviets' own understanding, and came in part to be reluctantly accepted in Western Europe and the Third World. The United States, however, immediately classified occupied Afghanistan as a 'threat to the Persian Gulf', and as such it was accorded a correspondingly high level of significance. Already in early 1980 this had emerged as the main difference between American and European appraisals of the situation.

However, the way in which the Afghanistan crisis was handled by the Islamic states, whose interests were bound to run parallel to those of the West, soon made evident the strong degree to which the Arab-Israeli conflict overlay the whole issue, preventing more far-reaching agreement, especially with the United States. Washington had to come to terms with the fact that, as a result of the long drawn-out Camp David Process, the conservative Arab Gulf states — the very states which, following the overthrow of the Shah of Iran, had been

19. The same applies to the whole Indian sub-continent. Misunderstandings between the United States on the one hand and Pakistan and India on the other were and continue to be the rule rather than the exception.

at the centre of American attention — had adopted an unequivocally firm position: against Israel, against Egypt and thus against the United States. It had become apparent once more that the United States was unable to exert enough pressure on Israel to bring about a greater willingness to compromise over the issues of Palestinian autonomy and the status of Jerusalem. Thus, at the beginning of the 1980s, the United States found itself in several ways excluded from the politics of the Persian Gulf, the area which, since 1973, had been the main focus of its interests in the Indian Ocean. It was regarded by Iran as enemy number one, it had no diplomatic relations with Iraq, and it was criticised on account of Israel by Saudi Arabia and the Emirates. These latter countries became increasingly impatient with the United States, which was but covertly appreciated as a protective power. Only the Sultanate of Oman still dared to adopt an openly pro-American stance.

The armed conflict between Iran and Iraq which began in September 1980 altered this picture somewhat, albeit only superficially. The United States had previously hoped for some improvement in its relations with Baghdad, in spite of differences over Israel, since Iraq was keen to find ways of offsetting the one-sidedness of its links with the Soviet Union. Washington now had to exercise restraint,[20] since any stance in favour of Iraq would have led to an upgrading of Iran's relationship with the Soviet Union. A development along these lines, discreetly encouraged by Moscow, could happen at any time. On the other hand, Saudi Arabia and the Emirates suddenly realized the value of a US guarantee to keep the Strait of Hormuz open. Yet this led not to a desire for a US military presence in the Gulf itself but to regional security arrangements among the Gulf states (excluding, but not directed against, Iraq). At the Islamic Summit Conference in Taif, Saudi Arabia, at the beginning of 1981, it was moreover clear that America's Middle East policy continued as before to meet with strong disapproval.

Looking at the other sub-regions of the Indian Ocean, it is Australia and South-East Asia (ASEAN) where the position and influence of the United States are both strongest and least endangered. In South Asia relations with India remain subject to constant disturbances, and Pakistan, although now again receiving considerably more attention from Washington in connection with the Persian Gulf, needs to keep other options open for itself. In the Red Sea area ties with Egypt are close, relations with Sudan are normal although somewhat erratically cultivated by the United States, and

20. This did not affect cautious steps towards a resumption of diplomatic relations.

North Yemen is a highly unstable partner. Somalia continues to be a problem case on account of its irredentist policies. In Eastern and Southern Africa, Kenya has, in view of its domestic problems, proved to be of only limited reliability, while the Republic of South Africa is an increasing burden; the Reagan Administration made several gestures, but these were met with growing mistrust from the 'frontline states'. With the islands of the Western Indian Ocean, the United States maintains only loose relations; Diego Garcia, in particular, tends to be a sore point in that area.

Thus US determination to strengthen its military presence in the Indian Ocean region, first apparent in the latter half of 1979, met with different responses in the region itself. In the pro-Western states it was more often than not welcome, while in those countries with leanings towards the Soviet Union, it tended accordingly to meet with a rebuff. Insofar as it was perceived in the context of lost American positions in Iran, the power build-up was condemned by the majority of states. Following the Soviet invasion of Afghanistan, the spectrum of opinion altered as a result of condemnation of the Soviet Union or at least disapproval of its behaviour, which was condoned by only a few Indian Ocean states, most of them African mainland or island states. Since then, the attempts of the two super-powers to extend their respective spheres of influence and their readiness to intervene have, to a quite unprecedented degree, become comparable with each other, so that they are now viewed in this respect as having 'equal status'.

In view of such a perception, founded mainly on the super-powers' demonstration of their military preparedness, other instruments by which they seek to further their influence take on added significance. In many cases, these could prove decisive in affecting the behaviour of littoral states *vis-à-vis* the competing power blocs and systems. Here the United States has so far had the advantage of being more willing and able to offer economic and humanitarian assistance alongside military aid. In most instances of acute need (natural disasters, refugee problems etc.), it has arrived promptly on the scene with both official and private aid. Most of the countries in the Indian Ocean region were hitherto fully conscious of this distinction but with the Reagan Administration, the question arose as to whether the United States would in future reduce or redistribute its non-military aid to the Third World and hence to the Indian Ocean region, on the basis of individual states' behaviour in the East-West conflict. Such a policy change could result in the United States forfeiting its important advantages in the competition between the super-powers, since the Soviet Union is mainly active with military aid, giving economic aid only very selectively. In this process the

Soviet Union and its allies could derive additional advantage from the asymmetrical situation which has developed from the fact that, in both the Arab-Israeli conflict and the confrontation between Black Africa and the Republic of South Africa, they are on the 'right' side.

In March 1981 the Congressional Research Service of the Library of Congress submitted to the House of Representatives' Foreign Affairs Committee a comprehensive report on the history of US relations with the Third World.[21] It had been drafted in 1980, after the Soviet invasion of Afghanistan. Four options were offered to Congress, listed without evaluative judgement, which could form a basis for future American policy towards the Soviet Union and the Third World:

1. *a Confrontation policy*,
2. *a Neocontainment policy*,
3. *a Flexible Response policy*, and
4. *an Economic Security policy*.

The basic features of these options are as follows:

Confrontation. This policy would aim to halt and push back Soviet expansion in the Third World and to re-establish US leadership by all appropriate means — military, economic, cultural, intelligence etc. The Persian Gulf would be a priority area, together with Central America and the Caribbean. The budgetary cost of this policy would be extremely high — as would the political cost, since the United States' allies would hardly be willing to go along with it.

Neocontainment. The main emphasis of this more restricted version of the above option would be on the military approach, including military assistance to individual Third World countries. Other means would mostly be abandoned. The policy would be limited geographically and on the whole would focus on the Gulf region and South-West Asia in general and, to a less extent, on Central America and North-East Asia. The allies would undoubtedly reject this option even more strongly than the former in view of its being largely confined to military means.

Flexible Response. This policy starts from the assumption that the Soviet Union is only expansionist within certain limits, and that limited co-operation is therefore possible between the two powers. In the Third World the United States should increasingly respond to the needs of those states with which it has common interests. In this

21. See *Soviet Policy and United States Response in the Third World*, Washington DC 1981 (US Government Printing Office).

option too, a priority is reinforcement of power in the Gulf region (and in the Indian Ocean region generally) using miltary means. Next would come Central America and the Caribbean, followed by the oil-producing countries of lesser significance such as Mexico, Nigeria and Indonesia. Economic assistance would be selectively increased and more attention would be paid to regional features. A policy of this type would be welcomed by the allies of the United States.

Economic Security. Priority would be given to securing US economic interests (raw materials, investments) principally by diversifying sources. The existing dependence on oil imports would be drastically reduced. The consolidation of United States military power in regions of the Third World is seen as counterproductive and too costly, and the Soviet Union is regarded as incapable of controlling the Third World by military means. Countries or regions with growth potential and with raw materials would receive priority, but some help would also be given to the poorer developing countries to ensure US influence there too. Such a policy would bring forth varying responses from the allies. On the one hand it would broadly correspond to the main policy guidelines followed in Europe and Japan, but on the other hand the reduction of US military protection in endangered areas of the Third World would give rise to much concern. Countries such as Saudi Arabia or Egypt would be left in a particularly vulnerable position.

On the basis of the above definitions, United States policy towards the Soviet Union and the Third World in the 1960s and 1970s would fall predominantly into the 'flexible response' category. However, towards the end of the 1970s, it was increasingly tending towards the 'neocontainment' model. The Reagan Administration came in under the banner of 'neocontainment' with some elements of 'confrontation' mixed in. A more precise analysis is not possible in this context. Future decisions taken by Washington will depend on Soviet activity in the Third World but, at the same time and by a process of osmosis, this activity will be influenced by those decisions.

(iii) *Diego Garcia and strategic positions at the beginning of the 1980s*. Since the end of the 1970s the nature of the involvement of both super-powers in the Indian Ocean region has undergone a qualitative change in the direction of stronger military postures. In the previous decade, security policy had been a much less important factor although, ever since the 'discovery' of the Indian Ocean in about 1970, this aspect had received a disproportionate amount of emphasis in political and academic statements in the East and West alike. Symptomatic of the increased importance attached to the military aspect was the decision by the United States to diversify the functions of the Diego Garcia base. This decision followed the Iranian crisis and was reinforced by the Afghan crisis.

Whereas previously some importance had been attached to not antagonising the Soviet Union and the Indian Ocean states and this had restricted the extension of the base, the United States appeared determined, once the situation had deteriorated in the Persian Gulf and surrounding area, fully to exploit the opportunities — limited by nature — offered on the island of Diego Garcia. This, moreover, was in keeping with the 'Carter Doctrine', which stressed the need for renewed reliance on US forces rather than on the role of friendly regional states.

As mentioned earlier, American interest in Diego Garcia goes back to the early 1960s.[22] This horseshoe-shaped atoll, approximately 23 km. long and 8 km. wide,[23] lies in the centre of the strategically important northern half of the Indian Ocean. It is 1,800 km. from India, 3,300 km. from both the Bab-el-Mandeb and Malacca Straits and 4,200 km. from Bahrain in the Persian Gulf. It belongs to the Chagos group of islands which form part of the British Indian Ocean Territory established in 1966. In a treaty with Britain, the United States specifically obtained the right to use the island for military purposes, while Britain is entitled to maintain a small military staff there. Around 1,000 inhabitants, who made a living from fishing and coconut products on Diego Garcia and the surrounding islands, were resettled in Mauritius, which received $1.8 million in compensation (the spending of which subsequently became a matter of dispute).

In 1968 the US Chief of Naval Operations, Admiral Moorer, suggested that Diego Garcia should be built up to provide a base for aerial reconnaissance, headquarters for a small permanent staff, and facilities for servicing aircraft-carriers on special occasions. Two further functions were added by the Joint Chiefs-of-Staff: the building of a modest communications centre and facilities for receiving strategic submarines. However, the Senate did not approve the

22. The following summary of developments up until the mid-seventies is principally based on the extensive source material given in M. Bezboruah, op. cit., pp. 51–91.

23. Another way of measuring the island, which only specifies the total length and average width, excluding the lagoon, makes the length 60 km. and the width approximately 400 m. (see map, p. 210).

plans, the main reason being that it did not think that an arms race with the Soviet Union should be initiated in the Indian Ocean. Instead, only the communications centre was to be set up. Between 1970 and 1972, $20 million were allocated for this purpose.[24] In early 1972 the Pentagon pressed for an extension of naval operations in the Indian Ocean: among the reasons mentioned were that the end of the Vietnam war was in sight, that the Soviet Union had made political and strategic gains as a result of the Indo-Pakistani war and that the Suez Canal was likely to to be re-opened. As a first move in this direction, the small naval unit stationed in Bahrain (MIDEASTFOR) was reinforced. The communications centre on Diego Garcia came into service at the beginning of 1973 under the Department of Defense as a link in the worldwide chain of such installations. Its principal function was to close a gap in the high-frequency belt and to transmit satellite information to the navy and air force.

The October 1973 war dramatically altered, for the first time, the strategic situation in the Indian Ocean, according it global significance. The US navy received instructions to conduct regular patrols; the Soviet navy was to be deprived of its capability, which it had demonstrated in 1971 and 1973, of neutralising a reinforced US naval presence by its operations. The difficulty experienced by the United States during the October war in moving supplies from the West to Israel further increased the future significance of the eastern route and hence of Diego Garcia.

For 1974, the Pentagon requested a further $29 million for improvements to Diego Garcia, which was mainly to be spent on logistical support for an aircraft-carrier task force. The Senate again refused to grant the funds. The request was repeated for 1975, plus an additional sum for the air force. The Senate approved about half the sum requested, but on condition that the whole scheme should receive prior approval from the President and should be discussed by both Houses in Congress. It was at this point that the idea was suggested of looking into the possibility of negotiating with the Soviet Union on bilateral arms limitation in the Indian Ocean. President Ford gave his approval in May 1975 but Senator Mansfield opposed the idea, whereupon Defense Minister Schlesinger made a surprise announcement, claiming that aerial photographs of Berbera in Somalia showed the advanced state of progress of the Soviet Union's 'parallel' project. The Senate now formally authorised half the sum requested by the Pentagon ($15 million) but referred the

24. By 1976, port facilities, an airfield, a fuel dump and barracks had also been built with these funds.

other half for resubmission in July 1976. In the mean time it was expected to become clear whether such restraint on the part of the United States was appreciated by the Indian Ocean littoral states, and whether or not the chances of arms control negotiations with the Soviet Union would increase as a result. Meanwhile plans for the enlargement of the Diego Garcia base were to be continued. This enlargement was to consist principally of installations providing logistic support for the navy and the air force, the dredging of the harbour, extension of runways, more accommodation and improvements to radio installations. Britain, the island's owner, agreed to these plans.

The Soviet Union's active policy towards Africa in 1975 and 1976 at first prevented any further progress towards bilateral negotiations on limiting military forces in the Indian Ocean, and in April 1976 the State Department issued a statement to that effect. This meant that there were no further obstacles to the remaining funds being made available. For Fiscal 1978 a further $6 million were requested. Work on the improvements was to be completed by 1980. A weakening of Western positions, not only in Africa but in other regions,[25] had caused Diego Garica's significance to be reassessed.

Meanwhile Diego Garcia was already being used as a base for long-distance reconnaissance aircraft (e.g. between the Philippines and Kenya). In 1977 there were 1,400 US troops (including construction workers) and twenty-five British military personnel on Diego Garcia and construction work was proceeding smoothly, even though in 1977 President Carter had proposed the 'complete demilitarisation' of the Indian Ocean (see below). It soon emerged that the United States and the Soviet Union did in fact acknowledge each other's strategic interests in the Indian Ocean, and that in the event of a reduction of military forces, Diego Garcia's role, at least as a centre for surveillance, would be retained.[26]

Carter's 'two-track' strategy — on the one hand a willingness to conduct limitation negotiations with the Soviet Union while, on the other hand, continuing the build-up on Diego Garcia — was pursued into the second half of 1979. In June of that year, at the summit meeting with Brezhnev in Vienna, the President promised that the bilateral negotiations would be 'promptly' resumed. At almost the same time the US Secretary of State and Defense

25. Bahrain also gave the Untied States notice to quit its base as did Thailand. Around 1977 it also seemed doubtful whether the Philippines would continue to allow the United States to use bases on its territory.

26. See J. Fuller, 'Dateline Diego Garcia: Paved-Over Paradise', *Foreign Policy*, no. 28, Autumn 1977, pp. 175–86.

Secretary announced a 'gradual but significant augmentation of US naval and air forces in the [Indian Ocean] region during the coming year'.[27] In fiscal year 1981 the government requested another $175 million for further work on Diego Garcia. Ultimately the hostages affair in Teheran in November 1979 and the invasion of Afghanistan a month later cleared the way for the United States to commit itself fully to Diego Garcia on account of the danger which, it was assumed, these developments constituted for the Gulf region.

Diego Garcia was of pivotal importance in the military and strategic measures — some short-term and others medium-term — decided upon at the beginning of 1980 (e.g. the securing of rights to use military facilities in the littoral states, the deployment of Marines, advance storage of arms on ships for use by the Rapid Deployment Force — RDF). Here, unlike the littoral states (Oman, Somalia, Kenya, Egypt) where political considerations admitted only limited measures in connection with facilities granted, former constraints limiting offensive capabilities on Diego Garcia were now dropped. The airstrip was to be expanded by 1982 to take B-52 bombers.[28] Seven floating arms depots were transferred to the waters around the atoll, and should remain there most of the time in future, thus requiring additional back-up facilities. The decision to place thirty naval units (including two aircraft-carrier task forces) on stand-by in the Gulf region for as long as the acute crisis lasted was another factor which raised considerably the supply and servicing functions envisaged for the atoll.[29] In August 1980 the *Washington Post* reported that Diego Garcia was to be further improved to the tune of $1,000 million(!).[30] A spokesman for the Pentagon commented on this report by saying that it was estimated that a total of $5,000 million was required over a five-year period for the United States' military presence in the Persian Gulf and Indian Ocean region — but gave no further details as to how this sum was to be spent.[31] The Reagan Administration set it at $237 million.[32]

It was certainly no coincidence that in July 1980, just as the United States — laying aside its former scruples — decided on maximum use of Diego Garcia, the OAU states unanimously demanded the

27. *The New York Times* (NYT), 28 Aug. 1979.

28. British approval for this was delayed until the summer of 1981.

29. For further details see House of Representatives, Committee of Armed Services, *Report of the Delegation to the Indian Ocean Area*, Washington DC 1980, pp. 11 f.

30. 7 August 1980, p. A1/7.

31. See *USWB*, 8.8.1980.

32. See *ibid.*, 13.3.1981.

return of the atoll to Mauritius, claiming that the military base represented a 'threat to Africa'.[33] It is a near-certainty that, in the context of their zone of peace policy, the majority of the Indian Ocean states, for whatever reasons, will endorse this demand. The Soviet Union and its allies will do all they can to encourage this. The United States, in its turn, will use 'Afghanistan' against the Soviet Union and the main outcome will be a situation of political stalemate.

It is still open to question whether the new 'Trident' nuclear ballistic missile submarines, which have recently come into service, will be considered for use in the Indian Ocean. Compared with the 'Poseidon' class, the 'Tridents', the MIRV missiles which have a much longer range, are also able to remain operating 'on station' for much longer periods. This would remove one reason which hitherto stood against the assumption — promoted mainly by the Soviet Union — that US submarines were being deployed in the Indian Ocean, namely the short stayover time as compared with the long journey from and back to base (Guam). If 'Tridents' were to be introduced into the Indian Ocean, this would certainly involve new functions for Diego Garcia (e.g. for rotating personnel). But it is equally certain that use of such an option by the United States would hardly remain secret for very long, and would give the Soviet Union substantial additional opportunities for exerting political influence on the Indian Ocean states. This is one more reason why the United States would need to weigh up any possible moves in this direction with much care.

Even without the submarine factor, the strategic position in the Indian Ocean exhibits a political asymmetry which is to the disadvantage of the United States, for the simple reason that the superpowers do not operate in a vacuum but subject to the piercing gaze and outspoken criticism of the Third World. The Soviet Union is able — even leaving aside Afghanistan — to demonstrate its military strength on a long-term basis from its own territory. Its advantage is that it is also an Asian power, a geographical advantage which is not perceived as a threat by many, perhaps even by the majority, of the states in the region. The military presence of the Soviet Union is also much less visible than the US presence, which requires much more effort for it to be built up. Thus, in the northwest Indian Ocean region, as far as military strike capability is concerned, the position of the Soviet Union is for the time being far superior to that of the United States and other Western defence capabilities combined. Moreover, in their implementation, the military measures decided upon under the Carter Administration

33. See *IHT*, 5.7.1980, p. 1.

have already run into considerable problems, not least because other zones of potential conflict are left more vulnerable as personnel and material shortages make themselves felt.[34] Even so, in the course of 1980, the United States did succeed in conquering a series of difficulties with greater assertiveness than had been foreseen in many quarters, and as a result it could not be denied that the measures acted as a deterrent.

However it is another negative factor in the balance that by further reinforcing its military presence near the Gulf region, the United States comes up against the desire of the littoral states to keep their distance from 'super-power rivalry', and the West's claims that it is in favour of non-alignment are scarcely made more credible in the process. A former US Under-Secretary of State, Mr Newsom, drew the Senate's attention to these points and, speaking of the Indian Ocean region, he added: 'In all countries there are images and political clichés about past colonisation and intervention which come to the fore when a Western country talks of securing facilities or establishing bases.'[35]

On the other hand, following the outbreak of the conflict between Iran and Iraq in September 1980, it became apparent that, in view of this new threat to their own security, the US presence in and around the Gulf was now regarded in a more favourable light by Saudi Arabia, the Emirates and other states of the region. The United States' evident readiness to guarantee the flow of oil through the Strait of Hormuz by the commitment of massive military resources did not fail to have a psychological impact in the Indian Ocean, all the more so in that it was not possible to regard this commitment merely in the context of 'super-power rivalry'. In the face of this acute crisis, there was also a quite unexpected demonstration of Western unity and co-operation. Moreover, the Iran-Iraq conflict has furnished an additional scenario to the list hitherto current among Third World Indian Ocean states: two non-aligned Islamic states are at war with each other while outside powers have so far been only peripherally involved. This conflict has brought out into the open the fact that there are threats to the economic nerve of the

34. See 'Can we Defend the Gulf?', *Newsweek*, 4.2.1980, pp. 11 f; J.K. Cooley, 'Indian Ocean Crises stretch Navy uncomfortably thin', *The Christian Science Monitor*, 31.3.1980, p. 8.

35. Testifying before the Senate Sub-committee on the Middle East and South Asia, in *USWB*, 8.2.1980, pp. 11–13. A year later, following the change of Administration in Washington, General Jones, Chairman of the Joint Chiefs-of-Staff, appearing before another Senate Committee, expressed a similar opinion when, *inter alia*, he said: 'There is some distrust of us over some of our policies for the area' (ibid., 17.3.1981, p. 17).

West (and of numerous Third World states too), which have their sole origin in regional tension, and this has caused the activities of outside powers in the Indian Ocean to appear in a new light. The 'zone of peace' has retreated one step further into the realm of utopia.

After the Reagan Administration came into office, the military build-up in the Gulf and Indian Ocean region received even greater priority, both within the United States, in the form of naval programmes, the creation of new transportation capacity and the accelerated preparation of the Rapid Deployment Force, as well as by seeking to improve the facilities offered by Egypt, Somalia, Kenya, and Oman and those on Diego Garcia. For the build-up in the region itself, over $2,000 million was earmarked over a five-year period beginning in 1981. This represented a 25 per cent rise on the appropriation voted under the Carter Administration.[36] The military aid programme was extended, especially for Kenya, Sudan, Egypt, Oman and Thailand. A new programme was prepared for Pakistan.[37] General Jones, Chairman of the Joint Chiefs-of-Staff, justified the measures to Congress on the basis of the need to counteract a military attack by the Soviet Union or its allies in the Gulf region. To this end, he argued that it was necessary to envisage a wide range of deployment modes 'to an extent perhaps unprecedented in our history'.[38] In October 1981, however, the carrier force was reduced to the single battle group that was deployed prior to the acute crisis in late 1979.

In late 1981, the *Sunday Times* of London published a report on a secret American 'Tripwire' plan enunciated by the then Secretary of State, Alexander Haig. It was supposedly designed to overcome logistical problems in the event of a Soviet invasion of Iran or any other Gulf state. The idea was to bring in a few hundred American soldiers close to Soviet targets; should they be attacked, there would be US retaliation in a place of American choosing.[38] In a scenario like this or one similar to it, there can be little doubt that Iran is an area where a direct military clash between the superpowers is most likely to occur. Indications are that the Soviets are equally aware of this, and are correspondingly wary.

36. ibid., 13.3.1981, p. 12.
37. ibid., 17.3.1981, p. 18.
38. See Rashna Writer, 'Strategische Dimensionen des Indischen Ozeans', *Europa-Archiv*, vol. 37, no. 11 (June 1982), p. 349.
39. '. . . The neo-conservatism of this period led to a reassertion of the role of the working class in the process of socialist transformation and to a reaffirmation of the indispensability of Marxist-Leninist doctrine *vis-à-vis* the variants of national socialism' (Beazley and Clark, op. cit., p. 67).

The US build-up was, and continues to be, strongly and widely criticized both within the United States and abroad. One argument used is that it is futile even to contemplate balancing the Soviet Union's geostrategic advantage, while in other quarters there are doubts as to US ability adequately to carry through the plan. Others have a fundamental objection to any increase in US arms expenditure for use in a Third World region. In fact US preoccupation with a whole host of military issues risks pushing the multiple threat to stability in the 'arc of crisis' in the Indian Ocean beyond the field of vision. And yet, particularly after the occupation of Afghanistan, the West must consider all aspects of the Soviet Union's political aims and strategy in the Gulf area including Moscow's capability for attack or subversion. The Soviet Union has made it clear that it claims a say in Gulf affairs. The means and methods of its future conduct can to some extent be deduced from the ways in which it has hitherto behaved in the Indian Ocean region.

(c) *The Soviet Union*

(i) *The ideological framework and the revolution from above.* Since the middle 1950s the premises underlying Soviet relations with the Third World, and thus with most of the Indian Ocean littoral states, and the characteristics of these relations have undergone repeated change. Under Khrushchev, special importance was attributed to ideological considerations, leading to a preference for those states which appeared to correspond most closely to the changing socialist concepts prevailing in Moscow during those years. Under Brezhnev and Kosygin, ideological experiments receded for a time in favour of more balanced relations with a greater number of Third World states. In the course of this development, plain utilitarian considerations of an economic and strategic nature gained the upper hand. An example of this new stance was provided by the change in Soviet relations with the non-Arab states of the Middle East and South Asia — Turkey, Iran, Pakistan — which were members of Western-oriented alliances and towards which Moscow made considerable overtures at that time.

In the first half of the 1970s this conservatism — together with the experience of setbacks, of which Egypt was the outstanding example — appears to have led to a renewed strengthening of ideological considerations, albeit this time more orthodox ones.[39] A tangible outcome of deliberate endeavours to form Moscow- aligned cadres, particularly in the armed forces, was the creation of several African and Asian régimes with 'Marxist-Leninist orientation'. A further outcome was an effective division of labour in the Socialist camp whereby friendly Third World countries (Cuba, Vietnam) and allies have taken over important tasks aimed at the 'construction of a socialist order' in these 'nationally liberated' and 'socially progressive' states.[40]

It was in connection with the strategic arms limitation talks (SALT) around 1969–70 that, for the first time, the Soviet Union began to be treated by the United States as a world power with equal rights. At the XXIV Party Congress in April 1971, Foreign Minister Gromyko declared that thereafter no question of any importance could be settled without the Soviet Union's participation or in a way which would be to its disadvantage.[41] Regarding the 'zones of national liberation' (i.e. the Third World), Soviet politicians and ideologues expected in the early 1970s a further shift of emphasis in favour of the Socialist bloc and against the capitalist-imperialist system. Internal and regional conflicts in the Third World were regarded as the inevitable birth-pangs of a new social and political order. The process of détente with the West was, however, to be insulated against these conflicts, since at that time détente influenced the central balance of forces to Moscow's advantage.[42]

After the setbacks with which the Soviet Union had had to contend at the beginning of the 1970s, the crises in Angola and Ethiopia offered from 1974 the first opportunity of demonstrating the new global reach and practical flexibility of the Socialist system. Backed by skilled diplomacy, the Soviets and their highly motivated Cuban assistants in revolution — taking into account the regional constellation, the predominant mood in Africa and the Third World as well as the West's indecisiveness — moved in troops and equipment, the quantity and composition of which were remarkably well-suited to military requirements.

The emergence of an increasing number of socialist-oriented states in the Third World seems to the Soviet Union to confirm the doctrine that, in accordance with the laws of history, an 'anti-imperialist vanguard' is now fighting on the side of socialism. (The Soviet claim that the non-aligned states should recognise the Socialist bloc as their natural ally falls under this heading.) As a

40. It is significant in this connection that the new Soviet constitution of 1977 contains a chapter on foreign policy which was not in the previous version of 1936. This chapter lays down *inter alia* the tasks of consolidating world socialism, of supporting national liberation movements and social change. See Aspaturian, op. cit., p. 3.

41. ibid., p. 1.

42. See B. Sen Gupta, *Soviet-Asian Relations in the 1970s and Beyond*, New York 1976.

result of this increase, ideological classification of Third World countries is made easier, for behind the vanguard there are states pursuing an increasingly anti-imperialist policy in the struggle for national and economic independence. The states or regimes still dependent on imperialism are now at the rear end of this formation.[43]

From the Soviet point of view, this development increases polarisation both globally, between the capitalist industrialised states and a growing section of the Third World, and, within the Third World states themselves (those which do not belong to the 'vanguard'), between governments and masses. To the extent that individual states are adopting a non-capitalist path of development, and that at an international level more and more countries of the Third World come to acknowledge the Socialist camp as their natural ally, the 'correlation of forces' is further shifted to the disadvantage of imperialism. The latter tries to stem the tide, even indulging in counter-revolutionary and interventionist activities, and is given backing by China. The forging of a link between these two power groups again represents a dangerous challenge to the Soviet-led camp. It is thus all the more urgent that all anti-imperialist powers in the Southern Hemisphere should close ranks and participate in the 'Socialist World System'.

It is therefore the responsibility of the Socialist camp — again according to the Soviet interpretation — to give constant active support to the just war of the exploited against the exploiters, the peoples' struggle for their liberation, since only by such assistance can the individual case be decided in favour of socialism and against imperialism. But when imperialism itself intervenes militarily (e.g. in order to secure advanced bases and — usually in direct connection with these — economic advantages) then, in its own state interest and for the sake of self-defence, the Soviet Union must join battle, not in a spirit of adventurism, certainly, but always after having carefully weighed up the forces involved. One significant factor in this connection is the enemy's degree of resoluteness and willpower[44]. From this follows the significance of military power:

43. Other Communist writers distinguish between the 'tendency to develop into a peoples' democracy' in Mozambique, Angola, Ethiopia and South Yemen and those countries which are still at the stage of 'national democratic development', e.g. Algeria. See H. Baumann, 'Die politischen Systeme in den afro-asiatischen Ländern', *Asien, Afrika, Lateinamerika*, vol. 8, no. 1 (1980), p. 94.

44. See Sen Gupta, op. cit., p. 21. See also H. Adomeit, *Das Vorgehen der Sowjetunion in internationalen Krisen und Konflikten*, Ebenhausen, March 1980 (Stiftung Wissenschaft und Politik, SWP-AP 2250).

as the most potent single factor in the multiple 'correlation of forces', it can be used to carry through decisions swiftly. Nonetheless, Soviet ideology is at pains not to lay too much emphasis on this factor and instead places in the centre of the picture the interaction of non-military forces — social, revolutionary and progressive — because in the final analysis it is only these which enable the laws of history to unfold.[45]

It is from this framework, in which ideology and power politics stand in relation to each other, that future patterns for Soviet dealings with the Third World emerge. The Soviet Union is able to give effective support to the forces of 'progress' in the Third World wherever these forces have gained a position of power within the state, even as a tiny minority, and wherever Soviet military power (or that of one of its allies) is sufficient to secure the socialist transformation of a state on a long-term basis 'after a careful evaluation of the objective forces'.

Soviet policy in the Indian Ocean region exhibits in typical fashion this mixture of ideology and power politics as it developed in the 1970s out of the Soviet twin claim to a say in global affairs and to its role of unrestricted leadership in the Socialist camp. In any assessment of Soviet conduct both these factors must be viewed together. Thus the Soviet Union's policy towards Afghanistan, in spite of appearances of 'peaceful coexistence', had for decades been founded on and supported by ideology. Had this not been so, the close Soviet links since the early 1960s with what later became the Khalk and Parcham factions would never have developed. It was this link which ultimately guaranteed the success of the 1978 coup.

Wherever there is a basis on which it can build, the Soviet Union attempts to forge ideological links of this kind. Setbacks have been numerous, for the power of nationalism as against 'internationalist' solidarity was frequently underestimated.[46] Where, on the other hand, the Soviet Union succeeds in influencing the social structures in individual developing countries according to ideological patterns, cadres emerge, willing to follow the Moscow line. However, to what extent these will withstand the temptation of falling back on attitudes of 'national communism' has not so far been adequately demonstrated.

Moscow's surest recipe for success in promoting revolution in the Third World is Communist infiltration of the armed forces, and

<hr>

45. See Aspaturian, op. cit., p. 10.
46. Cf. Soviet and Cuban efforts in the Horn of Africa in the spring of 1977 to set up a Socialist Federation comprising Ethiopia, Somalia and Eritrea.

conditions favour this wherever arms and military assistance is provided on a large scale over a long period of time. A publication in 1974 of the Moscow-oriented Communist Party of India entitled *Political Role of the Army in the Developing Countries* states: 'As a rule victory for the revolution is impossible in the face of opposing monolithic armed forces. For success it is essential to win over progressive and patriotic officers and men.'[47] Where this has been achieved, the ground can be rapidly prepared for a 'revolution from above', provided that Soviet military might assists in ensuring that the process is made 'irreversible'. Another Indian observer offered the following verdict on Afghanistan:

The April Revolution was indeed the first step in the direction of a military intervention. . . . [The Soviets] were aware of the need to protect the puppet government in Afghanistan with military force at some stage. They therefore kept themselves in readiness to provide such protection.[48]

Afghanistan established new standards for which the ground had to be ideologically prepared. A Soviet commentator wrote:

What kind of a revolution is it which has to be supported with the help of Soviet troops? What kind of a new government is it against which not only landowners but also peasants take up arms? These questions are quite legitimate. But, this commentator goes on, what was the 'political vanguard' in Afghanistan to do? 'Should it have waited until the political consciousness of millions had been awakened? No. We either had to bring in troops or else allow the Afghan revolution to go under. We decided in favour of troops. [. . .] There are certain situations in which non-intervention is a scandal and a betrayal. Such a situation was developing in Afghanistan.[49]

(ii) *Constants and variables of Soviet policy towards the littoral states.* 'Afghanistan' clarified many things. The military occupation of a non-aligned, strongly Islamic neighouring state, which had hitherto been predominantly neutral in the East-West conflict and which was situated close to the Persian Gulf, again showed both the limits of a policy of détente and the extent of Soviet confidence in

47. Quoted in A.G. Noorani, 'Lessons of Afghanistan', *The Indian Express*, 10.1.1980.

48. N. Joshi, 'Soviet Intervention in Afghanistan' in *Foreign Affairs Reports*, vol. 29, no. 7 (July 1980), p. 132.

49. Alexander Bovin in *Moscow News*, no. 16, 20.4.1980. Several extracts from this statement were also included in the 'Letter from Moscow' which Bovin and Primakov sent to *L'Unità*, the official Italian Communist Party newspaper. Its editor refuted the Soviet arguments in a vehement statement of principle in the issue of 25.4.1980. See 'Eine Polemik zwischen Moskau und der KPI über Afghanistan', in *Osteuropa*, vol. 29, no. 10 (Oct. 1980), pp. A457–63.

pursuing ideologically-founded goals that were achievable by force. But at the same time this action also showed evidence of a hitherto unsuspected accumulation of Soviet miscalculations with regard to reactions in the West and in the Third World, as well as to the consequences of occupying Afghanistan itself. The uncertainty which has emerged from the situation and the political and economic strains which are to be expected over a long period, represent for the time being a negative outcome for the Soviet Union in comparison with the situation before the Communist putsch of April 1978. Up to that point Soviet security was in no way threatened by Afghanistan; the formula of 'peaceful co-existence' guaranteed a high degree of Soviet influence (Western competition having long since ceased to be a relevant factor); in the Third World, and the Islamic world particularly, the Soviet Union had a reputation for respecting and dealing discreetly with other forms of government and belief and for well-calculated risk-taking, as in Africa. Since December 1979 all this has changed.[50]

The motives for Soviet behaviour may be at least partly located in the fact, already mentioned, that the Soviet Union's self-image had undergone a change according to the formula: world power plus ideological leadership equals a new quality of global influence. A Western interpretation of history would regard this as the temptation and arrogance of power, such as Henry Kissinger describes in his capacity as an historian (even if, as a politician, he himself was not always able to resist the tendency): 'The nemesis of power is that, except in the hands of a master, reliance upon it is more likely to produce a contest of arms than of self-restraint.'[51]

A glance back at some of the relevant trends and phases of Moscow's policy towards the Indian Ocean region in the 1970s contributes to the precision of our analysis of the constants and variables that make up Soviet conduct. In this decade, the elements of this policy evolved with remarkable swiftness, since in the Indian Ocean three different axes of conflict — East-West, North-South and Sino-Soviet — cut across and overlay one another. Long-term projections had to be adapted to unforeseen circumstances; the defence of the Soviet state evolved to embrace the defence of an ever wider glacis; and support given to distant allies in South-East Asia and in Africa extended ever farther the horizon of interests. The

50. The strategic advantages which accrued to the Soviet Union from the occupation of Afghanistan (see below) can hardly compensate for all the drawbacks.

51. Henry Kissinger, 'Bismarck: the White Revolution', *Daedalus*, vol. 97, no. 3 (Summer 1968), p. 919.

results of this state of affairs would not have been very encouraging for the Soviet Union had it not been able to draw strong and lasting political advantage from configurations which it had not created: from the anti-Western attitude which fuelled the Southern Africa syndrome and the much more explosive Arab-Israeli conflict.

In terms of top national security interests the Indian Ocean was still, around 1970, a low-priority region for the Soviet Union, just as it was for the United States. There was no state in the region which represented a direct threat since, already at the beginning of the 1960s, Iran had refused to have US bases on its soil and there was no longer an American military presence in Pakistan.[52] The only danger stressed by the Soviet Union at the time was linked to the possibility of the United States deploying strategic submarines in the northern Indian Ocean (see below). During this period Moscow had good relations with a series of Indian Ocean states, both littoral and hinterland — Afghanistan, India, Iraq, Egypt, Sudan, Somalia, North and South Yemen — and there was scope for further development. All these countries, moreover, were receiving Soviet military aid. A distinct improvement in previously strained relations with two allies of the West, Iran and Pakistan, was achieved, and this resulted in a partial neutralisation of the CENTO pact (see below). This development was first and foremost an outcome of improved economic relations with and credit assistance from the Soviet Union.

The way Soviet economic and military aid was distributed showed a clear emphasis in favour of the regions bordering on the Soviet Union in the Middle East and South Asia, extending as far as the Red Sea and the Horn of Africa, where Western-oriented Ethiopia also received Soviet economic aid and, to a limited degree, arms.[53] In Eastern and Southern Africa and the off-lying islands there was indeed some degree of political sympathy for the Soviet Union, but Chinese competition was already emerging alongside. On the Eastern flank of the Indian Ocean region, in South-East Asia, the Soviet Union, after its setback in Indonesia in 1965, had very little success in attempting to gain a new foothold, aside from establishing diplomatic relations with Malaysia and Singapore. The Vietnam war did however offer opportunities for furthering influence in the medium term. Australia, lastly, was an indisputable outpost of the West.

52. The U-2 incident in 1960, involving a US plane on mission from Peshawar in North Pakistan, brought to an end this covert operation.

53. However, the Suez Canal was closed, which diminished the value of this geographically defined sphere of influence between the Mediterranean and the Horn of Africa.

In 1969 Brezhnev had made his proposal for a Collective Security System for Asia,[54] in connection with the plan launched at around the same time by Kosygin for the creation of a zone of economic co-operation between the Soviet Union and Iran, Afghanistan, Pakistan and India. As a long-term strategy, the Collective Security System for Asia had diverse aims: against China and the West as enemies of Asian security; to establish the Soviet Union as an Asian as well as a European power;[55] to alter gradually the economic and social conditions in the area in its favour; to secure a corresponding influence in controversial Asian issues; and finally to put an end to China's and Japan's territorial claims against it.[56] From 1968 the Soviet Union had a regular, albeit limited, naval presence in the Indian Ocean and this was meant to have a political impact in the above context. It emerged from the various initiatives that Moscow's medium-term goal was to create a position of superiority for itself *vis-à-vis* China and the West in the area between its southern frontiers and the Indian Ocean. Military means would then be used to underpin and maintain this position.

Moreover, if these aims were viewed in the context of the Soviet Union's favourable position in Arab states at the beginning of the 1970s and in the light of a prospective re-opening of the Suez Canal, then, according to Richard Loewenthal, Moscow's strategy was 'aimed at creating beyond the Soviet Union's southern borders a zone of Soviet penetration different in nature from the Communist-controlled European glacis to the West but somewhat analagous in its imperial function — a zone of influence whose limits would stretch from the Mediterranean through the Red Sea and Persian Gulf to the Indian Ocean'.[57] In 1976 Loewenthal reached the conclusion that these aims, even though they had been pursued with a remarkable combination of political and economic means, had so far not been achieved. None of the important states of this region was, he argued, exclusively under Moscow's influence, so that to this extent Soviet 'counter-imperialism' lacked an empire.[58]

The most severe setback, for which the Soviet Union was not able to compensate during the 1970s, was Egypt's break with Moscow. This dragged on over several years and it was not until early in 1976

54. Cf. D. Braun and J. Glaubitz, 'Kollektive Sicherheit als Konzept Sowjetischer Asienpolitik', *Europa-Archiv*, vol. 29, no. 1 (Jan. 1974).

55. This intention was already noted in the Indian Foreign Ministry's annual report in 1970. Cf. Beazley and Clark, op. cit., p. 110.

56. The latter in parallel with Europe and CSCE.

57. 'Soviet "counter-imperialism" ', in *Problems of Communism*, vol. 25, no. 6 (Nov.-Dec. 1976), p. 55.

58. Ibid., p. 63.

that the bilateral treaty of friendship was also revoked (see below). Sudan also changed direction after an abortive coup in 1971 in which the Soviet Union had been implicated. Under Saudi Arabian influence, the Arab Republic of Yemen moved away from the Soviet Union to some extent. As a result of these developments, at the time of the re-opening of the Suez Canal in 1975, the strategically significant area around the Red Sea was largely free of Soviet dominance.

Soviet efforts to make a regional partner out of Iraq, replacing Egypt, were also unsuccessful. It is true that in 1972 a treaty was signed (see below) whereby close links were established between Iraq and Comecon, and by giving military aid the Soviet Union would obtain the right to use Iraqi airfields and dock in the Gulf harbour of Umm Qasr — but all this was counter-balanced by the resulting estrangement of Iran. The Soviet Union's endeavours to achieve a diplomatic balance remained unsuccessful, until a temporary understanding was reached between the enemies in March 1975. This understanding, to which the Soviet Union did not in fact contribute, changed the configuration of circumstances, but ultimately not to the Soviets' advantage. Iraq embarked on a course which involved cautious distancing from Moscow, later reinforced by a clash of interests in the southern part of the Arabian Peninsula and in the Horn of Africa (Eritrea, Somalia, South Yemen) as well as by Iraqi *raison d'état* connected with its domestic politics, its economic situation, its non-aligned status, and so on. A particularly low point was reached with Iraqi condemnation of the Soviet invasion of Afghanistan.[59]

By contrast, Soviet endeavours to secure influence fared considerably better in India, though not in South Asia generally. India's neighbours were all wary of her aspirations to have a position of dominance, and this was apparent in the foreign policy options which they chose to adopt. To counterbalance the Moscow-Delhi link, these states secured for themselves stronger ties with Washington and Peking. However, this did not represent a real setback for the Soviet Union, because not only does it consider its maintenance of a special relationship with India to be a cornerstone of its Asia policy but, because of India's influence in the Third World, it also supports by this friendship its policy towards the developing countries.[60] At the same time, the Soviet Union needs India's help in

59. See interview with Foreign Minister Hammadi in *Newsweek*, 25.2.1980.

60. India is invariably mentioned in every important Soviet statement made on relations with the Third World. In the political exhortations published for 1 May 1981, India was the only non-Socialist country mentioned by name. See *Times of India*, 13.4.81, p. 15.

the Sino-Soviet conflict. Soviet discomfort was clearly evident at every step that seemed to be leading towards a normalisation of relations between India and China — resumption of full diplomatic relations in 1976, a visit by the Indian Foreign Minister to Peking in the spring of 1979 followed by an obvious interest on China's part in improving relations. Soviet relief that so far none of these steps had actually led to a qualitative change was equally evident. A situation in which India requires Soviet backing against China (particularly against a US-backed China) is thus perpetuated, and moreover India in many foreign policy. issues almost automatically takes up a position against China, out of rivalry, thus supporting the Soviet Union.

Outside South Asia, this rivalry was most clearly visible in South-East Asia (the ASEAN states and Indochina). Because India, from early on, had had an interest in having a friendly state on the southern border of its potential enemy, China, it had built up its relations with Hanoi even before the end of the Vietnam war. When the war was over, and particularly after the fall of Saigon, these relations were stepped up and, in order to maintain them, India gave generous economic and technical aid to Vietnam, especially after 1977.[61] The Chinese 'punitive action' against Vietnam, in February and March 1979, was strongly condemned by India which, in the middle of 1980, recognised the Heng-Samrin regime in Cambodia. All of this fitted entirely with Soviet interests and at the same time had the effect that the ASEAN states and Australia again distanced themselves from India. As a result, polarisation in this part of Asia — where China, the ASEAN states and Australia equated 'Afghanistan' with the Vietnamese occupation of Cambodia — increased further.[62] Vietnam has thus been another pillar of the Soviet Union's policy towards Asia, at least since 1975 when it became clear that Hanoi had turned its back on Peking.[63] Since then

61. See D. Braun, *Indien und die Dritte Welt, Fallstudie zur Entwicklung von Süd-Süd Beziehungen*, Ebenhausen, July 1979 (Stiftung Wissenschaft und Politik, SWP-S 272), especially pp. 137 f.

62. In a speech at Alma Ata in August 1980, Brezhnev addressed the forces in Asia that were friendly and those that were hostile to the Soviet Union. Among the former he mentioned by name Mongolia, Vietnam, Laos, Cambodia, North Korea, Afghanistan and India, and among the latter, alongside China, Pakistan. Japan was referred to with scepticism and he was guarded on Iran.

63. See H. Bräker, 'Die Aufnahme Vietnams in den RGW und die Politik der Sowjetunion und der VR China in Südostasien', Cologne 1979 (Berichte des Bundesinstituts für ostwissenschaftliche und internationale Studien, no. 7).

the increasingly close co-operation between the two states (in mid-1978 Vietnam joined COMECON and at the end of the same year concluded a treaty of friendship) has been, for Vietnam as much as for the Soviet Union, a direct function of their conflict with China. Meanwhile, it would appear that this state of conflict will persist. Steps in the direction of a cautious *rapprochement* between the Soviet Union and China (initial talks were held in Moscow) were again brought to a standstill after the Soviet invasion of Afghanistan, and in Hanoi a series of purges removed from the Party and state leadership all those individuals who had shown any leanings towards a policy that would take greater account of Chinese interests. It thus appears that what China is rejecting is not so much Vietnamese striving for hegemony in Indochina itself as the close links — including their military aspects — maintained by Hanoi with the Soviet Union. This 'encirclement' is unacceptable to China, but by the same token the Chinese threat to Vietnam forces Hanoi to seek support outside the region. It is unlikely that this tangled state of affairs can be unravelled in the near future (see pp. 122 f.).

For the Soviet Union, close links with Vietnam, and thereby with Laos[64] and Cambodia, represent a significant strategic gain in the South China Sea, within reach both of the US bases in the Philippines and of the Malacca Straits and the Indian Ocean. Moreover, Moscow drew lasting ideological advantage from the fact that it had supported the 'right side' in an Asian *bellum justum* against the super-power America. Vietnam was subsequently to lean increasingly on the Soviet Union to the point where, in the words of a current Chinese dictum, it became 'the Cuba of Asia'. On the other hand, Vietnam's economic and organisational weakness in all areas other than the military is proving an increasing drain on Soviet resources. As a result of the guarded attitude of the ASEAN states, which turned increasingly against the Soviet Union after the invasion of Afghanistan, Moscow has suffered a net loss in the Indian Ocean region, the more so since this attitude on the part of the ASEAN states involves a more positive approach to China and causes them to turn increasingly to the United States.

At this point it should be stressed as a provisional conclusion that Soviet policy in South and South-East Asia since the beginning of the 1970s has been strongly influenced by the Sino-Soviet conflict. In

---

64. It is interesting to note that, in Brezhnev's report to the XXVI Party Congress of the CPSU in February 1981, Laos was the only other Third World country to be included, alongside Vietnam and Cuba, as a member of the 'Community of Socialist States'. This was no doubt intended as a warning to China.

South Asia, because of its strong links with India, the Soviet Union is in a favourable position. There is little likelihood of a significant *rapprochement* between India and China, and the varying attitudes of the smaller states in this sub-region are of little significance to the Soviet Union — with the sole exception of Pakistan. In South-East Asia, on the other hand, the Soviet Union backs Vietnam, which has been extremely isolated within the sub-region since its invasion of Cambodia. Its chances of surviving a confrontation with China in the long term are none too certain. With regard to Vietnam, China has a geographical advantage over the Soviet Union, just as in the case of Afghanistan geography favours the Soviet Union rather than China.

While, as described earlier, US interest in the Indian Ocean was — from around 1974 increasingly, and by the end of the decade almost exclusively — focused on the Persian Gulf, the Soviet field of activity has by contrast steadily widened. It is thus debated both in the Third World and in the West whether the Soviet Union will in the long term be in a position to maintain and consolidate its geographically distant 'acquisitions' in South-East Asia, in Southern Africa and perhaps also Ethiopia. This is likely to depend not least on the general approach and priorities of the Andropov leadership.[65] But it is most probable that the trend which became evident in the second half of the 1970s will continue. It is thus likely that the Soviet Union will do its best to secure its geographical glacis with a view to creating the 'zone of Soviet penetration' referred to above. Since the Iranian and Afghan crises, the conditions for such a strategy on the part of the Soviet Union have greatly improved and are certainly better now than they were in the mid-1970s.

It is true that with Afghanistan the Soviet Union created significant problems for itself in the short and medium term; but viewed in the long term, it is not unreasonable for Moscow to hope that it may ultimately succeed in pacifying the country. This hope seems all the more realistic given the unstable situation in the states which are Afghanistan's neighbours, Iran and Pakistan. Despite the size of the resistance movement in Afghanistan, which in the years following the occupation increased in terms of both numbers and calibre, it is hardly conceivable that an eventual 'political solution' would fail to guarantee the most important Soviet interests and above all a regime in Kabul which is not openly anti-Soviet. How much Sovietisation can be accomplished there in the long run is still an open question. At

65. See B. Meissner, 'Sowjetische Aussenpolitik und Afghanistan', in *Aussenpolitik*, vol. 31, no. 3 (1980), pp. 260–83.

the beginning of the 1980s both Iran and Pakistan lay more squarely in the Soviet zone of influence, and a wide array of political instruments, including subversion or scarcely concealed support for internal opposition groups, can be more effectively employed there than in previous years.[66] Iran is in such an exposed position on the Soviet Union's borders that it must be regarded as a primary target of Moscow's strivings for dominance. Yet the Soviet Union is most likely to exercise restraint until such time as changed internal as well as regional political conditions there allow it to make moves in that direction. In the mean time it has at its disposal a Communist party faithful to Moscow (Tudeh) which until very recently has been in tactical alliance with the ruling Islamic forces.

Since 1979–80 Moscow's shadow has been falling more than ever upon the Arab Gulf states. The regimes in these states fear direct Soviet military action much less than they fear internal instabilities which could be fostered by too obvious a Western military presence. At the same time, in the 'moderate' Gulf states those anti-Western 'radical' forces which are opposed to their own governments obtain encouragement from far-reaching parallels between Soviet and pan-Arab rejection of the Camp David process. This mixture of instability and resentment against the West is explosive, and opens up increasing opportunities for the Soviet Union to exert its influence in the future. In the Arabian peninsula it already has a solid bridgehead in South Yemen, a country which also receives support from Cuba and East Germany. The uncertainties which were prevalent there between 1976 and the beginning of 1978 seem to have been overcome. New possibilities for South Yemen to influence North Yemen have also emerged. The effects of a union between them or even only of increased co-operation would be enough to arouse fears in Saudi Arabia, given Aden's military strength.

The conflict between Iran and Iraq initially also seemed to be working to the advantage of the Soviet Union rather than to that of the United States. In early 1981 a French Middle East expert saw the situation as follows:

Owing to its alliance with Syria, the Soviet Union has again secured a foothold in the Middle East in a spectacular manner. It has thus improved the prospects of making its influence felt in efforts to resolve conflicts in the Gulf region. Some observers are for this reason already speaking of a 'new Yalta' in the East.[67]

66. See the circumstances surrounding the hi-jacking of a Pakistani plane to Kabul in March 1981.

67. P. Rondot, 'Irak gegen Iran: Krieg ohne Entscheidung?' in *Europa-Archiv*, vol. 36, no. 3 (Feb. 1981), p. 74. In this connection the question

In as much as the 'doctrine' for peace and security in the Gulf region, which Brezhnev proposed at the end of 1980 during his visit to Delhi,[68] was supposed to lead in this direction, it was certainly not judged a success. Even a commentator on Indian state radio was sceptical:

It is, however, mainly for the superpowers to discipline themselves on the line stipulated in the doctrine. [. . .] Frankly, current indications do not hold out much hope.[69]

With the Lebanon war in 1982 it turned out that the Soviet foothold in Syria was not secure enough in the Arab quicksand. Moscow's role was reduced to that of an angry spectator, watching from the sidelines as the United States' mediation went its way. However, it is too early to judge whether subsequent acts in this drama will not offer the Soviet Union the chance of a spectacular re-entry, on the lines of developments after the Arab defeat in 1967; Israel's predominance could once more open for it the doors of even conservative Arab countries. Regarding the Iran-Iraq conflict, it is still Moscow that enjoys near-normal bilateral relations with both warring parties whereas Washington does not.

It is thus that, in this area between Iran, the Arabian peninsula and the Red Sea, major interests of both super-powers overlap. So far there is no conclusive evidence to suggest that the Soviet Union's primary goal was to get Gulf oil for itself or even to influence its supply to the industrial states of the West. What it does want, however, on its own admission, is a political say in this area — something which it has so far been largely denied. In the West there are conflicting opinions over the associated issue of whether the Soviet Union should be brought in as co-guarantor in a Middle East peace solution. During the first year of the Carter administration, the United States actually took steps in this direction, but since then the tense climate of superpower relations has prevented any steps towards a solution, much less a 'new Yalta'.

(iii) *The military component.* In most Western analyses of the military element of Soviet policy in the Indian Ocean region, the navy has hitherto been placed so much to the fore — frequently it has been the only object under study — that the perspectives have

arises as to whether the treaty with Syria has not also created some problems for Moscow.

68. See *New York Times*, 11.12.1980, p. A12.

69. *Summary of World Broadcasts — Far East* (SWB-FE) 6601/A2/1, 15.12.1980.

become quite distorted. Naval power is a factor which, for reasons of history and tradition, Anglo-Saxon politicians and academics in particular tend to overemphasise even where, as is the case with the Soviet Union, this factor plays a much smaller role than do land-based forces. This remains essentially true despite the rapid build-up of the Soviet navy since the 1960s and the impressive figure of its strategist Admiral Gorshkov.

In the Soviet Union's two most important military operations in the Indian Ocean region so far — the Big Lift to Ethiopia at the end of 1977 and beginning of 1978 to win back the Ogaden, and the invasion of Afghanistan — the fleet thus played only a partial and supporting role. Nor does the important practice of using military aid to exert political influence have much to do with a naval presence. The same is true of the development of infrastructures on land — roads, airfields, military supply depots, etc. All these activities had been going on since Khrushchev's extended Afro-Asian policy without giving rise to anything like so much attention in the West as was aroused by the appearance of a small Soviet naval unit in the Indian Ocean in 1968.

According to a list drawn up by the US State Department in 1976, between 1955 and 1974 the following states in the Indian Ocean received significant military aid from the Soviet Union:[70]

	US$ (millions)
Egypt	3,450
Iraq	1,600
India	1,400
Indonesia	1,095
Iran	850
Afghanistan	490
Somalia	115
South Yemen	80
North Yemen	80
Sudan	60
Pakistan	60

In the following years the picture changed somewhat, primarily because of the withdrawal of both Indonesia (as long ago as 1965) and Egypt, and also because some of the African states bordering on the Indian Ocean came to be included.[71] Military ties with Iraq were

70. Bureau of Intelligence and Research, *Communist States and Developing Countries*, Report no. 198, 27.1.1976. Quoted in Bezboruah, op. cit., p. 134. (It goes without saying that these figures are only based on estimates and should thus be used with caution.)

71. Cf. W. Kühne, 'Schwarzafrika und die Sowjetunion. Die Bedeutung

maintained, despite the cooling off in political relations, and the air force facilities which Iraq afforded the Soviet Union have been of especial value to it until very recently. Activities of this type took place under cover of the bilateral treaty of friendship which was still in force.[72] Relations with India have, in this respect, remained consistent over the years and it continues to be high on the list of recipients of Soviet military aid. Afghanistan speaks for itself.

Insofar as Soviet military aid was intended to exert political and ideological influence, the results cannot have been entirely encouraging for the Soviet Union. Even in the case of friendly India, the limits are clearly defined. In foreign policy and defence matters India, as mentioned above, adopts a line of action largely parallel to that of the Soviet Union, but the substantial Soviet military aid did not bring about any progress in the direction of a change in India's political system. The same is true of Iraq. Moreover, both these states have been at pains to ensure, in India's case, that no Communist cells were formed in the armed forces and, in Iraq, that any such cells were immediately crushed. Yet these two states (and the same is true of Egypt and Indonesia) had established their respective links with the Soviet Union at a time when their own armed forces — and the nation-state itself — had already achieved a certain degree of consolidation. This does not apply to structurally weak states like Afghanistan, to those which came late to independence such as Mozambique and South Yemen, or to those where the composition of the army was strongly modified by revolutionary purges (Ethiopia). In countries like these the situation tends rather to be as follows:

The Soviet Union and its socialist friends have to attempt to gain more or less direct access not only to the areas that are important for the military survival of the allied regime but also to those which are of central significance for enabling the states in question to develop structures and policies in keeping with the ideology.[73]

The considerable number of Soviet, Cuban and East European military advisers (and 'internal security' advisers) in such states, as well as the training of cadres within the Socialist camp, creates

der Rüstungs- und Militärhilfe als Instrument der militärstrategischen, ökonomischen und ideologischen Einflusssicherung', in *Europa-Archiv*, vol. 35, no. 9 (May 1980), pp. 325–34; I. Clark, 'Soviet Arms Supplies and Indian Ocean Diplomacy', in L.W. Bowman and I. Clark (eds), *The Indian Ocean in Global Politics*, Boulder, Colo., 1981, pp. 149–71.

72. 'The Soviet Union signed . . . a further agreement, involving three bases, in December 1978', IISS, *The Military Balance 1980/81*, p. 39.

73. Kühne, op. cit., p. 331.

favourable conditions for this process. This is not least because, in most Third World countries for a long time to come, special tasks in the modernisation process and in nation-building are likely to continue being reserved for the armed forces.

In the 1950s and '60s, the military component of Soviet policy in the Indian Ocean region was still on the whole reactive *vis-à-vis* the overwhelming influence of the West. The Dulles policy of containment was having its effects: multilateral pacts were securing the presence of Western powers, and Great Britain and France still had considerable military rights and opportunities for influence which were a legacy from the colonial period.[74] By 1970 these circumstances had changed greatly: Great Britain had begun its retreat from east of Suez; France too, once its colonial possessions in the Western Indian Ocean had become politically independent, saw its military positions endangered; and the United States was embroiled in Vietnam. A notion of threat, still not clearly defined, was at this time taking shape in the West, and a Swiss political analyst, Jacques Freymond, expressed it as follows:

Although it does not see any direct military menace, the West is slowly coming to realize the threat hanging over its trade, its outlets, and its supplies of raw materials. It sees the oil-producing countries and the uncommitted nations gradually constituting a common front that, with the support of the big revolutionary powers, is forcing it on the defensive. The West therefore feels compelled to frame a policy valued for the whole of this 'southern front' in gestation . . .[75]

Because of this Western mood of uncertainty regarding a multiform threat orchestrated by the 'big revolutionary powers' (among which China was still unreservedly included), the presence of Soviet naval units in the Indian Ocean began to be regarded as an unmistakable symbol of the prevailing danger.

In all the Soviet Union's statements throughout the 1970s justifying the presence of its fleet in the Indian Ocean, there was constant reference to the threat to Soviet territory, posed in the first instance by American submarines with nuclear warheads operating from the Indian Ocean, combined with the offensive capability of US aircraft-carriers.[76] It is not clear how far such fears on the part of

74. The Khrushchev memoirs provide a significant insight into Soviet initiatives and perceptions at that time. They reflect both uncertainty with regard to unknown territories and the belief in a historic mission of the Soviet Union in connection with the African and Asian states then gaining their independence.

75. 'Western Europe and the Indian Ocean', in Cottrell and Burrell, op. cit., p. 426.

76. As early as 1964, in a memorandum to the United Nations the Soviet

the Soviet Union, which did not fail to have an effect in the Indian Ocean littoral states and in the West, were genuine, and to what extent they were put forward, then and now, as a pretext. In this connection it was the Australian communications base North-West Cape and Diego Garcia which were most often mentioned as links in a chain of US offensive strategy against which the Soviet Union was forced to take up a position. What seems most probable is that Moscow has never excluded a threat posed by nuclear submarines in the Indian Ocean, not least because such an option has never been expressly ruled out by Washington. It is just as likely, however, that up till now there have been no regular patrols by strategic submarines, because among other things additional strategic cover of the Soviet Union's territory from the Indian Ocean did not seem necessary; also because, given the limited number of strategic submarines available, such operations were not economic (the period of operational presence would be severely curtailed by the long journey to and fro).[77] It is thus an open question whether, as referred to above, the strategic premises for the United States will change in the 1980s to the point where, following the introduction of the 'Tridents' with their substantially greater range and on-station presence, the Indian Ocean will become more important as a zone of operations.

It remains to ask what, up till now, have been the reasons for the Soviet naval presence in the Indian Ocean. A direct threat to the Soviet Union's national security is obviously not the main reason. There seem rather to be a series of motives, all of which carry approximately equal weight, and one or another of which comes into the foreground according to politico-military dictates. Nonetheless, the reason which seems to take precedence over all others is the function of the navy in securing the Soviet Union's claim to be a global power. In this respect, it had a lot of ground to make up in the recent past, and no one could dispute its right to be present in the Oceans for the purpose of safeguarding its own interests. At the same time, this new capability created potential threats to Western interests.[78]

Union proposed that the Indian Ocean should be declared a nuclear-weapon-free-zone.

77. A useful summary and evaluation of the arguments advanced up to now are to be found in R.W. Jones, 'Ballistic Missile Submarines and Arms Control in the Indian Ocean', *Asian Survey*, vol. 20, no. 3 (1980), pp. 269–79.

78. See on this subject D. Mahncke and H.P. Schwarz (eds), *Seemacht und Aussenpolitik*, Frankfurt M. 1974. S.G. Gorshkov, *Seemacht Sowjet-*

One important political function of the Soviet navy in the Indian Ocean in the 1970s was to provide support for any regional states threatened with 'imperialist intervention'. Both in the 1971 Bengal conflict and in the 1973 October war, the Soviet fleet, after swift reinforcement, took up positions which countered US naval movements and at the same time could pass for examples of active support for the interests of Third World states.[79] Following the Iran crisis and the temporary reinforcement of the US navy to include two aircraft-carrier task forces, this function appeared unrealistic. In a scenario of American occupation of oilfields and of a subsequent intervention by Moscow, the Soviet navy would probably be given tasks only in connection with operations from the air to be conducted mainly from Soviet territory.

A more significant factor is likely to continue: support for regional client-states in clashes with their neighbours — a means also employed by the Western sea-powers. Thus in 1973 Moscow sent a naval contingent to Iraq during its border clash with Kuwait; yet at the same time it was making diplomatic efforts to defuse the conflict. In 1977 and 1978 the fleet provided support for the air force operations in the Ogaden war. Amphibious assault ships brought in matériel, and Soviet units operated just outside the harbour at Massawa which had been cut off by Eritrean rebels. At the beginning of 1981 the Soviet Union reinforced its naval presence in Mozambique (its treaty partner), in response to a South African incursion there (see p. 162). In the conflict between Iran and Iraq, the Soviet navy has so far not been able to have any political effect since officially it had to adopt a neutral stance in relation to the two sides.

During the 1970s the Soviet Union developed its network of agreements with Indian Ocean coastal states. By this means it obtained harbour facilities and landing rights in the Indian Ocean area and the adjacent strategic areas (the West coast of Africa and Vietnam). The heaviest build-up took place in Aden (and the surrounding area), in particular after the withdrawal of naval and air force equipment from Somalia at the end of 1977.[80] As part of the same process, the

Union (German translation), Hamburg 1978. M. McGwire and J. McDonnell (eds), *Soviet Naval Influence — Domestic and Foreign Dimensions*, New York 1977.

79. See W.F. Hickman, 'Soviet Naval Policy in the Indian Ocean', *U.S. Naval Institute Proceedings*, vol. 105, no. 918 (Aug. 1979), pp. 45 f.

80. In May 1979 the Soviet Union furnished evidence of its appreciation of the new strategic position by giving a naval demonstration off Aden. Aircraft from the carrier *Minsk* performed vertical take-offs and landings, and

Soviet Union provided South Yemen with an assortment of military equipment and, in view of its close ideological ties with this state, supported its army with military advisers, together with others from Cuba and East Germany.

So far the Soviet Union has no comparably versatile military facilities at its disposal anywhere in the Indian Ocean area. It is true that the Ethiopian ports of Assab and Massawa are open to its navy, but these lie in Eritrean territory and hence not far from the areas of fighting.[81] The Soviet Union makes use of harbours in Mozambique (Maputo, Beira, Nacala), which could come to play an important role if the conflict in Southern Africa were to intensify — there have been recent indications that events were moving in this direction. In India the Soviet navy has no exclusive right of access, but in the event of an international conflict it would most probably invoke the bilateral treaty (see below) under which it could obtain such rights, always provided that this were also in India's own interest. The possibility is there in any case. Apart from South Yemen, the Soviet Union has important military facilities for its navy and air force, outside the Indian Ocean, in Vietnam and hence within reach of the Malacca Straits and providing a geostrategic link between its Pacific harbours and the Indian Ocean (see Chapter 5).

To overestimate the Soviet fleet's potential for operation in the Indian Ocean, as is often done in the West, is just as unhelpful for an overall analysis as the (less frequent) contrary assumption. In any situation short of war, its chances are pretty good, and the political dividends stemming from its open support of client-states work particularly to its advantage. On the other hand, if there were a war, or in the unlikely scenario of an interruption of Western oil supplies, the geostrategic disadvantages of the Soviet navy would immediately come to the fore, namely, difficult maritime access to the Indian Ocean, lack of air cover, and so on. 'Now a powerful force in absolute terms, it does not yet match the West's greatly superior capacity for operating in distant waters', was the verdict of the International Institute for Strategic Studies in 1979. But the fact that the Soviet Union has an obvious determination to deploy its navy there must be taken into account. 'The major danger is that, at a time when third world conflicts are on the increase, greater Soviet naval strength creates a higher risk of clashes, accidental or deliberate,

the amphibious assault ship *Ivan Rogov*, with 400 marines on board, was put through its paces.

81. Only Massawa is a deep-sea port and is suitable for enlargement for military purposes. Since 1980 the Dahlak islands lying off Massawa have been extended for military purposes by the Soviet Union.

arising out of the super-powers' pursuit of their respective interests.'[82]

The substantial change in the strategic situation in the Indian Ocean, as it is perceived in the West at least since the Soviet invasion of Afghanistan, therefore rests, as we have said, upon the fact that, *vis-à-vis* the Gulf region, the land and air potential on Soviet territory has led to a sharp asymmetry between the super-powers.[83] The Soviet navy, which is concentrated in the north-western Indian Ocean, is merely one supplementary factor in this configuration. According to an assessment of the situation given by NATO HQ in April 1980,[84] the Soviet Union permanently maintains 850 fighter planes north of the Iranian frontier. In a crisis situation, more would be added to these and would be able to operate from airfields in the west of Afghanistan. Considerable reinforcements of this air power could be swiftly brought from Soviet military districts in Central Asia. A distance of approximately 1,100 km. separates the Baku area from Abadan/Basra. The strongest concentration of Soviet troops outside Europe — stronger even than that on the frontier with China — was at that time, according to the same assessment, stationed in the military districts of North Caucasus, Transcaucasus and Turkestan.[85]

In this area the Soviet Union is continuing to alter the military balance of forces to its own advantage. The United States navy is unable to form an effective counter-weight to this trend in the absence of secure and protected bases — although land-based US air forces launched from Egypt and Turkey could weaken the Soviet advantage. In any case, the Soviet Union is making increasing use of its geostrategic position and is leaving it to the other side to make itself *politically* vulnerable through its endeavours to obtain facilities in the Indian Ocean as well as by further extensions to Diego Garcia. The unstable situation within the Gulf states themselves, and the tensions between them, could further contribute to rapid changes in the regional constellation of forces without any direct involvement by the super-powers. The most unfavourable situation for the West would emerge if, in the course of such changes, the Soviet

82. *Strategic Survey 1979*, p. 24; see also R. Burt, 'Soviet Military Power: Growing, Troublesome', *International Herald Tribune*, 11.12.1980, p. 7.

83. See David Rees, *Afghanistan's Role in Soviet Strategy*, London, May 1980 (Conflict Studies, no. 118), pp. 14 f.

84. L. Rühl, 'Aufmarsch im Raum "40.40.20.70" ', *Die Zeit*, 25.4.1980, p. 5.

85. An assessment of the situation made at around the same time by the British military analyst John Erickson is given in the appendix.

Union were to obtain a legitimate say in Gulf affairs.[86] A development of this kind is certainly not out of the question, and it is one which the West would not be in a position to oppose by military means.

In any case, the Iranian and Afghan crises have, since 1979, served to throw light on those aspects to which the West had not previously given sufficient attention and which stem from the geographical proximity of the Soviet super-power to the Gulf region and the north-western part of the Indian Ocean. Not least among these aspects is the psychological factor. The Soviet Union's military power represents a threat — as the British 'fleet in being' did previously — by its mere presence and undoubted state of readiness on its southern frontiers.

(d) *Arms limitation negotiations, 1977–1978*

As has been established in earlier sections, the military potential and strategic options of the United States and the Soviet Union in the Gulf region are asymmetrical. This asymmetry is what principally accounts for the fact that, after 1979, when the Iranian and Afghan crises took place, the United States was no longer expected to return to the negotiating table which it left in February 1978 in what appeared at first to be a temporary and limited protest against the large-scale intervention by the Soviet Union and Cuba in the Horn of Africa.

At the time, the fourth round of bilateral negotiations on mutual limitation of military forces in and around the Indian Ocean was in progress.[87] The majority of the littoral states had welcomed these talks and regarded them as fitting in with their attempts to create a peace zone, and when the talks were broken off, they accordingly expressed their disappointment. Since then the Soviet Union has issued protests against this unilateral action by the United States and

0186. For example, if Teheran or Baghdad were to ask for help in the event of further entanglements between these two countries or as a result of a change of government in Iran following open civil war.

87. This theme is dealt with in more detail in Dieter Braun, *Grossmacht-interessen und Regionalpolitik am Indischen Ozean*, Ebenhausen, April 1978 (Stiftung Wissenschaft und Politik, SWP — S 263); Joel Larus, 'The end of Naval Détente in the Indian Ocean', *The World Today*, vol. 36, no. 4 (April 1980), pp. 126–32; Richard A. Best, Jr., 'Indian Ocean Arms Control', in *U.S. Naval Institute Proceedings*, vol. 106, no. 924 (February 1980), pp. 42–8; and in Richard Haass, 'Naval Arms Limitation in the Indian Ocean', *Survival*, vol. 20, no. 2 (April 1978), pp. 50–7.

has repeatedly made known its own readiness to resume the negotiations. At the summit meeting in Vienna in June 1979, President Carter promised the Soviet side that the talks would be reopened 'promptly'; and yet, already at that time, the United States was all set to move off in the opposite direction. It wanted to close the gap between itself and the Soviet Union, whose military advantage was now very obvious. As a result of the Soviet invasion of Afghanistan this advantage had become unequivocal, as the Soviet Union was now much closer, geographically, to the states of the north-west Indian Ocean littoral. For the United States the reasons for negotiating had ceased to exist.

A brief outline of the background and progress of this negotiating episode is required to place it in its proper historical perspective. Among other things, this will help to explain the marked change in atmosphere in overall relations between the super-powers which set in at the end of 1977 and for which a great many different factors were responsible. However, such an outline will also reveal that each super-power had its own way of looking at things where the Indian Ocean was concerned, and insofar as these approaches are characteristic, they are relevant to the political analysis.

At the beginning of the 1970s, both sides had already shown a degree of willingness to limit their military presence in and around the Indian Ocean. At the time, the region was a low priority for both Washington and Moscow and for this reason it appeared to be a suitable area for testing confidence-building measures. In the following years military potential on both sides grew slowly yet steadily, but this was not so much part of an action-reaction cycle as it was a consequence of the growth of the interests of each side within the area. In the mid-1970s the domestic debate in the United States on the further extension of Diego Garcia was symptomatic of a willingness on the part of 'liberal' politicians to begin limitation talks with the Soviet Union. Another factor which influenced these talks was the demand by the Indian Ocean states for a peace zone. The Soviet Union was also influenced by this circumstance, but its paramount concern must have been to exploit the general mood in the United States with a view to further increasing the existing asymmetry which was (and continues to be) characterised by the far greater dependence of the United States on maritime communications. By building up Berbera and other military installations in Somalia, the Soviet Union at this time created a counterweight to Diego Garcia, along with a bargaining counter for use in bilateral mutual limitation talks. The United States, on the other hand, assumed that, because of its close co-operation with Iran and Saudi Arabia, the Gulf region was adequately protected, and thus reinforcement of its own potential there did not seem necessary.

The intervention by the Soviet Union and Cuba in Angola delayed the opening of the talks, and they were finally begun shortly after President Carter came to office.[88] Codenames for the aim of the negotiations were 'stabilisation' of existing forces with subsequent 'reduction'. The first round of talks — which took place in Moscow in June 1977 — served to establish positions and, as a first attempt, to clarify concepts such as the geographical area to be covered by the negotiations, involvement of littoral states (e.g. Australia) and of military forces outside the Indian Ocean, the issue of 'bases' and of the right to use foreign 'facilities', transit arrangements, definitions of naval presence (e.g. measuring 'ship days'), and so on. Significant progress was made, as was confirmed by both sides after a second round in September 1977 in Washington. A draft was prepared for a preliminary agreement, aimed at 'freezing' naval force levels on both sides and stating the intention to make subsequent reductions. The Soviet Union was evidently prepared to accept Diego Garcia, and at that time there was still a chance that it might be able to influence the extent of future build-up on the island.

However, before the third round of talks in Berne in December 1977, the Soviet Union was forced to give up Berbera, which meant that it had lost its counterweight to Diego Garcia. This complicated the negotiations. Moscow now demanded drastic reductions in American activities on Diego Garcia and elsewhere in the Indian Ocean in order to restore the lost balance. The United States, now on the defensive, abandoned the medium-term goal of reduction and concentrated its efforts solely on stabilisation. The Soviet Union was still not discouraged by this, and an article which appeared in *Pravda* in January 1978[89] set out the Soviet position, and contained among other things a demand for the end of further extensions on Diego Garcia.

Meanwhile the Soviet Union and Cuba were in the process of giving massive support to Ethiopia, and when the fourth round of talks opened in Berne in February 1978, the American side stated that this behaviour was incompatible with the intention to limit forces. It therefore adjourned the proceedings. Two months later, however, Secretary of State Vance explained that the talks had merely been postponed and would be resumed, the aim being 'to

88. There was some confusion at the beginning because Carter spoke of 'complete demilitarisation' and because he had not adequately consulted US allies.

89. See S. Vladimirov, 'The Indian Ocean: an urgent problem', *Pravda-APN*, 18.1.1978, p. 4.

stabilise the military presence of both sides at the levels which prevailed until recent months, and then to consider possible reductions'.[90]

In the meantime, however, it was becoming clear that the United States no longer spoke with a single voice. The Pentagon, along with National Security Adviser Brzezinski, regarded Soviet policy in Africa as a threat. Defence Minister Brown said that he favoured a reinforced naval presence in the north-west Indian Ocean. It had also become clear at this time that it was quite impossible to reconcile Soviet activity, which involved the transportation by air of heavy weaponry and other equipment, with the hitherto prevailing categories of 'naval limitation'. *Pravda* retorted, in an article replying to these arguments,[91] that the renewed American arms build-up in the Indian Ocean constituted a threat to Soviet national security, since its territory lay within reach of strategic offensive weapons. In October 1978 the Head of the State Department Bureau of Politico-Military Affairs, L. Gelb, speaking to the House Armed Services Committee, again argued in favour of a resumption of talks. One of the reasons advanced by Gelb in support of his arguments was that Soviet naval strength had once more returned to its 'pre-Ethiopia' level. He said that 'an agreement would maintain the US force balance and would permit us to fulfil our security and foreign policy commitments in the area.'[92] Meanwhile the issue had become a hot potato in Washington, and the number of those opposed to any agreement on the Indian Ocean area had greatly increased, both inside and outside the Carter administration.

Yet in June 1979 in Vienna, President Carter promised the Soviet side that the talks would be resumed in the near future. This was just one of numerous contradictions in US foreign and security policy, since in the mean time, chiefly as a result of the Iranian crisis, plans to strengthen the American naval presence in the Indian Ocean were already quite far advanced in Washington. These plans even included a rapid deployment force with land-based support. In the summer of 1979 the US air force made demonstration visits to several Gulf states and in October that year the Middle East force operating from Bahrain was strengthened — an unequivocal sign of a military build-up by the United States.

From the spring of 1979 the Soviet Union had also been

90. United States Wireless Bulletin, 11.4.78. p. 4.

91. S. Dmitriyev, 'Facing a Choice', 21.8.1978, *The Current Digest of the Soviet Press*, vol. 31, no. 34 (Sept. 1978), p. 10.

92. 'Indian Ocean Arms Limitation Negotiations', in *Department of State Bulletin*, vol. 78, no. 2021 (Dec. 1978), pp. 54–5.

strengthening its presence. The aircraft-carrier *Minsk* visited several Indian Ocean ports including Port Louis in Mauritius, Maputo in Mozambique and Aden in South Yemen. In August the Soviet Union deployed units of its strategic submarine fleet and an *Echo* class II ship, carrying infantry and missiles and accompanied by a supply ship, docked in Aden.[93] At the same time, in its press and its diplomacy, the Soviet Union reverted to a sharply recriminatory tone which it had not used since 1976. An example of this was the approach of the Soviet diplomats at the United Nations meeting of littoral and hinterland states in July 1979.

That the endeavours of both sides towards limitation of forces ended in failure is evidence of one simple fact, namely that in spite of a desire for global détente, each of the super-powers essentially pursued its own specific and varied interests in the states around the Indian Ocean. On matters such as these, which are far more important to them than naval presence, agreement could not even be contemplated. In fact, this had been clear as early as 1973 when Brezhnev's visit to the United States in June — a high point in détente policy — was followed soon afterwards by the threat of military confrontation between the super-powers during the October war in the Middle East.[94] The example of the conflict on the Horn of Africa also served to show that the Soviet Union set a higher priority on military partisanship than on willingness to reach an agreement, while the United States for its part reinforced its position near the Gulf, now threatened by instability.

From this it once more emerges that mere partial arrangements for mutual restraint, even when they are embodied in a treaty, are bound to remain ineffective so long as a deeper mutual understanding by each of the other's global political aims and of the means of achieving them is lacking. At this point the limits of any 'détente' between antagonistic systems become apparent. Yet for the West it was both sobering and helpful to have gained more insight into this fact on account of the events of the 1970s in the Indian Ocean region.

(e) *Treaty policies: their uses and limitations as a means of securing influence*

Since the 1950s, both super-powers had been pursuing policies which

93. See Larus, op. cit., p. 131. According to Larus this class of submarine is the key element in combating aircraft-carriers.

94. 'It may be that we shall come to recognize that two such rivals could never in any case have cohabited on this basis for more than a fleeting moment, that projects for a solid and enduring partnership were from the beginning illusory' (Hedley Bull, op. cit., p. 447).

aimed at securing influence in the Indian Ocean region by means of multilateral and bilateral treaties with the littoral states. A policy of this kind was initiated by the United States in the Dulles era in an attempt to use a belt of states allied with the West as a means of containing both China and the Soviet Union. It was in the Indian Ocean area that the final touches were to be put to a process which was already under way in the Pacific and the Atlantic.

The schematic thinking that underlay US policy proved inadequate to meet the aspirations of the young nations in this part of the developing world and to allay their sense of threat. Both the Baghdad Pact (later known as the Central Treaty Organisation — CENTO)[95] and the South-East Asian Treaty Organisation (SEATO),[96] the two most important multilateral systems established in the Indian Ocean region in the mid-1950s, subsequently gave rise to numerous misunderstandings on both sides and were even deliberately misused.[97] The largest state in the area, the Indian Union, utterly repudiated both pacts, and a good deal of the tension and periodically renewed hostility between India and the United States can be shown to originate in this stance. A different story could be told of the 1952 ANZUS Treaty between Australia, New Zealand and the United States. This treaty, which at the outset barely affected the Indian Ocean, has retained its validity as a security pact among predominantly 'white' states, and its significance increased still further after the British pulled out of Asia.

The Soviet Union did not follow this American pattern of multilateral defence pacts[98] but when, considerably later than the United States, it began to extend its influence in this part of the world, it developed its own specific claim to legitimacy. After first spreading (in 1969) the idea of a Collective Security System for Asia, which aimed in the long term at a *pax sovietica*, the Soviet Union concluded in the 1970s a series of long-term bilateral treaties of friendship and co-operation with individual states of the Indian Ocean littoral — as

95. Great Britain, Turkey, Iran, Pakistan. The United States, though formally only associated, nonetheless played a full part in its activities.

96. United States, Britain, France, the Philippines, Thailand, Australia, New Zealand, Pakistan (the latter because of the geographical position of East Pakistan).

97. While the United States was interested, almost exclusively, in containing the Communist powers, the regional partners used the link with the United States to consolidate their positions *vis-à-vis* local rivals.

98. According to the peculiar logic of the Non-Aligned Movement, in which Indian influence was strong, these alliances alone were considered to cause 'alignment', in contrast to bilateral agreements with one of the great powers.

a means, so to speak, of consolidating single cornerstones of its future edifice.

Both the overwhelmingly negative reception which met the idea of the Collective Security System in Asia,[99] together with the experience of a sudden *volte face* by some of its treaty partners, must have proved just as disappointing for Moscow as did similar experiences for Washington. The Soviet Union too was in some ways a victim of fundamental errors of judgement with regard to Afro-Asian developments. However, this has not so far prevented it from continuing efforts to consolidate its influence wherever the nature and variety of its relations with a regional partner appeared to justify their elevation to a qualitatively higher level. In practice, this happened mostly when the partner in question felt acutely threatened by a stronger neighbour and thus welcomed Soviet backing.

The United States also concluded bilateral agreements with regional partners, for example Iran and Pakistan (also Turkey) in 1959, in order to strengthen US commitment to the CENTO states after the coup in Iraq, and then shortly afterwards with Bahrain to secure naval facilities (a treaty which was renewed in 1971 and 1977), with Thailand in the context of the Vietnam war (in which a Thai contingent fought on the American side), and in 1960 with Ethiopia in connection with Eritrea and Somalia.[100]

There followed a long interval before, in the middle of 1980, the United States embarked on a new series of bilateral agreements for the purpose of securing military facilities, this time with Oman, Kenya, Somalia and Egypt. This diplomatic effort by the United States, which was under pressure because of the Iranian and Afghan crises, showed just how difficult it has become in the changed global climate of the 1980s for a super-power to find any states at all in the Third World willing to sign a treaty. The price to be paid has risen enormously, as was proved at the beginning of 1980 when Pakistan declined US military and economic aid to a value of $400 million. Even in the cases just mentioned, the only states likely to be prepared to sign a treaty were those which hoped that ties with the United States would help them to ward off a severe threat to their national security posed by a stronger neighbour.

99. It was introduced into the bilateral treaties with Afghanistan and South Yemen, but not into those with other Asian states such as India, Vietnam and Iraq.

100. It is not precisely known on the basis of what agreements the United States co-operates militarily with Saudi-Arabia. The Saudi government takes care to reveal as little as possible in this matter for reasons of domestic and regional politics.

On the other hand, the United States was also not prepared (and had not always previously been prepared) to enter into definite commitments to offer protection or support to a treaty partner in a bilateral or multilateral alliance. Individual cases have remained ambiguous for decades as, for example, the US commitment to give support to Pakistan, especially after the 'Executive Agreement' of 1959, or to Thailand, after the 'Rusk-Tanat Agreement' of 1962. In these two cases there has always been some doubt on both sides as to the extent to which the undertakings previously given would in fact be honoured by the United States, and this ambivalence has undermined American credibility. Of the agreements signed in 1980, the same was particularly true of the one with Somalia which in the United States only passed through Congress after considerable opposition. This treaty was from the outset so burdened with political handicaps (Somali irredentist claims against not only Ethiopia but also Kenya) that US support for this particular state had to be qualified accordingly (see p. 154).

The two multilateral systems, SEATO and CENTO, were dissolved in the second half of the 1970s 'in view of changed circumstances' (SEATO)[101] and after the Iranian revolution (CENTO). (Ever since 1976 Pakistan had in fact been trying to leave CENTO and join the Non-Aligned movement.) Even after the break up of SEATO, South-East Asia did retain one treaty instrument intact, the South-East Asia Collective Defence Treaty. 'That document, whose strength was subject to dispute during the Vietnam War, remains the main military tie between America and Thailand.'[102] The ANZUS pact was once again upgraded as a result of the increased tension in the Gulf and in South-East Asia (Indochina), and its area of activity was specifically extended to include the Indian Ocean, where naval exercises were held.

A balance-sheet of thirty years of US treaty-making in the Indian Ocean area shows that, in the early stages, the 'American connection' was sought because the United States seemed to be strong and trustworthy, and because during the Cold War period there were areas in which its interests could be seen clearly to converge with those of the regional states. In the 1960s, the United States began to steer clear of treaty ties which involved too many constraints, and there was a growing desire among regional states to open up towards the Communist powers (interrupted in the case of China by the

101. 'Ministerrat der SEATO-Staaten, September 1975', in *Archiv der Gegenwart*, 15.9.1975 19728.

102. J.M. Collins, *US-Soviet Military Balance: Concepts and Capabilities 1960–1980*, New York 1980, p. 345.

Cultural Revolution), while the situation in Vietnam was making itself felt. The Nixon Doctrine reigned supreme for much of the 1970s, and then towards the end of the decade the polarisation between the United States and the Soviet Union suddenly intensified again, and this also had an impact on the region. In 1980 a whole series of Indian Ocean states were prepared to enter treaty commitments with the United States in order to protect themselves from any direct or indirect actions by the other super-power; yet at the same time, confidence in the ability and the will of the United States to provide such protection had distinctly waned, and moreover the general climate of opinion in the Third World was opposed to close ties with the super-powers.[103] On the other hand, there was considerable opposition within the United States itself to new treaty commitments overseas, in spite of a prevailing mood which increasingly favoured active preservation of interests. This situation resulted in agreements that were accompanied by scepticism from the outset, and which were restricted in their content to those few areas in which the interests of the super-power happened to coincide with those of the regional state in question.

The Soviet Union had begun its treaty-making policy with states in the Indian Ocean areas as early as 1921 when it signed its first agreements with its southern neighbours (which included Afghanistan and Iran), along with several other states. In the latter half of the 1920s these efforts were intensified, and with Afghanistan pacts of non-aggression and neutrality were signed in both 1926 and 1931. The aim was to initiate a network of treaties of this kind (also among the Soviet Union's partners themselves) which would form a *cordon sanitaire* against anti-Soviet activities by Western powers in Asia and the Middle East. Teheran renounced its 1921 treaty on several occasions, but Moscow would not recognise this move and it is thus assumed that the treaty remains in force. Article 6 of this treaty grants the Soviet Union the right to intervene in the event of a third power undertaking activities on Iranian soil which are regarded as a threat to Soviet security interests. The fall of the Shah can only have served to aggravate the risks for Iran resulting from this treaty claim. When Soviet relations with Afghanistan were activated after the Second World War, in 1955, Moscow confirmed that the non-aggression pact concluded in 1931 still remained in force.[104]

103. Cf. Shirin Tahir-Kheli, 'Proxies and Allies: the Case of Iran and Pakistan', *Orbis*, vol. 24, no. 2 (Summer 1980), pp. 339–52.
104. See A.G. Noorani, *Brezhnev Plan for Asian Security*, Bombay 1975, pp. 269 f. It may be noted that the preamble of the friendship treaty of 1978 also refers to these early treaties.

As an outcome of the strengthening of the Soviet Union's global position around 1970, a series of bilateral friendship and co-operation treaties were signed with states in the Third World. Between 1971 and 1980 eleven such treaties were concluded, eight with Indian Ocean littoral or hinterland states (two of these were subsequently unilaterally renounced).[105] Offers were made to other states which declined them. In the Indian Ocean region this is known to have happened with Pakistan and Indonesia. In most of the treaties signed, it can be assumed that the Soviet Union was the interested party, but in the cases of India and of Vietnam, the treaties were signed shortly before the outbreak of a war in which Soviet backing was an asset to the partner.

Although the form of all the treaties is similar (preamble, statement of common social and political concepts, a section on economic and other forms of co-operation, clauses on security policy, duration of the treaty), the differences between them are nonetheless considerable. Some allow the conclusion to be drawn that a regional partner successfully staked its own claims in the face of Soviet demands,[106] but in others the opposite would seem to apply. The treaty with Afghanistan, in particular, is redolent of a patron-client relationship. Another feature of some of the treaties is the inclusion of clauses which corresponded to the Soviet Union's general foreign policy interests at the time the agreement was made, e.g. the special emphasis in the treaty with South Yemen (October 1979) on international détente. An outstanding peculiarity is the 'withdrawal clause' in the treaty with Afghanistan. This is the only instance where provision is made for cancellation of the treaty, with six months notice, before the end of its period of validity (twenty years), which undoubtedly reflected Soviet uncertainty when signing the treaty at the end of 1978 as to whether the Communist experiment in Afghanistan might not be doomed to failure. (In the course of 1979, Moscow decided not to take advantage of this clause but instead to invoke the treaty as grounds for invasion.)

105. In order of conclusion these were Egypt 1971 (renounced 1976), India 1971, Iraq 1972, Somalia 1974 (renounced 1977), Angola 1976, Mozambique 1977, Vietnam 1978, Ethiopia 1978, Afghanistan 1978, South Yemen 1979, Syria 1980.

106. India provides the most striking example of this. Apart from the section dealing with security matters, this treaty is the least binding. However, Ethiopia, like Somalia before it, also seems to have successfully opposed the inclusion of provisions slanted to suit the interests of the Soviet Union. See Dieter Braun, *Patterns of Soviet Policies towards the Third World*, Ebenhausen, May 1977 (Stiftung Wissenschaft und Politik, SWP-AZ 2135) pp. 23 f.

Since the Soviet treaties entailed co-operation at more substantial levels than comparable US documents had done, and furthermore since they postulated or aimed at agreements or at least convergence on ideological and foreign policy goals, it was that much easier to recognise where the ideal clashed with the reality and where the treaty became increasingly irrelevant for one or both parties.

If the matter is viewed in this way, it can be seen that at the time of signing the treaty with Iraq in 1972 there was a fair amount of agreement in vital areas: Iraq was anti-Western, inclined towards the socialist social and economic model, supported opposition to feudal structures in the Arabian Peninsula, and so on. In the course of the 1970s, however, increasing divergence set in and Iraq adopted positions that in some cases ran counter to Soviet interests. This applied to its positions on Somalia, Eritrea, South Yemen and the April 1978 coup in Afghanistan. When the Soviet Union invaded Afghanistan, Iraq went as far as to denounce the action publicly. Moscow's implicit support for Khomeini since 1979 has served to break links still further. Iraq's military attack on Iran in September 1980 showed just how far Baghdad had meanwhile freed itself from its treaty obligations to Moscow, while the Soviet Union saw no alternative to observing strict neutrality between the opponents, as it had previously done in the face of growing tensions between Somalia and Ethiopia in 1977. Here developments had led to a *renversement des alliances* by the Soviet Union, and this possibility cannot be excluded in the case of Iraq and Iran.

The limits of this approach for the Soviet Union — which in its idiosyncratic and legalistic manner sets such great store by treaties — as a means of securing influence thus emerge clearly. National interests can very easily induce in their partners a disregard for the solemn formulae of treaties or encourage them to interpret these to suit themselves as soon as these interests cease to run parallel to those of the Soviet Union. And where such parallel interests do exist — as in the case of India, as long as China is perceived as a potential enemy — behaviour is influenced accordingly without there being any need for a treaty; but where this prerequisite falls away or fades into the background, a treaty provides the Soviet Union with no real grounds for appeal, as has been shown with Egypt, Somalia and Iraq.

It is probable that those regimes which have moved closest towards Marxist-Leninist principles (South Yemen, Afghanistan, Vietnam and, to a less extent, Ethiopia, Mozambique and Angola) will act on the whole in accordance with the treaties, since this corresponds to their general political preferences. But it is not the treaty itself which is the decisive factor, for it merely stakes out a framework and outlines a more or less less feasible programme for co-operation. Moreover, at the time of concluding a treaty, the Soviet Union must have been at pains not to make itself fully liable for the social development and internal stability of a partner not yet squarely placed in the Socialist bloc on a lasting basis. It is in this way that these treaties still differ markedly from those concluded with the Warsaw Pact countries and those which embody the Brezhnev doctrine.[107] Even so, as has already been pointed out, Vietnam was expressly mentioned at the XXVI CPSU congress as a member of the 'Socialist community of states' along with Cuba and Laos, the only other such states in the Third World.

The Soviet Union accords special interest to those articles of the treaties which deal with military co-operation. Apart from the treaty with India, all others refer to the continuation of agreements already concluded in this field. Again with the exception of the treaty with India, and of those (subsequently renounced) with Egypt and Somalia, all treaties make provision for military co-operation 'to guarantee the security of both partners'. It is on the basis of this bilateral commitment that the Soviet Union founds its claim to maintain its own military installations in these states, to station personnel there, and so on. And this makes for the possibility of using the treaty-partner's territory to further Soviet global strategy. At the beginning of the 1980s, the Soviet Union made particular use of this option in Afghanistan, Vietnam, South Yemen, and also increasingly in Ethiopia and Mozambique. Before the outbreak of war between Iran and Iraq, the latter was also being made use of in this way. This practice is more or less on a par with the arrangements concluded in 1980 by the United States to gain use of military facilities in the Indian Ocean littoral states. Both, moreover, are embodied in treaties that provide for co-operation without constituting alliances.[108]

This comparison between American and Soviet use of treaties has shown that there are obvious similarities of purpose in spite of the different character and tenor of these instruments. The United States, having gone ahead with treaty policy in the 1950s, today seems to take a more sober view of its practicality than the Soviet Union. Both have experienced failures, but both still go on wooing

107. W. Kühne, *Die Politik der Sowjetunion und Afrika. Bedingungen und Dynamik ihres ideologischen, ökonomischen und militärischen Engagements* (Stiftung Wissenschaft und Politik (ed.), Internationale Politik und Sicherheit, no. 10), Baden-Baden, forthcoming.

108. The Soviet treaty with Vietnam goes considerably further in terms of mutual obligations.

individual countries to sign contracts, the significance of which may quickly be overtaken by events. The Soviets, with their belief in an inexorable historical process working in their favour, may be duped more in the long run than the Americans, who in this respect have become more pragmatic.

The Non-Aligned movement is an important rallying ground for the superpowers' treaty partners. In most of its treaties the Soviet Union explicity 'respects' its partner's non-aligned stance. This principle may well turn out to be of practical significance for both the United States and the Soviet Union, at least in so far as a partner-state is able by invoking it to restrict the implications of its treaty ties with a super-power, especially in the military arena.

Chapter 4
OTHER OUTSIDE INTERESTS

(*a*) *China: strong influence with limited means*

Peking has been involved in political and strategic developments in the Indian Ocean for a long time. The maritime routes are increasingly frequented by Chinese merchant traffic but so far this has not led to any form of naval presence.[1] Military activities have been restricted to arms supplies and training assistance given to individual states in the region and, earlier, to numerous 'liberation organisations', rebel and separatist movements. This also involved the provision of infrastructure in the form of roads, bridges and railways for strategic purposes.

Pakistan is the only country with which, since the middle 1960s, there has been substantial co-operation in these fields on a lasting and regular basis.[2] Geostrategic considerations have always been the decisive factor here, since the security interests of the two states are closely linked. Pakistan is able to offer China access to the Indian Ocean via the Karakoram Highway, even though this access is by no means easy and would not be difficult to obstruct in the event of a conflict. Since the Soviet occupation of Afghanistan, the significance of this 800 km.-long high mountain road has increased and Soviet interest in cutting the connection by one means or another at some time in the future has doubtless increased too.

The main instruments used by China to gain influence in the Indian Ocean region were of a political and — allowing for its limited possibilities — an economic nature. It took advantage of opportunities there in the early 1950s, well before the Soviet Union, by cultivating relations with individual states, primarily with India and Indonesia. In 1955 the Bandung Conference enabled it to break through into the wider Afro-Asian sphere (Egypt, Syria, Yemen *et al.*). Despite its link with India, China lost no time in forging another link with India's rival Pakistan (in 1956) — also in spite of the latter's participation in the Baghdad Pact and in SEATO.[3] In the

1. It could be that some of the more modern Chinese submarines have spent time in the area but there is no proof of this.

2. Between 1967 and 1976 China supplied Pakistan with armaments to an estimated value of US$ 335 million, without receiving anything in return. House of Representatives, *Committee of Armed Services Report* (footnote 3), p. 21.

3. The Pakistani Prime Minister Suhrawardy visited Peking in September

joint communiqué of December 1956, it was stated that there existed 'no real conflict of interests between the two countries' — a notably far-sighted claim by both partners.[4]

A few years later the Sino-Soviet conflict emerged into the open and an important aim of Chinese policy in Asia was henceforth to label the Soviet Union as an outside power from Europe whose territorial possessions in Asia rested on a foundation of colonial usurpation. By the same token the Soviet Union sought to emphasise its Asiatic characteristics in order to be accepted as an Asian power as well as a European one. Only India was prepared to support this claim. Elsewhere in Asia it was ignored.

Right up to the beginning of the Cultural Revolution in 1966, which paralysed Chinese foreign policy for years, Peking succeeded in building up its influence in the Asian and African littoral and hinterland states of the Indian Ocean. India began to feel the full force of this after the Himalaya war when most of the Non-Aligned states on whose support it had counted adopted a neutral and in some cases even pro-Chinese attitude. This Chinese influence was based on very varied expectations in the partner-states:

— on ideologically motivated help against 'reactionary' neighbours or systems of colonial rule;[5]

— on the desire to provide a counterweight against a superior neighbour (Ceylon and Nepal against India);

— on a prescription for self-reliant economic development on the 'Chinese model' (Tanzania);

— and on expectations that good relations with Peking would serve to limit the extent to which China would give support to subversive forces in their own country (Burma, Thailand).

Even before the interlude of the Cultural Revolution, China experienced harsh setbacks. It had carried its revolutionary zeal too far. On two visits to Africa, to Somalia in 1964 and Tanzania in 1955, Chou En-lai had called for revolution, and this induced an attitude of caution in most African governments. The events surrounding the fall of Sukarno in 1965 led to a lasting feeling of ill-will towards China in Indonesia since China was held responsible for support given to the local Communists. The Chinese minority in the country came to bear the brunt of this ill-feeling. Soviet mediation

---

1956, and only three months later Chou En-lai paid a return visit to Karachi.

4. S.M. Burke, *Pakistan's Foreign Policy: an Historical Analysis*, London 1973, p. 215.

5. See Peking's role in the Afro-Asian solidarity organization in Cairo (later in Dar-es-Salaam) or Chinese support for Aden against Saudi Arabia.

during and after the 1965 armed conflict between India and Pakistan at the Tashkent Conference in January 1966 showed China that its Soviet rival was making headway even with its close partner Pakistan. The far-reaching Chinese withdrawal from the international political scene which followed, and then lasted until 1970–1, also helped to set the stage for a completely new start.

In 1971 the beginnings of China's *rapprochement* with the United States brought a new configuration of forces into being, at the international level generally but also more especially in the Third World region around the Indian Ocean, and this new set-up soon acquired lasting features. In the course of the 1970s this led to ever-increasing dovetailing of Chinese interests with those of a conglomeration of extremely heterogeneous states which, for a variety of different reasons, opposed an expansion of Soviet power. During most of the decade, China made use of the ideological 'three worlds theory', whereby both super-powers were classified together as constituting the first world, with all other developed industrialised states constituting the second, while China counted itself as belonging to the third. Since the establishment of full diplomatic relations with the United States in 1979, China's foreign policy has been primarily based on power politics, with the Soviet Union as its main opponent — all other considerations being subordinated to this one. Some recent modifications in connection with the Reagan Administration's Taiwan policy could, however, express Peking's desire for a more balanced stance between Washington and Moscow.

The extension of Soviet influence in the Indian Ocean region had already been described by China as 'encirclement' as early as 1969–70 and labelled accordingly as a 'new version of British imperialism'. It was asserted that 'social imperialism' (as the Chinese regularly characterise the imperialism of the Soviet Union), was seeking a maritime route from the Mediterranean through the Indian Ocean to the Western Pacific and the Sea of Japan.[6] Thus at the beginning of the 1970s China renewed its efforts in the littoral states of the Indian Ocean, and thereafter its endeavours were even more clearly directed against the Soviet Union, while the United States, the 'other super-power', was treated with indulgence. But this policy turned out to be not just reactive *vis-à-vis* Soviet activities but offensive in the diplomatic field. Peking consolidated its positions wherever the prevailing configuration of forces was in its favour, modified its support wherever Moscow brought its far

6. See *Peking Review*, 27.6.1969. See also in connection with this section K.R. Singh, *The Indian Ocean: Big Power Presence and Local Response*, New Delhi, 1978, pp. 81–96.

greater potential to bear, and furthermore used its geopolitical edge over the Soviet Union wherever possible. In January 1974, taking advantage of South Vietnam's weakness and before Hanoi had consolidated its power, China occupied the Paracel Islands in the South China Sea. This was an important move in a strategically and economically significant area.

In the non-communist areas of South-East Asia, as well as in Australia, the end of the Vietnam war also brought about a change in the previous appraisal of China as a revolutionary threat. The withdrawal of the United States had a sobering effect and gave rise to regional initiatives. In 1974 a Thai trade delegation visited Peking for the first time, shortly after the Prime Minister of Malaysia had also paid a visit. It is true that in the longer term the ASEAN states feared China's influence, particularly where Chinese ethnic minorities posed political problems on the home front (principally in Malaysia); yet a united Vietnam, supported by the Soviet Union, soon proved a more serious danger, especially after the occupation of Cambodia at the end of 1978. Since then common interests between the ASEAN states and Australia on the one hand and China on the other have grown considerably, and Peking even gives unmitigated support to the pro-Western outlook of this sub-region. Even so, the ASEAN states have lasting reservations with regard to China,[7] and these are linked with the hope that, in the medium term, it will in fact prove possible to achieve a reasonable understanding with Vietnam within the South-East Asian region.

After the mid-1970s and the change in the power structure of Bangladesh following Mujibur Rahman's death, there was a clear split in China's relations with the countries of South Asia. There has been little change in the strained relations with India, but with all the other states of this sub-region Peking has maintained good and, in some cases, very close relations (Bhutan, whose foreign policy is controlled by Delhi, being the one exception). As with Pakistan, relations with Nepal and Sri Lanka date back to the 1960s, which means that they have stood the test of time amid changing circumstances in both China and South Asia. To this end China was prepared to make a considerable financial outlay, and to assist development by various other means. It was also active in Afghanistan until 1978, where it was successful in the promotion of smaller development schemes.

7. Of interest in this connection was Prime Minister Zhao-Ziyang's assurance that China would in future ensure that party relations with Communists in ASEAN countries would no longer affect relations between the states. See *International Herald Tribune*, 2.2.1981, p. 1.

Chinese-Indian relations, which had thawed out somewhat around 1970 for the first time since the Himalaya war, froze again at the end of 1971 with the Indo-Pakistan War, after the signing of the Indo-Soviet treaty. In subsequent years Peking tried to isolate India in South Asia, to cause it harm by supporting guerrilla activities in the north-east of the country, and to discredit it internationally as a 'lackey of Moscow'. In 1976 both states yielded and full diplomatic relations were resumed. The fall of Indira Gandhi in March 1977 led to hopes in Peking that Indo-Soviet relations would be noticeably upset, but they turned out to be crisis-proof and were not even fundamentally disrupted by the Soviet invasion of Afghanistan. However, the Soviet occupation of Afghanistan caused a shift in Peking's South Asia strategy. In view of an expansionist Soviet Union, China deemed it necessary to encourage co-operation and understanding among South Asian countries rather than to build on their divisions. Such a policy had to focus on the strongest state, India, while trying to keep up good bilateral relations with India's neighbours. To this effect, Peking's leaders during 1981 visited the capitals of all the South Asian states except Bhutan.[8] This policy has been partly successful. One consequence was that China no longer supported Pakistan over Kashmir but stressed that this was an issue to be dealt with exclusively by the two contending parties — a step towards meeting Indian views.

In Afghanistan itself, before the putsch of April 1978, China had some political influence, mainly with the non-Pashtoon minorities. It is almost certain that, both before and after the Soviet invasion, the Chinese took advantage of this influence and other circumstances to provide weapons and training for the Afghan resistance. In so doing, however, it had to be careful of the sensitive political situation in Pakistan which has never admitted that this kind of support is provided from or by way of its territory. In and around Afghanistan, however, China does have the advantages of geographical proximity and ethnic links which it will use to influence events there. According to China, Moscow's operation in Afghanistan was part of a 'pincer movement' which will be continued towards the Gulf while Vietnam is threatening the ASEAN countries and the Malacca Strait.[9]

In the Gulf region,[10] between 1973 and 1978, the main emphasis

8. Foreign Minister Huang Hua was in India, Sri Lanka and the Maldives. Prime Minister Zhao Ziyang visited Pakistan, Nepal and Bangladesh.

9. *Beijing Review*, no. 26, 1.7.1980.

10. See on this subject L.C. Harris, 'China's Response to Perceived

of Chinese interests fell on Iran whose fundamentally anti-Soviet political and military position corresponded with Peking's view of the situation. But to establish links with Iran, China had had to abandon its support for the 'liberation front' in Dhofar, the PFLOAG (People's Front for the Liberation of Oman and the Arabian Gulf). The change of front was complete, since afterwards Iran dispatched a contingent of troops — and there is no doubt that it did so with Chinese approval — to combat this same rebel movement in Oman's Western province. Hua Kuo-feng's state visit to Teheran in August 1978 was one of the last to the Shah's tottering regime. Peking's relations with the Islamic republic which followed the Shah's fall were understandably rather difficult but, once a crisis had developed between Iran and the United States (after the taking of the hostages at the US embassy in Teheran in November 1979), China took up a position firmly opposed to American sanctions, having calculated that if it did not the Khomeini regime would set aside its endemic hostility to its powerful neighbour the Soviet Union and would channel all its energies into its struggle against the United States.

On the Arabian side of the Gulf, Chinese influence has so far been limited, chiefly due to Saudi Arabia's refusal to establish relations with 'godless' China (and, similarly, the Soviet Union). Saudi Arabia is one of the few states in the world which has continued to maintain full diplomatic relations with Taiwan. Until now, China's most important diplomatic base on this side of the Gulf has been Kuwait.

In the Red Sea and the Horn of Africa, by contrast, Chinese activities met with fewer constraints. In the Sudan, China derived lasting benefits from the abortive Communist putsch of 1971 and in Egypt from President Sadat's rejection of the Soviet Union. Peking's relations with Cairo since the 1950s have proved remarkably durable in spite of all the changes which have taken place in the two countries over this period.[11] In South Yemen, on the other hand, China lost influence when Aden realigned itself with Moscow (1977–8), and the same goes for Ethiopia. Somalia had, it is true, been receiving political support from the Chinese as early as the beginning of the 1960s, including backing for its claims to Greater Somalia, but Somalia's subsequent pro-Soviet period, which lasted until 1977,

Soviet Gains in the Middle East', *Asian Survey*, vol. 20, no. 4 (April 1980), pp. 362–72.

11. At the end of the 1970s, sales of Chinese armaments manufactured to a Soviet design provided a further economic link that was of benefit to both sides.

restricted Chinese room for manoeuvre. All the same, President Siad Barre did visit Peking in 1972. In the following years the Chinese built a strategically important road along the frontier with Ethiopia. This was an example of the unwavering and tenacious way China holds fast to relations which have once been set up, even when circumstances turn against them.

Here, as in Eastern and Southern Africa, the second half of the 1970s brought a distinct loss of influence for Peking. One reason for this was China's lack of capability to project its military power into distant regions and another factor was Peking's change of priorities in favour of concentrating on neighbouring regions (South Asia and South-East Asia). While Chinese participation in African affairs had reached a peak in 1974 — chiefly through its support for liberation movements fighting against white-ruled Southern Africa but also through the building, within this same context, of the Tanzam railway — the clashes which ensued as states were undergoing rapid change in this area restricted Chinese opportunities for influence. The Soviet Union proved itself unquestionably superior both in the deployment of military means and allies (especially Cuba) and in the political guidelines which it followed, which were mostly in harmony with the resolutions issued by the Organisation of African Unity.

Not until the outcome of the Zimbabwe conflict did China once more gain a political bonus in Africa. When he had won the elections in the new state, Robert Mugabe moved away from Moscow, which had supported his rival Joshua Nkomo, and maintained the links with Peking which he himself had been cultivating for some time. Overall, however, China must have learned that Africa is a particularly hard field to till and one where lasting relations are correspondingly laborious to maintain.[12] At the same time the realisation must have grown that the Soviet rival would not encounter easy success there either. Even so, there as in the rest of the Third World, Peking offers an alternative to countries which want to show, by cultivating their relations with China, that they are not being controlled by Moscow. If one takes as an index the number of state visits from Africa to Peking at the beginning of the 1980s — including those from the islands of the Western Indian Ocean — it would appear that this wish continues to be fairly widespread.

In conclusion it must be noted that Chinese policy towards the

12. The outstanding Tanzam railway project has so far brought China more problems than political gains, the major reason for this being that the railway (between Dar es Salaam in Tanzania and the Zambian Copperbelt) has been very inadequately maintained by the countries participating in the scheme.

Indian Ocean region, in keeping with Chinese policy generally, has undergone strong fluctuations in the last fifteen years. Goals have changed and instruments have turned out to be unsuited to the task, the more so where the geographically distant regions are concerned. Yet there have been constants: first, opposition to Soviet influence wherever this seemed feasible, and secondly, increased concentration on the politically and strategically important area close to its borders in South and South-East Asia. Bilateral relations with Pakistan since 1956 offer an example of remarkable steadfastness,[13] but this relationship still has to face the test of changed political conditions in the region at the beginning of the 1980s.

In the contest with the Soviet Union, China does not have the power to tip the balance in a material sense, but even so its specific weight as a regional power and as a factor in the global context is certainly not underestimated, at least not by the Soviet Union.

(*b*) *Japan: an economic power with vulnerable sea routes*

Because a great proportion of Japan's requirements in oil and other important raw materials come from the Indian Ocean region, and approximately half of its maritime trade passes through the Indian Ocean, its interests in the region are vital. Yet in spite of this level of dependence, Japan has no military instruments of any kind in the area with which to protect its imports, and would in any case be prevented by its constitution from contemplating such a projection of power. Japan thus relies for its protection on the forces of the United States and other Western powers, and during the 1970s it co-ordinated its own policies in this sphere more closely with those of the West.

A significant turning-point was the oil boycott by the OPEC states in 1973. This shattered Japan's confidence in secure supplies from the Arab exporting countries and at the same time revealed the limits of its solidarity with its ally the United States. On 22 November 1973, thirty-five days after the declaration of the boycott, Japan gave way and abandoned its hitherto neutral stand in the Middle East conflict. At that time it had petroleum reserves for only fifty-nine days, including the oil in tankers then on their way to Japan.[14]

In the following years Japan tried to diversify its oil supplies in all

13. In September 1980, President Zia ul-Haq called China 'the most staunch and reliable ally that Pakistan ever had' (*New York Times*, 28.9.80, p.E .2).

14. See M. Momoi, 'Japan and the Persian Gulf and the Indian Ocean', in A. Amirie (ed.), *The Persian Gulf and the Indian Ocean in International Politics*, Teheran 1975, p. 167.

kinds of ways. Even so, dependence on the Persian Gulf remained strong, at least 75 per cent, and the increasing fall-off in Iranian supplies from the beginning of 1979 (or the relinquishing of these supplies due to higher prices as well as the Teheran hostages affair) made the situation even worse. The war between Iran and Iraq that started in 1980 for a time reduced imports which had been considered secure, but supplies from other Gulf states promptly compensated for this fall-off. Meanwhile, according to government statistics, Japan now had reserves for 111 days, but still 72 per cent of its oil imports came through the Strait of Hormuz,[15] which shows how dependent it continues to be on supplies from the Southern Gulf and on free passage through the Indian Ocean.

In view of these facts and of the high level of activity of Japanese firms in the Gulf area, it is surprising how late Japanese foreign policy 'discovered' this region. In early 1978 a Japanese foreign minister, Mr Sonoda, visited the Gulf states for the first time, to be followed nine months later by Prime Minister Fukuda.[16] At the time the region had a 20 per cent share in Japanese foreign trade.[17]

This reserve, indeed total lack of political involvement, was symptomatic of the Japanese post-war 'posture'. The business sector discovered and secured markets and also, to a large extent, dictated the terms of trade, which were quite often to the disadvantage of the partner-states, while Tokyo's official diplomacy remained predominantly passive and accommodating.[18] In many littoral states of the Indian Ocean, which are inundated with credits binding them to take supplies of Japanese goods, this led in the 1960s and '70s to a pervasively negative image of Japan as an 'economic animal', interested only in selling and not in any more balanced form of development policy (technology transfer, sending out experts, etc.). From 1978 it would appear that Japan attempted to change this image.[19] Since then it has taken a more prominent stance on political

15. See *Neue Zürcher Zeitung*, 26.9.1980, p. 3.

16. This had the effect of strengthening Japan's support for Arab demands *vis-à-vis* Israel.

17. Up to the end of 1980, the most significant of the major Japanese projects in the Gulf region were a petrochemicals complex in Saudi-Arabia, a petrochemicals complex in Iran, an oil refinery in Kuwait, the development of off-shore oilfields and the construction of a terminal in Abu Dhabi, and an oil refinery in Oman.

18. It was only in 1974 that Japan set up a semi-official development assistance agency called 'Japanese International Cooperation Agency'. Previously there had only been a department with the function of briefing the Prime Minister.

19. See J. Glaubitz, 'Schwerpunkte der Aussenpolitik Japans', in M.

developments in the region generally, and in individual cases has adopted clear positions, as on Cambodia and Afghanistan. Underlying this was a foreign policy which, since the normalisation of relations with China, was increasingly fired by anti-Sovietism — a substantial motive for this being a Soviet policy towards Japan that was rather lacking in understanding. (In addition, Japan sometimes chooses to adopt positions in keeping with those of the United States, China, Australia and the ASEAN states.) Hand in hand with this went an economic and development policy towards the Indian Ocean states and the Third World generally which for the first time showed some understanding of the fundamental preconditions for this type of exchange (increased imports, joint ventures, greater technical assistance, etc.).[20]

Japanese relations with the two 'developed' Indian Ocean littoral states — Australia and South Africa — developed in a rather different fashion. With Australia it was first necessary to overcome the resentment which dated back to the experiences of the Second World War, after which there nevertheless grew up a 'symbiotic relationship characterised by a high level of interdependence'.[21] In 1977 a bilateral treaty was concluded providing for co-operation in political, economic and other fields. At the time of signing this treaty, Prime Minister Fraser was keen to stress that it had no exclusive character but was intended rather to strengthen peace and security in the Asian and Pacific area at large. For a long time Australia has been Japan's most important export market and although trade in the other direction would appear to be much smaller in terms of volume, it is nonetheless of appreciable importance for Japan's supplies of raw materials. Hence the link between Japan and Australia is of even more significance in the political and economic context of the Pacific region.

Relations with South Africa, on the other hand, are becoming ever more highly charged for Japan. Both sides have a strong interest in continued trade relations. Japan is South Africa's third biggest export market and South Africa is the fourth largest importer of

Pohl (ed.) *Japan 1978/79. Politik und Wirtschaft*, Hamburg 1979, pp. 110–33.

20. See D. Morris, 'Importing more from Africa', in *West Africa*, no. 3301, 27.10.1980, pp. 2122–38; regular reports on South and South-East Asia in *Far Eastern Economic Review*. Credits were given for a railway modernisation scheme in Pakistan to the value of 9 million yen (interest rate of 2.75 per cent, repayable over thirty years with ten years grace) — see *Times of India*, 21.10.1980, p. 9.

21. 'Australia-Japan Relations', *Australian Foreign Affairs Record*, April 1980, pp. 93–9.

Japanese goods. Japan mainly imports raw materials (platinum, chrome, asbestos, manganese, uranium) and avoids direct investments, but this problem seems to be circumvented by using the 'homelands' or Bantustans.[22] Although Japan has tried up to now to keep as low a profile as possible in South Africa, it is questionable how much longer this will be possible. In South Africa Japanese have 'white' status, in contrast to other Asians.[23] However, Black Africa expects solidarity from Japan, as an Asian state, in its struggle with South Africa. During a visit to Africa in 1974, Mr Kimura, then Japanese Foreign Minister, undertook that his country would cut back on economic links with South Africa, but since then Japan's dependence on these links has only become more evident.

One successful attempt to reduce the dilemma has been Japan's increasing economic involvement with Black Africa. In 1980 the volume of this trade was approximately equal to that with South Africa. Efforts are also being made to give verbal support to African political positions in the United Nations and other fora. Lastly, Japan is seeking alternative sources of raw materials, in Black Africa, South-East Asia and elsewhere. But for the time being the link with South Africa will remain as economically profitable as it is politically open to attack.

South-East Asia is of especial significance for Japan, first because of its position between the Pacific and the Indian Ocean, and secondly as a source of raw materials, as well as increasingly as a market. Although, after the occupation of Cambodia by Vietnam, Japan attempted to keep a foothold in Indochina, its interests have since further converged with the ASEAN states. Vietnam's pro-Soviet stance is threatening for Japan, since from there the Soviet Union could disrupt its links with the Indian Ocean. At the beginning of the 1980s, the Malacca Strait is within striking range of Soviet air and naval forces which could operate from Vietnam. At the beginning of the 1970s, Japan's main concern had been the Malaysian and Indonesian claim for control of the Malacca Strait (with Indonesia there was the added claim with regard to navigation around its islands). Later these preoccupations receded into the background, not least in view of the provisional results of the international law of the sea conference. Instead, a potential threat to vital sea routes has emerged from the Soviet Union in connection with the deterioration in relations between Moscow and Tokyo, especially since 1978. So far there are no signs that Japan is likely to participate

22. See E.A. Olsen, 'Building Bridges to Africa', *Africa Report*, vol. 25, no. 2 (March/April 1980), pp. 52–6.
23. Recently the Chinese from Taiwan also obtained this status.

in safeguarding these sea routes using its own military means, although the Reagan administration has stepped up pressure on it to do so: the United States expects stronger military readiness on the part of Japan as this would enable American forces to be moved from the North-West Pacific to the Indian Ocean.

Like its relations with Australia — indeed even more so — Japan's relations with the ASEAN states have been encumbered by the after-effects of the Second World War. Japanese economic expansion thus had especially negative effects in this region (hence the 'ugly Japanese').[24] Since 1978 the picture has changed somewhat: not fundamentally,[25] but there are signs of normalisation. The development of the ASEAN states is no longer conceivable without the Japanese contribution, which in 1978 represented 20 per cent of all Japanese foreign investment.[26]

Japanese firms have so far been the most successful in complying with the terms of investment in ASEAN countries and in winning through against American and European competition. (On the other hand, this in turn stimulated the interest of the ASEAN group in promoting economic links with the EEC to counteract their growing dependence on Japan.)

In the political sphere, Japan has been increasingly in agreement with the ASEAN states since 1978, as already mentioned. This was especially clear in the way the problems arising from the Cambodian crisis situation were dealt with. [27] Japan adopted a position in this context which was in contrast to that of India, and even more so after the Soviet invasion of Afghanistan. This was apparent when in March 1980 the special Japanese ambassador Sonoda visited New Delhi and the talks were described by the Indian side merely as 'open'.[28] When Foreign Minister Ito visited India in August 1980, the conflicting positions on Cambodia and Afghanistan came clearly to light: the verdict of the Indian press was: 'The nature of differences on these issues is such that it leaves no scope for a joint

24. Cf. the disturbances during the visit by Prime Minister Tanaka in 1974, particularly in Thailand.

25. The list of ASEAN complaints about Japan's official economic policy and concerning the business practices of its firms is long and likely to become even longer, given structural differences and dissimilar ways of approaching these matters.

26. See 'Japan and the Economic Development of the ASEAN countries', in *Exim Review*, vol. 1, no. 1 (1980), p. 6.

27. After a period of hesitation in 1979 when Japan attempted to maintain some form of economic ties with Vietnam. Afghanistan was the decisive factor here too.

28. See *Times of India*, 11.3.1980, p. 7.

initiative to solve these problems.'[29] As a result, the measure of mutual understanding during Ito's subsequent stay in Islamabad was all the greater.

Compared with the former Japanese tendency towards soft-pedalling in the diplomatic sphere, but also compared to aspects of the détente process in Western Europe and the correspondingly reserved treatment meted out there to the Soviet Union after the invasion of Afghanistan, the positions taken up by the Japanese government have been unequivocal. This has been welcomed in the ASEAN states, in Australia, in China and in the United States. The conclusion of the peace and friendship treaty between Japan and China in 1978 was an important element of the stronger anti-Soviet trend in Japanese foreign policy, and it thereby contributed substantially to shaping its general profile. Perhaps the most significant aspect of this development is that in Japan itself, where the Second World War left behind a deep trauma, it is only since the end of the 1970s that public opinion has been prepared to accept an active foreign policy that is not merely restricted to economic diplomacy.[30]

(c) *The United Kingdom: historical legacy both a burden and an advantage*

In 1967 Britain still maintained as many as 80,000 troops in Singapore and Malaysia, and another 30,000 in Aden and the Persian Gulf. More than one-tenth of British defence expenditure went on South-East Asia, and between 1948 and 1967 British forces took part in more than twenty local conflicts around the Indian Ocean.[31] Britain was a member of CENTO and SEATO. In 1964, after the conflict between India and China, Prime Minister Harold Wilson designated the Himalayas as Britain's strategic frontier. In 1965 the British Indian Ocean Territory (BIOT) was formed out of individual groups of islands in the Western and Central Indian Ocean, and Diego Garcia belonged to this territory.

But when Britain redirected its interests towards Europe, this, together with restrictions on government expenditure, led late in 1967 to a sudden decision by the Labour Government which amounted to complete military withdrawal from east of Suez by the

29. *Times of India*, 30.8.1980, p. 1.

30. Notable are the changed circumstances, compared to the Tanaka visit in 1974, of Prime Minister Suzuki's visit to the ASEAN states in January 1981.

31. See L.W. Martin, 'British Policy in the Indian Ocean', in Burrell and Cottrell, op. cit.

end of 1971. The Conservatives energetically opposed this decision
— principally with the argument that military means were required
to safeguard the considerable remaining British investments and
trading interests in the Indian Ocean states — but, when they came
to power in 1970, they were only able to modify these plans in a few
minor areas. In this context great significance was attached to the
recent appearance of the Soviet fleet in the Indian Ocean and a
concomitant of these developments was that around 1970 much
more attention began to be devoted to this area in discussions on
strategic matters and in the related literature.[32]

In South-East Asia and the Persian Gulf, the two regions in which
there was a sizeable military presence until 1971, the difficult transi-
tional phase was handled by Britain with remarkable diplomatic
skill. In particular, the creation of the United Arab Emirates (UAE)
in December 1971, together with the maintenance of an indirect
presence in the Sultanate of Oman, showed its capacity for a
constructive approach. In South-East Asia, the 'Five Power Defence
Pact' with Malaysia, Singapore, Australia and New Zealand was set
up on an *ad hoc* basis, and one consequence of this was limited
presence by the three British services. In the 1970s the significance of
the Pact gradually diminished — after 1975 British troops were no
longer stationed there — until 1980, when it was quite suddenly
revived on account of the changed strategic situation (see Part III).

The Tory government also attached great importance to
continued use of the South African military base at Simonstown at
the Cape of Good Hope and above all to military co-operation with
Pretoria. At the beginning of the 1970s the Commonwealth nearly
came to grief on this issue. It was only in 1975, after a new Labour
government had come into office, that a stop was put both to the use
of the base and to military co-operation — by which time the Suez
Canal had also been reopened.

Membership of the CENTO Pact (see Part II above) gave Britain a
further opportunity to put its Middle East experience to good use.
The annual naval manoeuvres (Midlink) in particular enabled the
British navy to co-operate with the US fleet in the Gulf region until
1977 and this practice was resumed in the autumn of 1980 to protect
the Straits of Hormuz. The British base in Bahrain had been handed
over for use by the Americans at the beginning of the 1970s and at the
end of the decade the small base previously belonging to the Royal
Air Force on the island of Masirah, off Oman, was similarly
transferred. The extension of Diego Garcia by the United States

32. See D. Braun, 'Der Indische Ozean in der sicherheitspolitischen
Diskussion', in *Europa-Archiv*, vol. 26, no. 18 (Sept. 1971).

went ahead (as described elsewhere) with British approval, and a small British liaison group remains stationed on the island.

In this way, Britain's security commitments in the Indian Ocean steadily declined in the course of the 1970s. The withdrawal was, as Laurence Martin has described,[33] 'incoherent and piecemeal — with little overall strategic philosophy'. In London the conviction was growing that British interests outside the Atlantic area would have to be safeguarded by means of diplomacy, investment and trade. Yet at the end of the decade turbulence in the Middle East once again forced an awareness of the, significance of military power. But for military deployment in this region 'Britain will have to rely chiefly on its American ally and confine its own military contribution to an auxiliary role of 'presence' and token participation at best.'[34]

This is a piece of British understatement, for those who criticised the way Britain lost its predominant role in the Indian Ocean most harshly were themselves British and by no means always of Conservative persuasion.[35] The British, in view of the still widespread consciousness of this tradition, tend to emphasise the 'erosion', while 'Indian Ocean outsiders', such as Germans, on the other hand note how persistent are the customs introduced by the British and the extent to which in the wide arc of the Indian Ocean littoral states there is still adherence to British standards, often at a barely conscious level. This is true even in spheres where this adherence is problematic, as for example in the stubborn retention of irrelevant English patterns in educational and legal systems.[36] But Britain had little influence over the way in which the native élites, the 'brown sahibs', wrote their own new constitutions or interpreted the ones the British had left behind; here negative legacies from the colonial period were frequently mixed with elements deriving from the need to consolidate power. Even so, there is no doubt that hitherto the positive aspects of the British institutional inheritance have predominated, and among these special significance has been

33. Laurence Martin, 'The Domestic Content of British Defence Policy', in Gregory Flynn (ed.), *The International Fabric of Western Security*, London 1981, p. 154.

34. Ibid.

35. See M. Lipton and J. Firn, *The Erosion of a Relationship — India and Britain since 1960*, London 1975, 427 pp.

36. This accounts for such oddities as a presidential decree issued in Pakistan in November 1980 abolishing 'My Lord' and 'Your Lordship' as forms of address in the law courts and causing them to be replaced by 'Sir' or the equivalent term in Urdu. *Dawn Overseas*, 15.11.1980, p. 3.

accorded to the principle of independent justice. However, there are few states — India is an exception — which have managed to retain down to the present day an army with a non-political role.

This kind of British influence continues to have an effect, especially in the context of the Commonwealth which, despite numerous pessimistic predictions at the beginning of the 1970s, was still going strong at the end of the decade without any sign that it had substantially weakened. This is no mean proof of Britain's ability — without a constitution, it is true, but not without conventions for the creation of a community — to maintain what it has brought into existence. In 1979 the number of states in the Commonwealth had risen to forty-one, and of these countries fifteen belonged to the littoral and hinterland states of the Indian Ocean.

The meeting of the Commonwealth Heads of Government held in Lusaka, Zambia, in August 1979 furnished impressive evidence of skilled use of this forum by British diplomacy to achieve a breakthrough in the Zimbabwe question, which had become bogged down. Contrary to most predictions, Prime Minister Thatcher, with guidance from Australian Prime Minister Fraser and the leaders of the 'front-line states' (chiefly the Presidents of Tanzania and Zambia), succeeded in getting the participants to commit themselves to a common stand.[37] In his concluding speech, President Kaunda of Zambia spoke of 'epoch-making decisions'. Britain was given a mandate for a new Zimbabwe initiative and, thanks to the negotiating skill of its Foreign Minister Lord Carrington, the constitutional conference held in London the following month was successful. On the basis of a compromise agenda which enabled both sides to take part, it was decided to hold elections in Rhodesia in which 20 per cent of seats would be reserved for the country's white population.[38] Britain had shown that its frequently invoked 'special relationship' to its former colonies still had some substance.

This relationship was again put to the test a few months later when the Soviet Union invaded Afghanistan. Immediately after the invasion, Lord Carrington travelled to the states in the region which were affected by it — notably Pakistan and India. To the new Indian government, whose assessment of the situation was at variance with that of most other Third World states, Lord Carrington explained the differing British position and, in the course

37. Although Britain is frequently criticised by Black Africans on account of its close economic links with South Africa, in 1978 the volume of its trade with Black Africa was more than double that with South Africa (*Financial Times*, 1.8.1979, p. 18).

38. See *Africa Research Bulletin*, vol. 16, no. 8/9 (Sept./Oct. 1979).

of the discussions, explained the reasons for arms deliveries to Pakistan. He was unable to convince the Indian side, and yet, for reasons of tradition, he was given a better hearing in Delhi than was accorded to, for example, spokesmen for the United States' government.[39] But the case of Afghanistan also showed once again, this time with particular clarity, how far India, once the most important British bastion in the region, had moved away from British positions on foreign policy and security matters, despite substantial economic aid[40] and relations on many other levels. India's ties with the Soviet Union survived the crisis surrounding Afghanistan, but at the cost of the interests it had held in common with the West and the Third World.

In the following months, Britain attempted to win over its partners in the West and in various parts of the Third World to the proposal that Afghanistan should be 'neutralised' (the Carrington Plan). But the Soviet Union's position meant that this plan had no chance of fulfilment; yet, during a period of considerable confusion in the West, it did serve as a useful instrument for countering the Soviet occupation, at least at the diplomatic level.

Britain's intense diplomatic preoccupation with the many and varied consequences of the occupation of Afghanistan was reflected in a very detailed Parliamentary report, drawn up with the assistance of academic experts and published as early as July 1980.[41] One of its conclusions was that there was 'no evidence that the invasion of Afghanistan was part of a Soviet grand strategy to extend its influence to the Gulf and threaten Western oil supplies. Nevertheless, the Committee noted the Soviet definition of détente, the opportunist trend of Soviet tactics and the now-proven capability of the Soviet military command successfully to undertake such an invasion.'[42]

The events in Afghanistan at the end of 1979 also brought in their wake intense British diplomacy in the Gulf. In January 1980 Lord Carrington visited Oman, Saudi Arabia and Turkey in addition to South Asia. Douglas Hurd, a minister of state in the Foreign Office,

39. See 'Enttäuschung für Lord Carrington in Indien', *Neue Zürcher Zeitung*, 20.1.1980, p. 3.

40. India received far more financial help from Britain than from any other source: in 1979/80 it received 62 per cent of total bilateral payments. Britain also has more investments there than any other country. More than a quarter of all India's business contracts were concluded with British firms. By the same token, at the beginning of the eighties, India was Britain's third trading partner in the world (*Le Monde*, 16.4.1980, p. 6).

41. See House of Commons, Foreign Affairs Committee, *5th Report, Afghanistan*.

42. ibid. p. xxx.

went to Bahrain, Qatar and the UAE, and General Tomlinson
(responsible for training) went on a tour which took in Kuwait,
Bahrain, Qatar and Saudi Arabia.[43] There is a special tradition of
British responsibility for the strategically vital Sultanate of Oman,
and the military presence there, which is small but reckoned to be
efficient, was stepped up in the course of 1980 because of the
unstable situation in Iran and the threat from across the border in
South Yemen, i.e. even before the conflict between Iran and Iraq
focussed Western attention on the Strait of Hormuz.

After this event, Britain dispatched several naval units to the
vicinity of the Gulf, and in October 1980 held joint naval
manoeuvres with the US fleet there.[44] Diplomatic contacts with the
Arab Gulf states were stepped up, and the head of the British navy,
Admiral Sir Terence Lewin, visited Oman and the UAE with the aim
of strengthening military co-operation.[45] These activities were part
of a concentrated effort by the West to consolidate its position in the
southern part of the Gulf and to safeguard it in the face of the Iran-
Iraq conflict. The danger to the oil supplies of the Western industrialised states from unforeseeable developments in the northern
part of the Gulf had significantly promoted a closer understanding
both between the United States and Western Europe and among the
most important West European partners.[46]

There is thus no doubt that Britain's security policies regarding the
Indian Ocean region in the 1970s were largely conducted parallel to
the interests of the United States. In this period, as earlier, the
Americans, giving the British historical bonus its due significance,
must frequently have followed advice from London. Conservative
governments continued to see eye-to-eye with Washington, but even
under Labour governments there was remarkably little disagreement
when it came to fundamentals. On top of this, the British Left
cultivated special relations with many of the Indian Ocean littoral

43. At the beginning of 1980 there were British officers seconded to most
of the Gulf states. The highest number was in Oman (around 140) and there
were about as many more directly commissioned by Oman. According to a
press report in 1981, in Kuwait, Bahrain, Qatar, Saudi Arabia, Oman and
the United Arab Emirates, there was a total of 311 instructors, most of them
officers on secondment. No precise figures are available for the numbers of
directly commissioned numbers of British personnel serving in these countries. *Neue Zürcher Zeitung*, 14.4.1981, p. 4.
44. *Frankfurter Allgemeine Zeitung*, 22.10.1980, p. 3. Altogether
twenty-five ships took part.
45. *Dawn*, 5.11.1980, p. 1.
46. See L. Downie Jr., 'Allies Using Quiet Links in Gulf War', *International Herald Tribune*, 21.10.1980, pp. 1–2.

states, whose élites had often learned to look at the world through British eyes. Meanwhile, Britain has become a temporary or permanent home for a large number of individuals from the Indian Ocean area, and the domestic and regional politics of their countries of origin (the activity of Pakistani opposition groups is a case in point) often have to be dealt with on British soil — something which has taken place so far with only minimal violence.

Both tendencies in Britain, the one predominantly a function of power politics and the other clearly founded on ideological motives, together with the presence of large numbers of people from the Indian Ocean region, have combined to create a situation in which London has become the 'secret capital' of the Indian Ocean region, with a role that is hard to evaluate.

(d) *France: claim to special status*

France's attitude towards the Indian Ocean region since decolonisation displays some trends that are typical of its foreign and security policies as well as of its attitude towards the Third World:
— its approach has all the elements of that of a great power;
— it emphasises its complete independence *vis-à-vis* other powers with interests in the region;
— it adheres to positions that are important from an economic and security point of view even in the face of negative reactions in the Third World; and yet
— it is willing to adapt to Third World demands, and in this respect tends towards opportunism.

Whereas about 1970 Britain reacted strongly to Soviet expansion and issued warnings to the Western world while still going ahead with its own withdrawal from east of Suez, France appeared unperturbed by this development. Michel Debré, then Minister of State for Defence,[47] expressed the view that the Soviet Union's expansion was the kind of conduct to be expected of a great power and should cause neither fear nor surprise.[48] Around the same time (but in another context) he explained that France would maintain its capability to intervene in areas where it had interests and commitments.[49] When the military situation between the super-powers in the Indian Ocean first began to deteriorate during the conflict between India and Pakistan over East Bengal, France promptly increased

47. As well as the Deputy for Réunion in the French Parliament.
48. *Le Monde*, 27.8.1970.
49. *Revue de Défense Nationale*, vol. 28, no. 8 (Aug./Sept. 1970), pp. 1245 f.

its own naval presence and an extra five warships with a marine unit were dispatched as a '*mission de présence française en Océan Indien*'.[50]

Consistently throughout the 1970s, France maintained its claim to behave like a great power with a capability to intervene, although geographically this was largely confined to the Western Indian Ocean. This distinctly affected the extent to which there was a military balance in the region during the crises which took place around 1980 involving Iran, Afghanistan and the Iran-Iraq war. Outside the military sphere — in which, when a crisis did arise, a certain amount of coordination with US forces took place almost as a matter of course — France chiefly demonstrated its independence in two ways. First, it gave rhetorical support to the independent and non-aligned positions of states on the Indian Ocean littoral, emphasising its own aloofness from politics based on military blocs. And secondly it made commercial deals in arms and in the nuclear field, using its own 'independence' (as a non-signatory of the Non-Proliferation Treaty) to legitimise the conclusion of a great variety of supply and co-operation agreements with many different partners: with India as well as Pakistan, with Iran as well as Iraq, and so on. France even supported the 'Indian Ocean Peace Zone', the demand of the littoral states for the military withdrawal of outside powers — on the understanding, of course, that it would not itself be affected by such demands, since its own presence in the Indian Ocean was 'traditional', being founded on its territorial possessions.[51]

France's possessions and direct responsibilities in the Western Indian Ocean area shrank during the 1970s as former colonial territories (the Comoros and Djibouti) became independent, and agreements covering the use of military facilities were terminated (Madagascar). The island of Réunion is the most important remaining French possession. It is an overseas department and, as such, a constituent part of the Republic. Situated about 700 km. east of Madagascar, the island has half a million inhabitants. It is of only limited use to the French navy because of its unsuitable coastline, but following Madagascar's refusal in 1973–4 to allow a French military presence to remain on its soil — a development which took France quite by surprise — it inevitably acquired additional strategic significance. After Djibouti became independent, the headquarters of the French Indian Ocean forces was also transferred there. Possession

50. *Le Monde*, 15.1.1972, p. 9.
51. See R. Koven, 'France considering call to demilitarise Persian Gulf region', *Washington Post*, 6.7.1980, p. A 14.

of this island by France has not gone unchallenged. Various OAU resolutions have demanded self-determination and independence for Réunion as part of Africa, but France can assume that in the medium term at least, the majority of the islanders will regard belonging to it as more of an advantage than a disadvantage.

The position of the island of Mayotte is more complicated. Mayotte was formerly part of the Comoro group of islands and was to have been granted independence along with the rest, but this it vociferously opposed. In 1976, in a referendum conducted by Paris, the population of about 40,000 voted in favour of retaining links with France as a *collectivité spéciale*, a status created *ad hoc* by Paris. Mayotte had been a French colony as early as 1843 and most of its inhabitants were Christians, whereas the other Comoro islands were only colonised in 1912 and are now predominantly Muslim. This cultural antithesis helped France to justify its presence and to disregard what were in this case emphatic demands from the OAU for the withdrawal of the colonial power.

The status in international law of four very small islands in the Mozambique Channel[52] is somewhat different. These islands have no indigenous population and are claimed by Madagascar. In November 1980 the United Nations Political Committee voted by 83–13 with thirty-two abstentions in favour of the islands being transferred to Madagascar. France declared that the resolution was an 'interference in its internal affairs' and that Madagascar had no legitimate claim to the islands, that colonisation was not a relevant issue here, and that in consequence Paris fully upheld its claim to sovereignty.[53] France has small airfields on these islands as well as other facilities of military utility. According to a Reuter report from Paris, the islands play a 'key role' in the surveillance of the Mozambique Channel; they 'complement France's network of outposts and landing fields — aircraft are able to take on reinforcements there.'[54] Besides being of military significance, the islands have become of economic importance following the discovery in 1979 of manganese nodules in the area. France declared a 200-mile exclusive economic zone around them, and the already mentioned support for Madagascar's claim against France in the United Nations should also be viewed in this context.[55] Moreover, as a

52. Glorieuses, Juan de Nova, Bassas da India, Europa.

53. *Le Monde*, 27.11.1980, p. 9.

54. *Nachrichtenspiegel I*, 5.8.1979, Presse- und Informationsdienst der Bundesregierung, Bonn.

55. See V. Thompson, 'Madagascar', in *Africa South of the Sahara 1980–81*, London 1980, pp. 599 f.

result of France's Indian Ocean possessions, the French 200-mile economic zone is exceptionally large (3 million km^2 out of a total area of 11 million km^2). A well-informed French writer therefore considers this whole aspect to be a major reason for France's continuing to cling to what remain of its colonies.[56]

In Djibouti, on the Horn of Africa, the transition to independence in 1977 was remarkably smooth, particularly in view of the tense situation in the region at that time. Its port was an important transit point for Ethiopian goods which were sent on by rail to Addis Ababa. The area was claimed by Somalia on account of the sector of the population who were of Somali origin (viz. the Issas; the Afars are part of an ethnic group that extends into Ethiopia). Djibouti's proximity to the insurgency in Eritrea brought it indirectly into the conflict. After the Soviet Union had withdrawn from Somalia, Djibouti became caught up in super-power rivalry in the Indian Ocean because of its strategic situation across the water from Aden and its proximity to the Bab-el-Mandeb Strait.

Contrary to many expectations, the transition proved straightforward, with France maintaining what was by now a formally agreed presence. The ethnic conflicts which had been anticipated did not materialise and France has so far maintained order. This role was made especially difficult when activity in the port declined sharply as a result of the regional conflict; and once it had become independent, Djibouti, as a member of the Arab League, had to renounce its commercial ties with Israel which had previously been important. At the beginning of the 1980s, France was maintaining a permanent military presence there of approximately 4,000 men, including detachments of the Foreign Legion and the aircrew of a Mirage squadron.[57] This is by far the largest Western military presence close to the Gulf as well as to the Bab-el-Mandeb Strait and the Soviet installations there. Several units of the French Indian Ocean fleet regularly use Djibouti's (not very modern) docking facilities, and during the period of increased tension in the Gulf region US units did so too. The port was also visited by several Soviet naval units.[58] So long as France is able to hold on to this position, it can claim a key strategic position which is of paramount importance

56. See J.-P. Gomane, 'France and the Indian Ocean', in Bowman and Clark, op. cit., pp. 201 f.

57. These forces must also be seen in the context of France's capability to intervene in Africa.

58. See *International Herald Tribune*, 10.6.80, p. 1. and Philippe Decraene, 'Djibouti: naissance d'une nation', in *Le Monde*, 4 and 5.7.1980.

for the West as a whole, but those in power in Paris can certainly have few illusions about its vulnerability. In any event, the build-up of US forces in the north-western part of the Indian Ocean is being observed from Djibouti with an appropriate degree of attention.

In the spring of 1981, French Indian Ocean forces in the strategic triangle between Djibouti, Réunion and Mayotte (including the Mozambique Channel) consisted of some twenty vessels, the most important of these being a guided missile frigate (the *Duquesne*), five other frigates and five minesweepers.[59] With the outbreak of fighting between Iran and Iraq and the ensuing threat to the Strait of Hormuz, several additional naval units, including the *Suffren*, France's most modern guided missile frigate, were sent to the area, where they were involved in 'increased technical consultations' with other naval formations from the West (the United States, Britain and Australia).[60] France had never concealed that it regarded keeping open and protecting the oil routes as a vital factor in safeguarding its national security. Even at times during the 1970s when there were no crises, there was still quite a significant naval presence of about fifteen units. As before, it bolstered France's pretensions to a position of power along 'its' sea routes and served its policy of showing the flag from the Gulf and the Rea Sea, down the east coast of Africa as far as the more distant French possessions in the Southern Indian Ocean and the Antarctic.[61]

The French argue that this kind of display of military strength also automatically gives them the right to a political say in certain areas of interest which include the Western Indian Ocean. But another intrinsic part of its policy is the promotion of Francophone culture, a task always painstakingly carried out by Paris[62] in areas where traces from the colonial period remain, not least in those places (Mauritius and the Seychelles) where the British inherited a Gallic legacy from earlier French colonisers.

In the northern and eastern sub-regions of the Indian Ocean, the prerequisite French tradition was lacking.[63] Indochina, where this did exist, belonged to the Pacific region. Nevertheless, in the 1970s France put much effort into extending its activities, both political

59. See *New York Times*, 7.5,1981, p. A 5.

60. *Le Monde*, 29.10.1980. p. 10.

61. Kerguelen Archipelago; the islands of St Paul, Amsterdam and Crozet; Adélie Land (Antarctica).

62. Paris is assisted *inter alia* by research institutions in the universities, particularly in Aix-en-Provence where considerable opportunities exist for research on the Indian Ocean in various disciplines.

63. Except in tiny enclaves such as Pondicherry in South-Eastern India.

and economic, into areas where the predominant influence was Anglo-Saxon. It thus went into the Gulf region (where for decades cultural activities had been fostered in Iran, with the result that French had become the preferred foreign language of its upper stratum), into the Indian sub-continent and, from the late 1970s, into the ASEAN states, which had become of economic interest. In the Gulf and the Indian sub-continent both the methods of gaining political entry referred to above — economic co-operation and a common interest in being independent of the super-powers — were brought into play, especially in the sensitive areas of military equipment and nuclear energy. These instruments complemented each other.

The energy crisis of 1973–4 led France, which is heavily dependent on oil, to attempt in the manner for which it had been notorious in the 1960s and which it subsequently repeated under different guises, to get European support for its national interests and, having once obtained it, to venture on a policy of limited confrontation with the United States. At that time it was thought that bilateral supply agreements with individual oil-producing countries lessened dependence on multinational oil companies, and promises to supply arms and nuclear technology offered strong inducements to that end. This policy was to some extent successful, not least because France publicly supported the Arab cause against Israel ('barter Palestine for petroleum')[64]. But perhaps more often than not it became bogged down at the very outset, either because the United States exerted strong counter-pressure, or because France's 'non-aligned' positions were not shared by its European partners, or because political developments inhibited the development of major co-operation projects already under way, as with Iran and Iraq.

President Giscard d'Estaing's two state visits in 1980, to India and to the Gulf states, made this abundantly clear. The Indian visit in January of that year was overshadowed by the Soviet Union's occupation of Afghanistan which had just taken place. France showed great understanding of India's reluctance to condemn the Soviet Union, not the least of its reasons being the prospect of making major arms deliveries to India. This was reflected in the 'joint declaration' in which, under the banners of détente (France) and non-alignment (India), both sides stressed their 'particular responsibility' *vis-à-vis* the 'intervention' (referring to the activities of the Soviet Union) or 'interference' (a reference to those of the United States) on the part of the super-powers. Super-power

64. See W. Schütze, 'Neuorientierungen in der Aussenpolitik Frankreichs', *Europa-Archiv*, vol. 35, no. 23 (Dec. 1980), pp. 701–10.

'rivalry' must be countered, it was argued; moreover, the 'legitimate security interests of every state in the region' (an Indian euphemism for the Soviet Union's action) should be respected.[65] The President's trip to the Gulf in March 1980 also took place in the context of French endeavours to keep this vitally important sub-region out of the confrontation between East and West. Political concessions towards the Palestine Liberation Organisation and the establishment of a special relationship with Iraq were supposed to strengthen the basis of this policy. France had clearly distanced itself from the United States, while on the other hand the Euro-Arab dialogue was to be stepped up.

The emphasis on 'non-alignment' was tempered by France as well as by the Arab Gulf states when Iraq and Iran began their border war in the autumn of 1980. France recognised that its dominant security interests would be served by joining in Western endeavours to shield the southern end of the Gulf, and with it the Hormuz Strait in particular, against the instabilities resulting from the conflict. However, Paris acknowledged in addition 'that the room for manoeuvre for individual initiatives *vis-à-vis* the Soviet Union has become very limited and that the co-ordination of Western positions has priority'.[66] This meant the end — temporarily — of France's policy of 'mediation' between the super-powers. The post-Gaullist concept had turned out to be untenable at a time of acute East-West crisis.[67]

France was nonetheless able to close its 1980 Indian Ocean balance in credit. It had acquired important new spheres of influence which it has since been in a position to consolidate. The discreet assistance given by French security forces during the occupation of the mosque in Mecca at the end of 1979 paid off, and collaboration in this sector continued. France vigorously promoted itself to the Saudis as an alternative to the United States in the armaments field and, in view of inevitable tensions and ill-feeling between the United States and Saudi Arabia (over Israel, oil policy, etc.),[68] there was a wide range of activities in this sphere. However, given the critical shortage of personnel and technical know-how, it remains unclear whether and to what extent Saudi Arabia — and the Emirates, which are

65. *Le Monde*, 29.1.1980. p. 11.

66. Schütze, op. cit., p. 709.

67. During the 1962 Cuban crisis, de Gaulle himself was remarkably quick to side with the United States.

68. See U. Braun, 'Saudi-Arabiens veränderter Standort: Auswirkungen für den Westen', *Europa-Archiv*, vol. 35, no. 17 (Sept. 1980) pp. 539–46.

involved in a similar exercise — are in a position to diversify their defence arrangements in this way.

For this reason France had, many years previously, looked further east towards Pakistan, which promised to fill such lacunae. In the 1970s it appeared on the scene there — and at the same time in India — willing to supply arms and to enter into partnership to develop nuclear technology. According to plans made in Paris, Pakistan would supply to the Arab Gulf states pilots who were able to operate French flight systems (particularly the Mirage). The idea was discussed as early as 1973 during the state visit to Paris of Z.A. Bhutto, then Prime Minister of Pakistan.[69] The United States viewed this imminent challenge to its role as sole arms supplier to the Gulf with disfavour;[70] yet French and Pakistani plans were only fulfilled to a limited extent. In 1977–8 even the delivery to Pakistan of a French reprocessing plant for spent nuclear fuel was cancelled by France following American pressure. In India, on the other hand, France took part at an early stage in the construction of an experimental fast-breeder reactor of French design, and gave some assistance to the aerospace industry.

In early 1982, France and India concluded a deal — still not finalised at the time of writing — for the delivery and manufacture under license of 150 Mirage–2000 planes, from which France would earn more than $3,000 million. A special feature of the agreement is that this new Mirage system would be introduced in India in 1985, nearly simultaneously with its introduction into the French air force. This would be a very special case of high technology transfer to a Third World country.

Also in 1982, the French agreed to deliver enriched uranium for a US-built reactor in India, stepping into the place of Washington which wanted to retreat from the agreement because of the strict American legislation regarding non-proliferation. But in this highly sensitive area where the question of international safeguards is involved, it seems that France, as a member of the nuclear 'Suppliers Club', and India in its quest for total national independence are encountering difficulties in bridging their divergent interests and obligations. Some limits to French preparedness to assist the national aspirations of other nations in this particular field have thus become apparent.

Otherwise, the matter-of-factness with which France exports military equipment to any country which can pay for it has until now only occasionally led to resentment in the Indian Ocean area, as for

69. See *Le Monde*, 27.7.1973.
70. See *International Herald Tribune*, 18.9.73 and 4.1.1974.

example in India during the East Bengal crisis (when France gave up its arms trade with Pakistan in August 1971 only after strong protests from India), in Black Africa, where massive protests led it to discontinue its exports to South Africa in 1977,[71] and in Iran in 1980–1 owing to France's support for Iraq. On the whole, France has managed to make its openness to all parties in precisely these sensitive economic sectors credible as a principle of French policy — a principle which facilitates diversification for the recipient-countries and which is meant to lessen their dependence on the super-powers. In this France also upholds its claim to a special status, and appears — again in its own way — more of a known quantity than the other Western powers.

(e) *West Germany: many approaches but still no policy*

Unlike Britain and France, West Germany does not have — and has not had since the end of the First World War — any possessions in or around the Indian Ocean. It is less dependent on oil from the Persian Gulf than Japan, importing in 1980 about 45 per cent of its supplies from that region, a percentage which is on the decline.[72] Rivalry with other countries no longer provides one of the principal political motivations of its foreign policy.[73] But even if it had not done so before, after the invasion of Afghanistan at the end of 1979 Bonn certainly considered Soviet expansion in the vicinity of the Gulf to be a potential threat. In the Federal Republic, in contrast to the other outside powers considered here, the Indian Ocean, as an emerging focus of attention in international relations, had hitherto hardly been the object of much thought, let alone action, in official foreign policy or in political science. German publications on this topic have so far been few and far between, and their quality has hardly been outstanding. Not even the rudiments of a German 'Indian Ocean policy' exist in the early 1980s.

In the security-related sphere, the German Federal constitution precludes contributions to military defence outside the NATO area. Whereas within NATO's ministerial council some thought had been

71. This did not apply to all co-operation in this sphere. This is expected to change under the Mitterrand government.

72. In September 1980, the first month in which no oil was expected from Iran, West Germany imported a total of 7.7 million tonnes of which 3.3 million came from the Gulf states and no less than 2.1 million of this from Saudi Arabia alone. See Bundesministerium für Wirtschaft, *BMWi-Tagesnachrichten*, no. 7996, 28.10.1980, p. 3.

73. Until the beginning of the 1970s, rivalry with East Germany was still a strong motivating factor.

given in the past to the possibilities of extending NATO's area of activity, there was a discussion in the German press in the autumn of 1980 about whether it would be compatible with the spirit and the letter of its constitutional law for the Federal Republic to take part in an international military force overseas.[74] The Social-Democratic/Liberal coalition in Bonn answered in the negative but the issue is likely to be taken up again if the international environment and the conditions under which the Federal Republic conducts its activities continue to change as much in the 1980s and '90s as they have since the 1960s. This seems likely since instability is bound to increase in geographical areas of prime importance for the Federal Republic, which is itself poorly endowed with raw materials. Out of this situation could arise dangers which would have been unimaginable at the time when the constitution was being conceived. In any event, it is impossible to rule out a military contribution from the Federal Republic within the framework of an expanded commitment to intervene on the part of NATO, or within another collective alliance system, however little any Federal German government, given the country's vulnerable position and the burden of the German past, may be expected to volunteer for tasks commensurate with a development of this kind.

It was therefore not surprising that when a formation of German warships[75] was sent to the Indian Ocean for the first time (in the spring and summer of 1980), calling at several littoral states (Pakistan, India, Sri Lanka and Kenya, as well as Diego Garcia), there was something of a stir. The question was raised as to whether such a move was linked with a decision to abandon the principle of restricting activities to the NATO area. The Federal Government firmly denied any such claim and stressed that it had the right to use the high seas and moreover, that it was necessary from time to time to practise operating in tropical waters. However, these operations, which had been planned back in 1978, coincided exactly with a state of tension in the Indian Ocean. Additional orders were then given to the commanding officer of the formation 'which were designed to rule out any operational connection with the presence of other nations in the Indian Ocean'. The 'area of tension around the Persian Gulf was not entered.'[76]

Because of its particular sensitivity, the Federal Republic has up

74. See G. Gillessen, 'Das Grundgesetz sagt nichts über den Indischen Ozean', *Frankfurter Allgemeine Zeitung*, 3.10.1980.
75. Two destroyers, a tanker and a supply ship.
76. W. Reiss, 'Deutscher Flottenverband im Indischen Ozean', *Marine-forum*, 1981 1/2 (Jan./Feb.), pp. 4–10.

till now imposed very far-reaching restrictions upon itself regarding the supplying of weapons and equipment which could be used for military purposes. Outside the NATO sphere[77] such items are not supplied to 'areas of tension'. Yet, on the one hand it was never clear what precisely was to be classified as a military item, given the great many uses to which equipment (for example, in the vehicle and appliance sectors) could be put. On the other hand the definition of areas of tension[78] also caused endless problems. Discussions on this issue reached a temporary climax in 1980–1 when Saudi Arabia requested delivery of considerable quantities of the most up-to-date systems, notably Leopard II tanks. The advantages and disadvantages of a restrictive export policy were weighed up in an active public debate: this discussion is still going on, but there are indications that those in favour of continuing with a policy of restraint in this sphere are still in a strong position. The situation is somewhat different when it comes to orders for German shipyards because here employment is an important consideration and because on the whole warships are of little use for domestic purposes (i.e. repression). In any event, Bonn has been made highly conscious of the need to draw up new guidelines for the 1980s.

The Federal Republic has no historical obligations, prerogatives or burdens anywhere in the Indian Ocean region. Colonial East Africa (today mainland Tanzania) is entirely a thing of the past,[79] but up to the end of the 1970s, at least, the fact that during the inter-war period and up till after the beginning of the Second World War the German Reich had built up political, economic and cultural positions on the land bridge stretching from Turkey across Persia to Afghanistan (links which it was possible to revive in the 1950s) was not without significance. Already during the First World War, Britain had been worried about German 'adventures' in Afghanistan (the von Hentig mission). In the 1920s and '30s, Berlin strove to build up lines of communication along this Asiatic West-East axis, which included a Lufthansa air link as far as China. When the war broke out in 1939 there were ten times as many Germans in Afghanistan as there were British: they were serving as advisers (some of them in the army), engineers and technical instructors. The Third Reich's efficient construction team, the 'Todt Organisation',

77. And also those industrial countries which co-operate closely with the West, such as Australia, New Zealand and Japan.

78. The term originated from the predicament in 1965 of having to provide a conceptual basis for the breaking off of supplies to Israel.

79. Namibia, which is not of relevance in the Indian Ocean context, is probably a borderline case where German links are concerned.

built several roads and fortifications, and Siemens and Telefunken established telephone and radio communications.[80] On the British side of the Khyber Pass, anti-tank obstacles were hurriedly built in 1941,[81] because of the fear that the Germans might advance from the Caucasus across Persia. In that same year Iran was occupied by both Russia from one side and Britain and the United States from the other in accordance with a pact of 1907 which had likewise come into being because of a commonly perceived threat from Germany (the Baghdad railway).

In the 1950s and '60s West Germany was able to re-establish many of its old economic and cultural ties[82] in Iran and Afghanistan. The German presence was strong and had more substantial foundations in these countries than in the former British and French colonies which had become independent. In Afghanistan for example the instruction and further vocational training of the top echelons of the police force had since 1955 been entirely in German hands, and after the 1978 coup this tradition devolved upon East Germany. The fall of the Shah and the changes in Afghanistan at about the same time put an end to these special connections which had been in existence for decades.

In keeping with West Germany's interests and its conception of itself, relations with the Indian Ocean area evolved on the basis of bilateral official representation and economic expansion, which were frequently very much interrelated. In contrast to Japan (see above), the West German political presence was clearly shaped and strengthened by the provision of development aid and by semi-official organisations (e.g. those dealing with cultural and educational exchange). Thus in the 1960s and '70s, West Germany was one of the leading economic partners of the Indian Ocean countries as a group. This was because of both its economic competitiveness and the image it projected of itself as a Western industrial state encouraging development. These activities included countries with strong Anglo-Saxon or French traditions.[83]

West Germany soon became one of the most important maritime users of the Indian Ocean and of the Malacca Straits as a gateway to the Pacific. In its transport links with the Indian Ocean states, the

80. See M. Hauner, 'The Significance of Afghanistan: Lessons from the Past', *Round Table*, vol. 70, no. 270 (July 1980), pp. 240–4.

81. The remains of these can still be seen.

82. E.g. the large secondary school in Kabul, which had been founded as early as the 1920s.

83. But on the Arabian side of the Persian Gulf it took a very long time to catch up with Britain and the United States.

shipping of crude oil from the Persian Gulf through the Suez Canal, as well as around the Southern tip of Africa, acquired priority in the 1970s. In trade, German exports to oil-producing countries have, in some instances, risen by leaps and bounds since the first oil crisis. Exports to Iraq, for example, rose by 740 per cent in 1974 and even more steeply the following year.[84] As a result, West Germany was for several years Iraq's most important trading partner. The petro-dollars of other Gulf states were invested in German firms, though not to the extent of gaining a controlling interest; the decline of the US dollar, and continuing confidence in the stability of the German economy, were the reasons underlying this trend. The Iranian revolution brought heavy losses; German firms were expropriated and large orders were discontinued. However, all Western industrial countries were affected, and substantial economic losses were suffered by the Soviet Union too.[85]

The border war between Iran and Iraq also hit German economic interests, but because West Germany had smaller oil import quotas, its interests were less seriously affected than those of some of Baghdad's other partners. The conflict otherwise resulted in some disillusionment for German foreign policy. Until the eruption of the war, West Germany, like France, had made a special effort to develop closer political relations with Iraq, having calculated that this was a country with the potential for becoming a leading power among Arab and non-aligned countries.

Another reassessment was required in regard to India. After the Soviet invasion of Afghanistan, Bonn had considered India particularly well qualified to influence the Soviet Union. By the end of 1980 this view had already been proved wrong by India's vacillating, pro-Soviet attitude. However, India continued to be a key Third World country in the eyes of German diplomacy and for various industrial sectors in the Federal Republic; in the 1950s and '60s it had even occupied an especially prominent position, but later both countries developed other foreign policy priorities. German industry was unable to adapt to India's restrictive legislation, and various attempts to improve the quality of economic relations have so far failed because of bureaucratic hurdles in Delhi.[86]

84. According to the West German economics minister Friderichs on his return from a trip to Baghdad and Kuwait, in *BPA-Nachrichten*, 15.11.1975.

85. Nevertheless, in 1980 German exports rose compared with the previous year (US $1,400 million as against $1,170 million). See VWD (*Vereinigte Wirtschaftsdienste*), 6.5.1981.

86. Exploration of the sea-bed could turn out to be an interesting area of

In this respect, West Germany fared much better with the ASEAN countries. In the 1970s, bilateral relations initially formed the main emphasis. These relations were then substantially underpinned by the institutionalisation of links at organisational level between the EEC and ASEAN. German diplomacy made a valuable contribution to setting up this model for North-South co-operation, which was extended beyond the economic into the political sphere as well. The high point so far was in March 1980 when the Foreign Ministers of both organisations signed several agreements in Kuala Lumpur (on this occasion it was confirmed that the parties held similar views on the two main political problems of Asia at the time, namely Afghanistan and Cambodia).

Despite their structural diversity, ASEAN countries have stood their ground well during the economic crisis, which is closely linked to oil price increases (Indonesia and Malaysia are themselves not insignificant producers of oil). They are obviously interested in counterbalancing their trade with the United States and Japan, and in 1979 the EEC, with 15 per cent of ASEAN's foreign trade, lay behind Japan (25 per cent) and the United States (18 per cent). The equivalent figures for investments were 32 per cent for Japan, 16 per cent for the United States, and 14 per cent for the EEC.[87] ASEAN countries have an abundant supply of natural raw materials, the extraction and processing of which could be partly financed by EEC countries and could to some extent be facilitated by know-how from the EEC member-states. The partnership which is now getting under way shows signs of durability. In this context Bonn continually refers to its own political objectives which are to integrate developing countries into the world economy and to promote regional co-operation in the Third World, in response to the efforts of outside powers to achieve dominance there.[88]

On the opposite shores of the Indian Ocean, in Eastern and Southern Africa, on the other hand, West Germany is coming up against increasingly awkward problems. The crux of these problems lies in the permanent state of tension between Black Africa and the Republic of South Africa, which rose sharply following the collapse of Portugal's colonial empire. Here the dilemma for Bonn is similar to that of most other industralised countries which have until now

co-operation. Under a 1981 agreement, West Germany is to supply India with an exploration vessel and other appropriate equipment.

87. See *Süddeutsche Zeitung/Die Presse*, supplement on ASEAN, 13.11.1980, p. 11.

88. See Foreign Minister Genscher's speech in Kuala Lumpur, *Bulletin der Bundesregierung*, 11.3.1980, pp. 218 f.

endeavoured more or less successfully to find acceptable compromise solutions in their relations with both sides (see the sections on Japan and Britain). Beyond the borders of South Africa, in Namibia and Zimbabwe, such solutions have been successful or had at least reached the negotiating stage at the beginning of the 1980s. Indeed, with Namibia West Germany has played a considerable role in the search for a solution.

The touchstone of West Germany's relations with Black Africa in the 1980s will probably be its policy towards South Africa. In multilateral bodies such as the United Nations and the Organisation of African Unity, West Germany regularly came under attack in the 1970s because of the steady increase in its economic and technological activities in South Africa. Nuclear energy was one area which came in for particularly heavy criticism. In comparison, Bonn's bilateral relations with the most important Black African states have so far been less difficult than its multilateral ones, chiefly thanks to trade and foreign aid. Because the climate in Southern Africa can be expected to worsen, new and severe tests are undoubtedly on the agenda. Meanwhile the East-West conflict has spread still further — in Southern Africa and the Horn of Africa. West Germany will undoubtedly keep a close watch on East German activities there, including those in the military sphere.

In Africa too, as well as in the Indian Ocean region at large, Bonn must therefore adapt to political concepts which are adequate to take into account the inevitable further overlapping and deepening of the different types of conflict — East-West, North-South, South-South and Sino-Soviet — which are being played out there. This will then oblige it more and more frequently to take up a position in regional disputes in accordance with its own analysis of the situation and then to put this position forward within the framework of the decision-making processes of the EEC and the Atlantic Alliance.

In effect, this means the 'end of the post-war era', or in other words the end of the period in which the scope for action by Germany was determined on the basis of extrapolation from past experience, its limits being self-imposed. In addition, Bonn will have no choice but to comprehend and deal with this large region according to the way in which the region understands itself, for the level of common interests in the states around the Indian Ocean has increased. Geopolitical changes and the growing involvement of outside powers are contributing to this development. West Germany must endeavour to take a more synoptical view of events there than it has done previously. A possible first move in that direction was a conference of German heads of mission, covering the area between Cairo and Delhi, held early in 1981 at Islamabad and attended by the

Federal Republic's Foreign Minister; this type of consultation may serve to counteract the prevailing way of thinking in narrow geographical reference terms. The 'arc of crisis', with its web of instabilities, largely follows the shores of the Indian Ocean. In its dealings with this typical Third World region, West Germany's ability to judge developments had been restricted by its relative lack of colonial experience. This period should now belong to the past. In the 1980s, Bonn is confronted with the need and the opportunity to define its interests more sharply, and to act accordingly.

Part III
INTERACTION BETWEEN EXTERNAL AND REGIONAL POLITICAL AND STRATEGIC INTERESTS

Chapter 5

(*a*) *Australia's regional involvement and its alliance with the West*

Up until the end of the 1960s, Australia considered itself a country looking towards the Pacific and closely associated with the United States in this extended region, the latter protecting it militarily. Its west coast facing the Indian Ocean appeared to be protected by Britain's strong position in that region. However, the announcement of Britain's withdrawal from east of Suez occurred at the same time as Western Australia was being developed economically, with the result that Australia's Indian Ocean coast and its ports gained in significance. The appearance of a regular Soviet naval presence in the Indian Ocean during this same period was perceived as a threat of a new kind.[1] Over the next few years, the conservative Australian government looked for increased support from the United States, but did not always find the response it hoped for.

Since this important turning-point, the political and strategic equilibrium between the super-powers in the Indian Ocean area has been a top foreign policy issue in Canberra. Of all the countries bordering on the Indian Ocean, Australia can be compared in this respect only with India which has an equally strong interest, albeit for different reasons, in the configuration of forces in this region.[2]

The 1972–5 Labor government headed by Gough Whitlam emphasised those aspects of its foreign policy position which had clearly differed from former conservative ones. This had the effect of delineating Australia's foreign policy in a new perspective but

1. See K.C. Beazley and I. Clark (eds), op. cit. pp. 127 f.
2. Between 1974 and 1978, Iran was also greatly preoccupied with such matters.

115

without having to remove the mainstay of its ties with the United States. On the contrary, these ties remained decisive, although Washington now had to put up with stronger criticism. Whitlam stressed his country's solidarity with the aims of Asian countries and the Non-Aligned. The conservatives (i.e. the Liberal Party) had rejected the concept of the 'Indian Ocean Peace Zone', but Australia now took a positive stand towards it and became a member of the Ad Hoc Committee (see p. 176). The fundamental incompatibility of this position with Australia's continuing membership of the ANZUS Pact[3] and with the obligations connected with that membership — in particular the existence of American military installations on Australian soil — was pushed aside. Whitlam wanted to steer a course that would place the Asiatic and Pacific area surrounding Australia — 'our region' as he called it — into the foreground for the first time. This approach was one-sided, but it was basically correct. Australia had to find an identity which was in keeping with its geopolitical position, by establishing a greater degree of detachment from the United States and Britain and by increasing regional co-operation.

The security link with the United States continued to be obligatory for Australia even during this phase. For although it has a slowly increasing coloured population,[4] it will continue to consider itself a part of the West for the foreseeable future. Its ties with the United States are a yardstick of the insecurity to which it considers itself prone as a geographically isolated, sparsely populated country rich in natural resources, with a 'white' level of development in a world which is overpopulated and increasingly short of raw materials.

Whitlam had tried, under the umbrella of the United States, to get an undertaking from both super-powers that they would limit their presence by mutual agreement in 'his region', which included the Indian Ocean — but in vain. However from the end of 1975 the new government (the conservatives and the Country Party) under Prime Minister Malcolm Fraser changed course. It was now argued that the relative strength of the super-powers in the Indian Ocean had been upset by Soviet expansion and that the United States should immediately set about strengthening its presence there so as to redress the balance. In advancing this thesis, Fraser was going against the political and strategic assessment made in his own

3. ANZUS — Australia, New Zealand and the United States — was set up in 1952.
4. Estimates for the year 2000 put its share at about 5 per cent of the population.

country[5] — and in the United States, as was particularly obvious when, soon after taking office, President Carter appealed to the Soviet Union in March 1977 for a 'complete demilitarisation of the Indian Ocean' (see Chapter 3 above). As a consequence of these developments, there was also a change in the tone of official Australian pronouncements. The new line of argument — which also determined Australia's position in the United Nations — was that it was desirable to have a balance of forces between the super-powers at the lowest possible level. At the end of 1977, according to statements made by its Defence Minister, Australia did not see itself exposed to any 'clearly perceived threat', and defence expenditure remained limited accordingly.[6]

The next change of course was taken in 1978–9 and was connected with Vietnam's occupation of Cambodia and increased military co-operation between Hanoi and Moscow, which included the use of Vietnamese — formerly American — bases at Cam Ranh Bay and Danang. The change became even more pronounced following the Iranian crisis, and finally the Soviet occupation of Afghanistan. Australia took its stand firmly alongside the ASEAN countries in agreement with the United States as well as with Japan and China. Over Afghanistan, it opposed the position adopted by West European countries and particularly by France and West Germany on the grounds that it was too hesitant.[7] By the beginning of the 1980s — after the conservatives had won a second victory at the polls — Australia had in any case largely returned to its position of ten years previously; it was unmistakably on the side of the United States and clearly opposed to the Soviet Union. The 'balance at the lowest possible level' formula became less important in this context. In relation to the Indian Ocean region, however, there had in the meantime been many changes which also led to the formulation of new Australian foreign and security policy priorities for the new decade:[8]

— Over 50% of Australia's imports and exports (by tonnage) passed through the Indian Ocean (but only about 14 per cent of its trade was with the littoral states).

— Australia's oil import requirements have been increasing since the mid-1970s when they made up 25 per cent of total requirements,

5. See the 1976 report of the Senate Standing Committee on Foreign Affairs and Defence under the chairmanship of Senator Sim (Liberal Party), *Australia and the Indian Ocean Region*, Canberra 1976.

6. *FEER*, 2.12.1977, pp. 34 f.

7. However, Australia did send a team to the Olympic Games in Moscow.

8. See K.C. Beazley and I. Clark (eds), op. cit.

and they are expected to reach 65 per cent of Australia's requirements by the middle of the 1980s. In 1980 the largest proportion of
its oil imports came from the Persian Gulf.
— At the same time, Australia's exports to Gulf states rose to offset
its imports from this region. Raw materials and goods from Western
Australia formed a high percentage of these exports. On the other
hand, Western Australia is much more dependent on imported oil
(which accounted for 72 per cent of its requirements at the end of the
1970s) than the other federal states.
— In the 1970s, Western Australia's mineral wealth became increasingly significant. This mainly consisted of ore which was shipped to
Japan.
— Western Australia had clearly increased in importance for this
reason, and this was reflected in the decision to strengthen the
military infrastructure there (e.g. with the naval base at Cockburn
Sound, south of Perth).
— Heard Island in the southern Indian Ocean as well as the
Christmas and Cocos Islands in the eastern Indian Ocean belong to
Australia. From the mid-1970s the latter group was integrated more
fully into Australia's military infrastructure, especially that of the
air force. The US air force also used this infrastructure. A 200-mile
fishing zone around these islands was declared in 1979.[9]
— The probable outcome of the international conference on the law
of the sea will extend Australia's jurisdiction to cover a 200-mile
economic zone. This will also increase the responsibilities of the
coastguard service, which until 1980 had only twelve high speed
launches to cover 15,000 km. of coastline.
During the 1970s Australia emphasised several key political and
economic factors in the Indian Ocean region, which with few exceptions are likely to be valid in the 1980s. Among the exceptions is the
close co-operation which Whitlam cultivated with India between
1972 and 1975, chiefly in the political sphere. This was mainly
related to the super-powers and the Peace Zone. Under Fraser
— following a short period of better relations with Prime Minister
Morarji Desai — these ties again loosened. This was unavoidable
given the differing positions on international issues held respectively
in Canberra and New Delhi. In South Asia, Australia did however
maintain quite good relations with Bangladesh, which dated back to
the Bengal war of independence in 1971. Bangladesh was subsequently to become one of the few target-countries of Australian
development assistance in the Indian Ocean area.

9. See Department of Foreign Affairs Backgrounder (Canberra),
no. 285, 27.5.1981, p. ix.

By about 1980, Australia's main interests in the Indian Ocean area lay in two sub-regions — the ASEAN countries and Southern Africa. The reasons in the former case were chiefly economic and strategic, while in the latter they were predominantly political.

As we saw earlier, Australian diplomacy and Prime Minister Fraser himself played an important part in settling the issue of Zimbabwe on independence in 1979–80. Over racial conflicts in Southern Africa, the conservatives continued Whitlam's policy of solidarity with the Third World but implemented it in a slightly more restricted way. As early as the beginning of 1976, Fraser recognised the Neto government in Angola. In 1978 Canberra was opposed to France, Belgium and the United States acting to save Mobuto in Zaire. Mozambique was given economic aid, and the South West Africa People's Organization (SWAPO) was recognised as an important political force in Namibia. At the beginning of 1979 the decision was taken to send an Australian contingent as a peace-keeping force to Namibia if the situation required it, and both South Africa and SWAPO agreed to this. Pretoria's apartheid policy has been and continues to be strongly condemned. Yet bilateral economic ties continue, although diplomatic relations have been reduced to the necessary minimum.

What are the reasons for such a conspicuous involvement in an area so far removed from Australia's own immediate sphere of interest? Canberra takes the view that any radicalisation in Southern Africa stemming from racial and economic discrimination benefits the Soviet Union and that it is therefore important to encourage moderate political forces there and to condemn any kind of external military intervention. It maintains that a failure to prevent the radicalisation of Black governments and movements would mean setbacks for the West in Southern Africa which would in turn lead to repercussions in other parts of the Indian Ocean region. In addition, interests of a different kind are certainly also involved, given the problems Australia had with what remain of its aborigines, with its former colony Papua New Guinea, and with racial prejudice among broad sections of the white population.[10]

Australia's relations with South-East Asia are more complex. Only those aspects in which political and strategic elements are paramount will be considered here. The economic component would be just as important for a comprehensive evaluation, and in this connection Australia finds itself subject to strong attacks from

10. See H.S. Albinski, 'Australia and the Indian Ocean' in Bowman and Clark, op. cit., p. 74 f.

ASEAN countries because of its protectionist policies (for which it in its turn reproaches the EEC).

Within the framework of the Commonwealth, Australia since the beginning of the 1970s has been co-operating in defence matters with Malaysia and Singapore (see p. 93) and more extensively with Indonesia. The fall of Saigon in 1975 had strong repercussions in Australia and in the ASEAN countries. As it had weakened the United States as a potential protective power, the outcome was a *rapprochement* between the non-communist states of the region. The first signs of this *rapprochement* were set out in the Australian Defence White Paper of 1976.[11] However, it took the aggravation of the situation in Indochina before, both in ASEAN countries (mainly Malaysia and Indonesia) and in the Australian Labor Party, hopes lessened that Vietnam would be willing to co-operate. The 1978 treaty between Vietnam and the Soviet Union was interpreted both in ASEAN capitals and in Canberra as a new threat which had to be taken seriously. A militarily powerful Vietnam backed by the full force of a super-power altered the strategic situation in the area between the Indian Ocean and the Pacific.

The Soviet occupation of Afghanistan provided the extra impetus required to increase defence efforts both in ASEAN and in Australia. At the end of 1980, Prime Minister Fraser proposed to Singapore and Malaysia a revival of the five-power agreement which had been concluded in 1971 with Britain and New Zealand and which provided for training facilities in Australia, joint manoeuvres and an integrated air defence system.[12] The Australian Defence Minister gave a detailed explanation to parliament of the situation and the plans for co-operation with Australia's ASEAN neighbours. Such co-operation was to be seen as 'a process of demonstrating the underlying solidarity of the region in support of strategic interests that are shared'; 'the abiding security interests that we share with our regional neighbours call for continuing consultation and co-operation in the defence field.'[13] Although many of these intentions are likely to remain mere rhetoric, the degree of harmonisation taking place and the amount of information being disclosed in relation to precisely those military topics which had hitherto been

11. See D.J. Killen (Defence Minister), *Australian Defence*, Canberra, 1976 (Government Printing Service).

12. The first meeting of representatives from Britain, Australia, New Zealand, Singapore and Malaysia took place in January 1981 in Kuala Lumpur. Air and land manoeuvres started soon after.

13. See Department of Foreign Affairs Backgrounder (Canberra), no. 264, 10.12.1980.

dealt with cautiously in this region is nevertheless remarkable. The late 1970s brought forth changes in this sphere which could in no way have been foreseen at the beginning of the decade.

With the more critical global situation at the beginning of the 1980s, Australia considered, to a greater extent than previously, that the best guarantee of its security lay in the ANZUS Pact. At a meeting of foreign ministers from the three Pact member-countries in Washington in February 1980, the Indian Ocean was included in future ANZUS activities under the heading 'additional measures of military co-operation'. Australia subsequently dispatched some naval units and the aircraft-carrier *Melbourne* to the Strait of Hormuz and took part in joint naval exercises there and in the eastern Indian Ocean.

In addition, Australia fell in with American requests to incorporate the Darwin air force base into the strategic B-52 bomber network[14] and appeared prepared in principle to open the naval base at Cockburn Sound on the Indian Ocean to the US navy, possibly with a view to the more long-term home-porting of personnel. By the same token, Australia's air force took part in long-distance reconnaissance over the Indian Ocean from Diego Garcia.

Nonetheless Australia's most important contribution to 'collective security', now as before, is that it makes available military installations which are of great value to the United States in the supra-regional strategic balance of the super-powers. The three most important of these have been in operation from the late 1960s, since when they have constantly been extended. They are:
— the Exmouth communications centre (North-West Cape) which specialises *inter alia* in very low-frequency communication with submerged submarines;
— the Nurrungar early warning satellite station which has the task of detecting enemy missile attacks;
— the Pine Gap reconnaissance station which is linked to a geostationary satellite looking into Soviet and Chinese territory.[15]

There appears to be no disagreement among the experts as to the global strategic significance of these installations. In Australia itself there were initial protests, especially from the Labor Party, against the country's resulting involvement in the strategic confrontation between the super-powers and the resulting threat to national security. Yet even the Whitlam government had never called these

14. Cf. the agreement of 11 March 1981, the text of which is in Department of Foreign Affairs Backgrounder no. 274, 11.3.1981, p. viii.

15. See D. Ball 'American Bases: Implications for Australia's Security', *Current Affairs Bulletin* (Sydney), vol. 55, no. 5 (October 1978), pp. 4–14.

facilities into question, but rather had only claimed Australian 'sovereign rights' over them. The United States acceded to this, but it appears certain to experts that the many varied and overlapping functions of these complex installations, which are connected to a worldwide American communications and surveillance network, could scarcely be controlled by Australian liaison personnel. Critical Australian observers like Desmond Ball are therefore afraid that these installations could be put to numerous uses against the national interest and are demanding an investigation into the consequences of their being dismantled as the result of pressure from Canberra.[16] Up till now, no Australian government, not even Gough Whitlam's, has seriously considered this option. At the beginning of 1981, Canberra again agreed to Pine Gap's operations being enlarged, and this is obviously directly connected with the threat and deterrence potential of the super-powers.[17] At the same time however, the leader of the parliamentary opposition, Mr Hayden, demanded a revision of the agreement with the United States which covered the use of the North West Cape centre. He argued that it was essential to ensure that all orders issued from there had been approved in advance by the Australian government; if the United States did not accept this condition, a future Labor government would require that the station's activities be discontinued.[18] It is highly unlikely that the United States would accede to such a demand, and whether a Labor government would then proceed accordingly seems doubtful.

The United States could in the last resort withdraw further into the Pacific, but if it did so Australia would lose its important role as Washington's ally and would find itself exposed to the dangers of becoming isolated in an increasingly incalculable environment. In many respects it seems apt to compare Australia's position with that of West Germany which is also in the dilemma of being particularly exposed to the potentially hostile power because of American protection.

(b) South-East Asia: increasing polarisation and the shadow of China

From the Bandung Conference in 1955 until the mid-1970s there was a basic mood prevailing among the newly created nation-states of Africa and Asia — particularly in South-East Asia because of the United States' involvement in Vietnam — which President Suharto

16. ibid.
17. See *The Times*, 7.2.1981, p. 5.
18. See *SZ*, 16–17. 4.1981, p. 8.

of Indonesia expressed in his speech to the Non-Aligned Conference in Lusaka in 1970:

'From this forum we express the hope that the major powers will cease to play power-politics that are merely designed to take advantage of the weakness of the developing nations. [. . .] It is only our right if we express the hope that the Nixon Doctrine, or what is known as the Brezhnev Doctrine, or the Lin Piao Manifesto and the like, should not be utilized as an excuse to justify interference in the internal affairs of a country.'[19]

In a document published exactly ten years later, Singapore's Ministry of Foreign Affairs attacked 'a new imperialism' which had 'started its offensive in Kampuchea'.[20] Using ideology as a justification, Vietnam as well as Cuba had interfered in the affairs of other developing countries. The second half of the 1970s was in fact increasingly marked by Third World conflicts of this kind, chiefly in Africa and in South-East Asia. Through the support they gave to the opponents, the great powers certainly exercised a great deal of influence over the extent to which polarisation occurred; yet the reasons for the conflicts were intra-regional, with historical and ethnic roots in the region concerned, and were based on contrasting political and social objectives. In South-East Asia, Vietnam steadfastly established a position of leadership in Indochina, which after 1979 it endeavoured to consolidate. This, combined with an ideological sense of mission, was the primary cause of conflict at the beginning of the 1980s. All other conflicting elements, and the strategic interests of the super-powers as well, related to the 'Cambodia syndrome'.

South-East Asia is the bridge between the extended maritime and political systems of the Pacific and the Indian Ocean. From the beginning of the 1970s, the significance of this threshold has increased, particularly for the two super-powers, but also for Japan and Britain. As explained elsewhere, the reasons for this are various. When, at the end of 1971, Malaysia and Indonesia declared the Straits of Malacca to be their joint waterway, the main foreign users were as one in rejecting this claim by referring to the right of unhindered passage. Only China, because of its fundamental opposition to 'super-power hegemony', supported the two local states, and it was all the easier for Peking to adopt this position as its own shipping was as yet only slightly affected. Although Malaysia and Indonesia (Singapore had no part in this move) would not have

19. Quoted in G.J. Pauker, 'Indonesian Perspectives on the Indian Ocean' in Burrell and Cottrell, op. cit., p. 228.

20. Quoted in P. Lyon, 'Vietnam's Tense Triangle', *South* (London), Jan./Feb. 1981, p. 13.

been in a position either individually or jointly to apply sanctions to give weight to their demand for the recognition of national defence rights over the use of the Malacca Straits, they nevertheless provoked a great deal of diplomatic activity from Washington, Moscow, Tokyo and London.[21] In the step taken by the two local states, foreign powers saw a challenge to traditional rights to the use of the high seas similar to that contained in the proposal of littoral Indian Ocean states for the creation of an 'Indian Ocean Peace Zone', which was being announced to the United Nations at that time (see p. 74). They accordingly voted against it there too, and at first took up similarly negative positions, whereas China supported this proposal as well.

The 'Kuala Lumpur Declaration' was also made at the end of 1971. In this declaration, the foreign ministers of the countries belonging to ASEAN[22] proposed that South-East Asia should be recognised internationally as a 'zone of peace, freedom and neutrality' (see Chapter 6 below). The coincidence of all three initiatives — the national claims over the Straits of Malacca, the Indian Ocean Peace Zone and the South-East Asia Peace Zone — gave expression at that juncture to the attitude among Indian Ocean countries, mentioned at the beginning of this section, regarding new figurations in the presence of the great powers. Against these, it was hoped that, in keeping with newly tested models of Third World solidarity (i.e. at the 1970 Non-Aligned summit), it would be possible to band together and push through their own sovereignty claims.

Regarding South-East Asia, irreconcilable conceptual differences emerged in 1976 at the Non-Aligned summit in Colombo. The two communist neighbours, Vietnam and Laos, denied the ASEAN countries the right to speak on their behalf and thus prevented the inclusion in the conference's communiqué of the Peace Zone proposal for South-East Asia, in accordance with the Kuala Lumpur declaration. Vietnam and Laos subsequently demanded that American and Japanese influence be substantially reduced in the ASEAN area and put forward their own version of regional co-operation, which involved concluding bilateral agreements based on concepts which were incompatible with those of ASEAN. Last but not least, it was by this time (1978) clear how the foreign policy

21. See B. Sen Gupta, T.T. Poulose and H. Bhatia, *The Malacca Straits and the Indian Ocean* (New Delhi 1974), p. 128.

22. In 1967, Indonesia, Malaysia, Singapore, Thailand and the Philippines came together and formed this grouping. At the time it was no more than a very loose community of interests.

priorities of both sides had developed. ASEAN's were pro-Western, with cautious overtures towards China, and those of Vietnam and Laos were pro-Soviet, critical of the United States, and strongly anti-Chinese. The Cambodian crisis was to complicate matters still further.

Burma, a South-East Asian state on the Indian Ocean, insisted on taking an outsider's position throughout this period — until around the end of the 1970s. The government in Rangoon was and will probably continue to be prevented from exercising power over large areas of the country because of ethnic and other militantly separatist interests. In this connection, Chinese influence is significant. It compels every Burmese government to keep on the right side of Peking, and it would not be feasible for Burma to ally itself with powers hostile to China. Yet Burma can in no way be described as China's satellite. Its startling resignation from the Non-Aligned movement after the Havana summit in September 1979, on the grounds that the movement had departed too far from its principles, was based on its own decision. At the end of the 1970s Burma was taking similar positions to ASEAN on important foreign policy issues, particularly on Cambodia, and had also gradually drawn closer to the West and to Japan.

In South-East Asia, the interaction of external and regional interests took place in a typical manner. It is important in this context that China considers itself a regional power *vis-à-vis* South-East Asia — a view that is reciprocated. Geopolitical factors, historical events and the presence of Chinese minorities in Indochina, as well as in ASEAN countries and in Burma, are a constant reminder of the proximity of the empire of 1,000 million Chinese.

Following the military withdrawal of the United States from Vietnam (and thus also from Thailand), it was not immediately clear to what extent and in what way this great power, now badly shaken, would in the future still be committed in and to South-East Asia. In fact it took several years before this situation became any clearer. Important events in this context were the new agreement on military bases made with the Philippines in January 1979 and, later the same year, the American decision not to withdraw any of its troops from South Korea.[23] In the meantime, however, the Sino-Soviet conflict had become the dominant element of outside influence in the sub-region, and it is likely to remain so in the 1980s.

Cambodia was the catalyst here. China did not want Cambodia's incorporation into an Indochina dominated by Hanoi, and so from

23. For a concise account of these and subsequent events, cf Leifer, op. cit.

the outset supported the Khmer Rouge, in so far as they were nationalistic and anti-Vietnamese. (Other groupings in the anti-American front, on the other hand, were willing to collaborate with Vietnam, and they subsequently formed the cadres in Vietnamese-occupied Cambodia.) After Pol Pot had taken over in Phnom Penh in 1975, Hanoi hoped for the opportunity to be able to incorporate Cambodia into a socialist Indochinese confederation under its own control (an equivalent agreement along these lines was concluded with Laos in 1977). China did its utmost to oppose this, and from the end of 1977 opposition to Hanoi thus prevailed as the decisive factor within the Khmer Rouge. In 1978 its close ties with China were undoubtedly consolidated and skirmishes on the border with Vietnam increased.

In the autumn of 1978, Vietnam's Prime Minister Pham Van Dong visited several ASEAN countries and gave assurances that Vietnam had no plans to invade its neighbour. Only weeks later, however, Hanoi concluded a treaty of friendship and mutual assistance with the Soviet Union, an obvious case of reassurance against any measures the Chinese might take and comparable in this respect to the Indo-Soviet treaty concluded during the 1971 East Bengal crisis. By the beginning of 1979, Vietnamese troops had already occupied Cambodia. The reaction to this from the ASEAN countries and from Burma was extremely bitter, and they emphasised the breach of trust that had occurred following Pham Van Dong's visit. Indeed this incident undoubtedly had lasting repercussions, and it is also likely to cause any future Vietnamese assurances to be treated with the greatest reserve.

The occupation of Cambodia, subsequent Chinese 'punitive action' in February-March 1979, and the new threat to Thailand which arose from the loss of its historic buffer area, placed the non-communist countries of South East Asia in a new position. The ASEAN countries succeeded in finding a common approach, but not without some difficulty since each country had a different perception of the threat and of its own foreign and security priorities. Thailand and Singapore responded with an outright condemnation of Vietnam, and demanded its complete withdrawal from Cambodia before the start of any negotiations. This response largely coincided with China's position — although Singapore in particular was by no means acting out of pro-Chinese motives. Malaysia, Indonesia and also the Philippines, on the other hand, advocated a more moderate course which would make it easier for Vietnam to accept a compromise solution. These countries considered that it was China, particularly in the light of its 'punitive action', that posed the greater threat, whereas they did not want to deter Vietnam from entering into partnership with them sometime in the future, even if it became the supreme power throughout the whole of Indochina. A semi-official Indonesian assessment of the situation made in 1979 was symptomatic of this attitude:

ASEAN has adopted a neutral attitude, with regard to both the conflict between Vietnam and Kampuchea and the conflict between China and Vietnam. ASEAN's neutrality is intended to reduce the involvement of Great Powers in the region. On the one hand, this neutral stance seeks to prevent Vietnam from feeling cornered which could drive it further into the Soviet sphere of influence and thus enlarge the presence of the Soviet Union in Southeast Asia. On the other hand, there is anxiety as to China's intentions, especially its long-range intentions, which as yet remain unclear and indefinite. Thus the best course for ASEAN is seen as trying to limit the involvement of China in the region.[24]

However, the need for solidarity with Thailand, the new frontline state, was an issue central to the continued existence of ASEAN, and required its members to adopt a more clearly defined position. This was furthered by the Soviet occupation of Afghanistan and by Vietnam's violation of the frontier and its incursion into Thai territory in June 1980. Both events seemed to suggest a pattern, namely a lack of respect for the integrity of non-communist countries which for strategic as well as for ideological reasons were exposed to the risk of seizure or which at the very least were expected to conform to certain standards of good conduct as perceived by the 'socialist camp'. The three Indochinese countries had given a signal to that effect in a joint communiqué in which they had immediately and expressly hailed the Afghanistan operation as a victory for the common cause. The communiqué stated that the solidarity of the states of Indochina combined with the 'bulwark of world revolution' was invincible; it could 'change the balance of forces' in South-East Asia 'in favour of . . . national independence and social progress'.[25]

For ASEAN it was high time in 1980 to draw the line. Diplomacy alone was not adequate to counter manifest intimidation. Their own forces were in no way adequate to engage in active opposition.[26] To begin with, it seemed China and the United States were inevitably involved in efforts to protect Thailand. However, for ASEAN it was

24. J. Wanandi, *Security Dimensions of the Asia-Pacific Region in the 1980's*, Centre for Strategic and International Studies, Jakarta, 1979, p. 8.
25. FEER, 18.1.1980, p. 12.
26. All the same, ASEAN countries steadily increased their defence expenditure in recent years, drastically in some areas and chiefly for air forces. Yet were they to unite, which is hardly to be expected, these forces would long remain obviously inferior to those of Vietnam.

just as important to maintain a military counterweight to the Soviet Union's increased presence (using Vietnamese installations) in the Pacific and Indian Oceans. Here the interests of ASEAN countries coincided with those of the United States, China, Japan, Australia and Western European countries. Polarisation along the line of conflict between East and West had intensified and as a result the Sino-Soviet conflict was largely subsumed. A new type of constellation had emerged in this area.

Future developments will depend primarily on Hanoi. In the medium term it could be that the trend towards far-reaching independence from Moscow will win through, as has been predicted by many experts on South-East Asia,[27] and in fact this seems inevitable given the implications of militant Vietnamese nationalism. Contacts could then be in the offing which would transcend ideological divisions in this sub-region. Such a development is most clearly desired in Jakarta and in Kuala Lumpur. A prerequisite for this would be for the Cambodia problem to be resolved in such a way as to maintain a security function for Vietnam in Indochina, yet with compromise formulae which would enable ASEAN to save face. Then again, Peking might feel obliged gradually to reduce the pressure which it has exerted on Vietnam since the 'punitive action' of 1979. This school of thought starts from the assumption that China is primarily afraid of the Soviet Union's influence (which has been consolidated by treaties) on its southern flank, i.e. from Indochina, and that an Indochina led by a nationalist, communist Vietnam, which is essentially independent of Moscow, is no more than a secondary concern.

Others argue against this view. It is maintained that by no later than the time of its admission to Comecon in June 1978,[28] Vietnam had on its own initiative moved so far into the Soviet embrace that it would be very difficult for it to free itself, even if the direct threat from China were reduced. This alliance is now of the utmost strategic importance for the Soviet Union. Since 1978 a variety of compelling factors have considerably strengthened Hanoi's alignment with Moscow. Its desire for leadership in Indochina imposes considerable economic burdens, notably the expense of maintaining a grossly oversized army. Even if Cambodia were to be pacified, this would not substantially alter the situation. Comparisons with Cuba

27. The author's comments here are based in part on numerous conversations held in Asian capitals and in Australia in recent years.

28. See H. Bräker, op. cit. Bräker cites 1973 as the year when Vietnam started to move from a position of equidistance from the two communist powers to its close relationship with Moscow.

spring to mind even if one does not simply repeat the Chinese slogan 'the Cuba of Asia'. Only the Soviet Union is in a position to guarantee the funds[29] which, at the beginning of the 1980s, were not able to preserve the Vietnamese economy from stagnation and even from recession. These are the effects of an ideologically based economic and social policy which, following an experimental phase lasting until 1977, has become ever more dogmatic.

Those who belong to this school of thought believe that the alliance between Vietnam and the Soviet Union is permanently sealed, that China will consequently remain hostile, and that in addition Thailand will be in constant danger. In a global political situation of heightened East-West antagonism, or at least of continuing confrontation, South-East Asia will therefore remain a region in which both the Sino-Soviet conflict and the contrasting political and strategic interests of the West (including Japan and Australia) and the Soviet-led bloc will continue to be apparent.

Developments so far seem to bear out the views of this second school of thought. Yet here as elsewhere there are numerous imponderables, and predictable outcomes are unlikely. What is clear, bearing in mind that China is also a regional power in South-East Asia, is that regional politics rather than external influences will be the main decisive factor. The situation in the region could evolve in a variety of different ways. For example, there could be leadership changes in Vietnam, perhaps due to internal disparities (the South is apparently proving difficult to integrate), or there could be instability in ASEAN countries (Thailand and the Philippines seem the most susceptible to this but it applies to Indonesia too). In the medium term there could be internal changes in China as well, and these could have repercussions on its foreign policy. Should Cambodia be 'liberated' under Vietnamese domination and be recognised internationally, following India's example, this will alter the configuration in the region. The re-appearance of Prince Sihanouk as the new leader of anti-Vietnamese Cambodian resistance has made Hanoi's task harder; its main asset remains the negative image of the Khmer Rouge.

At present the striking military imbalance in South-East Asia inevitably forces countries to take sides. ASEAN on the whole needs American support, and Thailand also needs that of the Chinese. A Vietnamese advance towards Thailand would probably trigger Chinese action — most likely against Laos too. In that case the Soviet Union as party to a treaty could hardly stand by and watch yet

29. Estimates put present Soviet assistance to Indochina at US $2.5–3 million per day.

again, and the scene would be set for a (probably limited) Sino-Soviet conflict. To what extent the United States would then become involved would undoubtedly depend very much on the configuration of forces in the Pacific at that particular juncture; but in any event escalations with repercussions in the Indian Ocean as well as in Europe would certainly be inevitable.

In the event of a conflict, Soviet use of the Vietnamese Cam Ranh and Danang bases (and probably of the Cambodian port of Kompong Som) would be of consequence.[30] As revealed by the presence of the aircraft-carrier *Minsk* and other Soviet naval units in the Gulf of Siam in October 1980, the Soviet Union now claims the right to confront and rival American military power even in areas where the latter hitherto had strategic advantage. The alliance with Vietnam is thus of great value to the Soviet Union as a global power both for offensive and defensive purposes, and because Vietnam provides a connection between its Pacific coast and the Indian Ocean. It is a double advantage to have dealings with a regime in power in Hanoi, which because of its ideological persuasion and resulting world view is so closely aligned with Moscow. Of all Third World countries, this previously applied only to Cuba.

(c) *South Asia: India's quest for supremacy and Afghanistan as a catalyst*

Under Nehru, India pursued a globally oriented foreign policy with an eye on the power blocs of East and West and usually at a careful distance from them. But under Indira Gandhi priorities were changed. By the time of the emergence of Bangladesh, if not earlier,[31] the consolidation and protection of its dominating position in its own sub-region, along with the elimination of Pakistan's long-standing claim to the greatest possible parity with India, in particular had become the primary goal. Western states with interests in the region had, until the end of 1971, still largely followed the precept of treating the two unequal legacies of British India fundamentally in the same way, whereas from as early as 1955 the Soviet Union had persistently taken account of India's natural pre-eminence. Then

---

30. The Vietnamese Foreign Minister has repeatedly stated that for the time being Vietnam did not want to permit the Soviets to establish proper bases, but that visiting warships were normal; and that otherwise everything depended on how the international situation developed in the future.

31. See D. Braun, 'Die Staatsgründung von Bangladesch', in *Die Internationale Politik 1970–1972* (Jahrbücher des Forschungsinstituts der Deutschen Gesellschaft für Auswärtige Politik), Munich 1976, p. 413–28.

after its rival had been divided into two separate states, India's main goal appeared to be within reach: this was to keep all outside powers at such a distance from the territory to which it laid claim that they could no longer influence the balance of power in that area against India's interests. In 1972–3 the United States and Britain seemed prepared to accept this, while China at the time lacked the power to interfere.

Previously, during the Bengal crisis, there had been a trial of strength between India and the Soviet Union, on the one side, and Pakistan, supported only half-heartedly by the United States and China, on the other. The Indian Ocean had been drawn into super-power rivalry for the first time. The United States sent a task force centred around the aircraft-carrier *Enterprise* to the Bay of Bengal. The Soviet Union immediately followed suit by reinforcing its Indian Ocean fleet, and demonstrated interpositioning for the benefit of its client. Indo-Soviet co-operation also proved itself in the United Nations when China, represented for the first time, adopted a position in line with that of the United States in the Security Council and yet was unable to avert an Indian victory over its ally Pakistan.

As a result of this short conflict in which India's small navy also got the better of Pakistan's even smaller one, the Indian Ocean had become an additional theatre for military conflict and therefore, from the point of view of India and Pakistan, an area in which to use seapower. Up till then the strategic perspective of both countries had been totally fixed on their national borders, and in particular on Kashmir and on India's Himalayan frontier with China. The naval balance of power between the United States and the Soviet Union also acquired particular significance as a result. India was reassured that the United States presence was balanced by that of the Soviet Union, and Pakistan *vice versa*.

Sri Lanka's Zone of Peace proposal in December 1971 (see Chapter 6) was accordingly not understood by India, either at that time or subsequently, as a demand in the strictly literal sense for an end to the permanent military presence of outside powers; rather it implied a recognition that both super-powers had limited security interests in and around the Indian Ocean. The establishment of bases was condemned, since it was argued that this would inevitably lead to escalation and would increase tension.[32] Pakistan on the other hand has constantly been endeavouring to prevent India from

32. See R. Sawhny (Brig.-Gen. retd.,) staff member of the Institute for Defence Studies and Analysis in Delhi which is close to the government), 'Die Strategische Lage im Indischen Ozean, mit indischen Augen gesehen', *Marine Rundschau*, vol. 68, no. 11 (Nov. 1971).

superiority in naval and other military hardware in the absence of a foreign (i.e. American) counterbalancing force.

The naval limitation talks between the super-powers (see p. 68) in 1977–8 appeared to go a considerable way towards meeting India's desire to assert its own position of superiority and these talks accordingly provoked Pakistani misgivings. From 1979, however, as crises developed in the Horn of Africa, over Iran and Afghanistan and in the northern part of the Persian Gulf, escalating tension between East and West gave rise to a new situation. India did not stand a chance of bringing its influence to bear on these developments, which were of a global importance, and of counteracting the rapid military build-up in the Indian Ocean, either on its own or as a leader of the Non-Aligned. To the extent that India tried to do so, it rather created a danger of isolating itself. Indian public opinion was not insensitive to this: 'Threatened is not only India's primacy in the region, but also the foundations of India's power.'[33] In the late 1970s, the political and strategic premises thus also changed quite drastically in the South Asian sub-region.

During the 1970s, India's conduct towards the smaller neighbours turned out not to be without its problems. Indira Gandhi's aim of achieving for India a commanding position (usually referred to in New Delhi as 'pre-eminence') which could no longer be subjected to outside influence, continued to recede into the distance because of various developments. Thus India's explosion of a nuclear device in May 1974 increased the latent fears of its neighbours and especially of Pakistan, sparked off reactions at various levels,[34] and gave stimulus to the tendency towards a renewed search for protection from outside the region.[35] Pakistan's determination to press ahead with its own nuclear development was strengthened, and by the beginning of the 1980s it was evidently almost in a position to demonstrate its status as a nuclear threshold power. India could not fail to respond to such a development, thereby causing the situation to escalate still further.

Various attempts by Indira Gandhi's government to use pressure to achieve Indian supremacy only led to increased resistance and to acts of defiance. Her government's replacement by the Janata government in March 1977 resulted in not insignificant improvements in this sphere as the new leadership in Delhi had made greater

33. B. Sen Gupta, D. Bobb, 'In Danger of Isolation', *India Today* (New Delhi), 1–15.12.1980, pp. 48–58.

34. For instance, Sri Lanka was as a result confirmed in its demand to extend the denuclearisation of the Indian Ocean to cover all littoral states.

35. See D. Braun, 'Implications of India's Nuclear Policy for the Region', in Amirie (ed), op. cit.

concessions to India's neighbours part of its political programme. Pakistan, Nepal, Bangladesh and Sri Lanka became more willing to co-operate with India now that it seemed less intent on making its power felt and psychological barriers were reduced.[36] Yet this policy was never popular with India's self-confident élite, and Indira Gandhi, in her bid to return to power, was able to make capital out of denouncing this 'soft' policy of 'selling off India's interests'. Once back in power, she deliberately altered the emphasis, and the distance between India and its neighbours quickly grew again.

As a result, there was also a return to the earlier situation whereby India voted differently from all its neighbours (partly even including Bhutan) on important foreign policy issues, e.g. in 1980 on Afghanistan and Cambodia. India's isolation grew and led in a number of ways to increasing polarisation in the region. Pakistan turned towards the Islamic states, China and the United States. Bangladesh likewise increased its ties with those countries at the expense of its understanding with Delhi. Nepal, in stressing its demand for a Zone of Peace (see p. 173), also brought out an anti-Indian and pro-Chinese element. Sri Lanka's position grew more akin to that of the ASEAN countries, which was in essence pro-Western, than to India's. In any event, the centrifugal forces away from the geopolitical influence of South Asia with India as its 'natural centre' made themselves more strongly felt than ever, even if in the end they could not enable any of these countries to escape from the existing situation, which is geographically, historically, culturally and ethnically determined. There were some changes in this pattern from 1981. Both at the Non-Aligned Foreign Ministers' conference in New Delhi (Feb. 1981) and on Mrs Gandhi's later visit to the Gulf, there was a special Indian effort to find acceptable formulae on conflicting issues, including Afghanistan. Delhi had obviously recognised the dangers of isolation, *vis-à-vis* the Non-Aligned movement as well as within South Asia. Consequently there was a noticeable shift of policy, which brought India at least some steps closer to its neighbours.[37]

The interaction of South Asia with outside interests could only be judged on the basis of these intra-regional developments. For the

36. See D. Braun, 'Changes in South Asian Intra-regional and External Relationships' in *The World Today*, vol. 34, no. 10, pp. 390–400.

37. In April 1981, following an initiative from Bangladesh, the permanent secretaries from the Foreign Ministries of all South Asian countries met in Colombo to explore chances for regional co-operation, and a second meeting at the same level was arranged. However positively these developments are viewed in principle, it was clear that the persistence of severe clashes of interests, especially between India and its neighbours, set narrow limits for the time being on all efforts to find common ground.

West, the sub-continent was hardly a focus of attention for most of the 1970s. Because of the energy crisis of 1973–4, the Persian Gulf had been pushed to the fore; later it was to be Africa's turn and then again that of South-East Asia.

The nuclear issue was for many years the only topic which could attract attention to India as well as Pakistan (though always attention of a negative kind) from the United States. In the later 1970s, the Carter administration in particular but also the appropriate Congressional committees in Washington saw to it that the non-proliferation issue was given absolute priority as against all other political aims in the sub-continent. The outcome, however, was that the United States only succeeded in falling between all the existing stools and in alienating both India and Pakistan. It did not come one step closer to its aim of achieving non-proliferation or at least of encouraging it to the maximum extent possible. On the contrary its activity in this sphere favoured autarchic aspirations in both countries which in India had already been for decades the basis of its nuclear policy. It then took the Soviet invasion of Afghanistan before the White House could win through against Congress with the demand to deliver (contractually guaranteed) enriched uranium to India, using the traditional argument that new political priorities now called for this change. This also served to undermine still further the credibility of the previously dogmatic American nuclear policy. As a result of this same occurrence, Islamabad's nuclear programme lost some of its significance for the United States because Pakistan now threatened to become the next domino after Afghanistan. The Reagan administration heavily backed Pakistan and attempted to bring Congress round accordingly.[38]

For decades, Afghanistan was not itself a factor in the political and strategic equation between the United States and the Soviet Union in Asia. Around 1960 it was even a unique example of peaceful competition in a situation of Cold War. The Soviet Union sponsored projects in the north of the kingdom and the United States in the south, and their respective newly-constructed roads joined up.[39] As the Vietnam war intensified, the United States reduced its involvement, whereas that of the Soviet Union increased in

38. In April 1981, Congress was asked to make aid for Pakistan available if the President certified that its absence would 'jeopardise the common defence and security' (*IHT*, 23.4.1981, p. 1)

39. Khrushchev relates in his memoirs that Soviet road construction also had 'great strategic significance because it would have allowed us to transport troops and supplies in the event of war with either Pakistan or Iran'. *Khrushchev Remembers*, vol. 2 (Penguin Books, 1977), p. 351.

comparison with the activities of other countries. In the 1970s, in accordance with the Nixon Doctrine, the United States believed that its interests in Afghanistan were being well protected not least because Iran was striving for regional dominance. Indeed, between 1975 and 1977 Iran's proximity made itself felt in a way which was liable to interfere with the Soviet Union's concept for Asia. Moreover, during this period Iran was also in some agreement on regional issues with India, which had already previously become pretty heavily involved in Afghanistan.[40] After his violent seizure of power in 1973; President Daoud did not pursue pro-Soviet policies for very long; from 1975 he followed other priorities, and this led the Soviet Union *inter alia* to give even stronger backing to a merging of the Khalk and the Parcham, the two traditionally hostile communist groupings. The latter development led eventually — probably without direct Soviet involvement — to the communist putsch of April 1978. Yet the Soviet Union's immediate recognition of the new shift of power and the subsequent signing of a bilateral treaty were implicitly connected with its readiness to preserve the socialist system of rule even if this meant using its own military force.

The Soviet invasion of Afghanistan altered the political and strategic background not just in the Gulf region but to an even greater extent in South Asia. The event itself can only be understood in its two aspects. Looking at the deteriorating situation in Iran, especially after the taking of hostages at the United States embassy in November 1979, the Soviet Union was obviously reckoning on an American response involving the use of force, since this would immediately have pushed its own operations in Afghanistan out of the focus of world attention. Yet the Iranian revolution and its accompanying turmoil had already left Afghanistan exposed; and the United States had not only failed to establish a counterweight but, after the assassination of its ambassador in Kabul in March 1979, had largely frozen relations with Afghanistan. As a result, Western interests were represented on only a modest scale mainly by West Germany and France.

On top of this, American relations with Pakistan reached a low ebb in 1979 — chiefly over the nuclear issue — and in November that year, the United States embassy in Islamabad burnt down.[41] At

40. During this period the proposal for an 'Asian Common Market' was being investigated by Iran. India was the most important supporter of the idea; consequently the proposal had only a lukewarm response from Pakistan.

41. Pakistani security forces only received orders to go into action when American personnel in the building were in acute personal danger.

the time of the Soviet invasion of Afghanistan, American diplomacy was therefore capable of only an extremely limited degree of action in the whole area between Baghdad (with which the United States had no diplomatic relations) and Delhi (with which its relations were once again very bad). The United States military presence in the Indian Ocean could do nothing to compensate for this situation. It is against this dramatic background that American responses at the beginning of 1980, especially the Carter Doctrine, must be analysed.

Pakistan found itself directly threatened as a result of the Soviet occupation of Afghanistan, and in the period that followed tried out its options. However, none of them — neither its ties with the United States, nor the Islamic card, nor the 'regional solution' as perceived by India — proved truly viable. Nor did the Non-Aligned provide Pakistan with any practical support. China certainly remained its staunchest ally, but had no means in this situation of giving effective assistance. Pakistani diplomacy attempted to some extent, and with great adroitness, to combine individual options, for example increased American willingness to give support with financial assistance from the Arab oil states, especially Saudi Arabia. The Indian option, the way it seemed available at the time, soon proved politically unacceptable, since it would have meant an adjustment to India's priorities (also largely Soviet priorities).

Meanwhile, Pakistan found itself under considerable pressure from the Soviet Union both to recognise the Karmal regime and to prevent the infiltration of resistance fighters into Afghanistan. The Soviet Union had many and varied opportunities for exerting pressure, and could in both the short and the long term jeopardise the continued existence of the Pakistani state with its minority problems. These are epitomised in the province of Baluchistan where for many years the demand by Pakistan's central government for full integration has met with clear resistance. However, the Soviet occupation of Afghanistan has checked the readiness in that province to play the 'Moscow card'.[42] In any event, a collapse of the unpopular military regime and the coming to power in Islamabad of a civilian government which would sanction the Soviet hold over Afghanistan remains within the realms of possibility. India, understandably after its advances were rejected, has proved to be of little assistance. The director of the Delhi Institute for Defence Studies and Analysis, which is close to the government, wrote in the summer of 1980:

42. The oft-quoted article by the American writer Selig Harrison, 'Nightmare in Baluchistan' (*Foreign Policy*, no. 32, 1978, p. 136–61), is symptomatic of much reporting of this topic which tends to overestimate the revolutionary potential there.

. . . a coup by officers with Left-of-Centre orientation on the pattern of the Ethiopian coup — could take Pakistan on a different course, help to consolidate the state and open up a new chapter in the orientation of Pakistan and its relationship with neighbouring states.[43]

It was therefore only natural that Islamabad tried at a very early stage to enter into talks with its formidable opponent, the Soviet Union, and to seek compromises which might come close to Soviet demands without completely complying with them (the resolutions of the Islamic Conference in 1980 were just one factor which stood in the way of this approach). The United Nations was to be brought in and negotiations were to be conducted not with the government in Kabul but with the government party; but the Soviet Union showed no genuine willingness to accommodate Pakistan.

Meanwhile, with the arrival of the new administration in Washington, Pakistan's value to the United States increased. Its proximity to the Gulf and Islamabad's close relations with Riyadh were important factors here. After a long period, Pakistan was once more able to move the American option much further to the fore, while carefully safeguarding its non-aligned status. But whatever external changes may occur, Pakistan's internal situation will continue to be precarious, not least because of the great burden imposed by refugees from Afghanistan.

India was also greatly handicapped by Afghanistan. Outwardly at least its relations with the Soviet Union hardly seemed to have suffered, and indeed they were strengthened during President Brezhnev's visit to Delhi in December 1980, by substantial Soviet promises of further economic and military assistance. However at the same time, India lost some credibility with non-aligned states, as well as with Islamic countries and in the West, particularly because of what was by now its obvious inability to influence the Soviet Union's conduct *vis-à-vis* Afghanistan. This frustrating experience may well have subsequently damaged the atmosphere (if nothing more) of Delhi's relations with Moscow.

India's options were clearly restricted within the triangle of forces formed by the Soviet Union, the United States and China. Delhi's deep-seated fear of being treated by the great powers first and foremost as an object of their mutual rivalry, rather than as the centre of a separate established sphere of interests with a say in the adjacent areas of Asia and the Indian Ocean, was greatly aroused by the developments there since 1979. This mainly had repercussions in

43. K. Subrahmanyam, 'The Afghan Situation and India's National Interest', in *Foreign Affairs Reports*, (Indian Council of World Affairs, Delhi), vol. 29, no. 8 (Aug. 1980).

relation to Washington where even under the Carter administration but more so initially under Reagan, no attempt was made to conceal the low priority which India was accorded on a global scale. There was a shift after President Reagan and Mrs Gandhi had met in 1981 at Cancún, Mexico, after which the two countries tried to br¹dge some of their differences. The United States saw the advantage of giving India a chance to move nearer towards a position of equi-distance between the superpowers, whereas India was mainly interested in having increased access to financial markets controlled by the United States, in order to promote its economic development. There is no breakthrough in sight because too many issues of a more or less fundamental nature separate the two countries, but the out-look at the time of writing is for less bilateral friction than in the decade following 1971.

One cause of continuing friction appears to be the sensitive issue of Diego Garcia. In fact, since 1980 at least, New Delhi would seem to have come to terms with the continued existence of this US base lying about 1,600 km from Southern India. Yet internationally the topic has been kept highly charged by continuous Soviet propaganda, because of the definite place this island has acquired in diplomatic demands for a peace zone (see pp. 172 f.). For a long time the position against Diego Garcia (with or without directly naming it) has been ritually reiterated in joint Indo-Soviet state-ments. Pakistan's contrasting assessment of the strategic situation in the Indian Ocean and of the significance of Diego Garcia requires no further analysis.[44]

Sri Lanka, the country which lies closest to Diego Garcia and which under earlier governments had always shared India's objec-tions, altered the direction of its foreign policy from 1977 under the conservative government of President Jayewardene in such a way that it was much more in harmony with that of the ASEAN countries than of India. (This could change again under a government of a different political hue in Colombo.) At the end of 1980 there were press reports which suggested that Sri Lanka might even be prepared to grant the United States rights for military facilities. Such a far-reaching departure from its earlier international initiatives — Sri Lanka had introduced the Peace Zone plan at the United Nations in 1971 — is hardly to be expected. Colombo was to be the venue for a big Indian Ocean conference to include all the major powers, which was called by the littoral states for 1981 and then postponed to 1984.

Nearly all the islands in the Indian Ocean have acquired strategic

44. See Imroze Sagar, 'Indian-Soviet Naval Interests and Collaboration', *Strategic Studies* (Islamabad), vol. 2, no. 4 (summer 1979), pp. 79–89.

significance in the 1970s. This also applies to the Maldives, an archipelago of tiny islands spread out on a north-south axis to the west of Sri Lanka and close to the Chagos archipelago (with Diego Garcia). After British withdrawal from the Maldivian island of Gan, where there had been a modest Royal Air Force staging-post, the Soviet Union showed its interest in it, and other regional and non-regional states — with India prominent among them — immediately followed suit. It turned out that in cases like this it is just as important to keep others out as it is to occupy some particular strategic spot oneself. As mentioned elsewhere, even the Chinese Foreign Minister Huang Hua paid a visit to the little island republic in 1981. It looks as if — as a result of much mutual mistrust in a number of capitals — the Maldives will be able to continue enjoying a peaceful existence.

In sum, it emerges that the interaction between regional and external political and strategic interests in South Asia was and is likely to remain largely a function of two developments; first the prevailing relationship between India and its neighbours, including their respective foreign policy options, and secondly relations between the three great powers with influence in South Asia — the Soviet Union, the United States and China. Any hardening of attitude in the regional sphere leads the weaker countries to seek greater external backing; and any intensification of the East-West and the Sino-Soviet conflicts makes this kind of support correspondingly more divisive within South Asia. The Soviet Union's occupation of Afghanistan was the catalyst which gravely disturbed the previous, if precarious, regional order. India's return at about the same time to a quest for supremacy in the sub-continent increased trends towards polarisation. It is all too clear that the virulent domestic social and economic conflicts which exist in every country in South Asia do not encourage a readiness on the part of governments to reconcile differences with neighbouring states, but rather the contrary. However, this is not the place to pursue that line of reasoning.

(d) The Persian Gulf:[46] no longer a Western domain

No sub-region in the world has changed its character and its global political status in the course of a decade — 1970–80 — so much as

45. The same applied to the proposed lease of big oil storage installations near Trincomalee to an American company: the Colombo government withdrew its approval after Indian concern that the United States might thus gain a covert military foothold. *Times of India*, 7.3.1982, p. 7.

46. The term is still a matter of dispute between Iran, which favours the

the Gulf region.[47] Initially there was uncertainty over the possible consequences of the impending withdrawal of Britain, the prevailing administrative power, from the Emirates in view of a host of intra- and supra-regional conflicts, overt and potential. The three major powers in the region — Iran, Iraq and Saudi Arabia — ordered their internal and security affairs along very different lines. For the first time, Iran announced its claim to play a leading role throughout the Gulf. The civil war in Yemen had brought the virulence of disruptive social, tribal and ideological forces to the region's awareness and its later repercussions affected the Gulf.[48] The founding of the United Arab Emirates (UAE) at the end of 1971 was, given the differences between the constituent parts, an experiment in nation-building the success of which was unpredictable. Territorial claims were made up and down the Gulf. In many cases controversies arose in connection with oil production rights. Iraq laid claim to Kuwait; Iran demanded a revision of sovereignty rights over the Shatt al-Arab waterway forming the border between Iran and Iraq and also claimed Bahrain. At the time when the UAE was being founded, Teheran was securing for itself three strategically important small islands in the southern part of the Gulf.[49]

At the same time it was clear at the beginning of the 1970s that the economies of Western industrial countries, and of Japan in particular, were heavily dependent on the continuation of secure supplies of oil from the Gulf. The Soviet Union gave Iraq the backing it required to nationalise its oil installations, and it supported efforts there, as well as in South Yemen, to change conservative systems of rule on the Arab side of the Gulf. The East-West conflict created a pattern of polarisation. Iran, Saudi Arabia and the Emirates — with the partial exception of Kuwait — lined up on the side of the West, and Iraq and South Yemen sided with the East. The West looked on the widespread instability in what was already a vitally important region with concern but without too much alarm; this was primarily because the entire balance of power both regionally and

Persian Gulf, and the Arab littoral states which regard it as the Arabian Gulf. The geographical term used internationally has not so far featured in this political squabble.

47. In writing this section, the author received advice from Ursula Braun, Munich (see also the bibliography).

48. One factor here was the liberation front (PFLOAG), which was backed by the Soviet Union and China and which has been operating out of South Yemen in Dhofar, a province of the Omani Sultanate.

49. Greater Tanb, Lesser Tanb and Abu Musa, all of which had previously been regarded as belonging to two Arab emirates.

globally was still to the West's advantage. At the same time, the collective power of Third World countries (in this context chiefly the OPEC states) *vis-à-vis* the established financial and economic powers of the Western world had not yet become manifest, the swiftly growing future dependence of the United States on oil from the Gulf was still not apparent in Washington. And finally the connection between the Arab-Israeli conflict and political events in the Gulf, above all the phenomenon of an 'Islamic International', was also still hidden in the future.

By the end of this decade and at the beginning of the 1980s, the Gulf region was the focus of attention, expectations and fears not only in the West but also in large parts of the Third World. Regionally as well as globally, the 'correlation of forces' had altered considerably in favour of Moscow — and its interpretation of this concept — although the Soviet Union still had no direct access to any Gulf state in the sense of having a client regime. Yet Soviet geographical proximity and its military potential had become an important political factor. The East-West conflict was therefore concentrated in a dramatic way in the Gulf and in the geopolitical and geostrategic area surrounding it. This area now included Turkey, Israel, Egypt, Pakistan, the southern part of the Soviet Union and the north-west Indian Ocean.

The regional instabilities of the early 1970s had led to developments quite different from those which had been conceivable at that time. The most fundamental change came about as a result of developments in Iran at the beginning of 1979. Although the 'Islamic Revolution' led to great unrest in the Gulf region and to new alignments, the largest country in the region had left the stage at least for a time in the sense that it was no longer an active participant in regional developments. The Iran-Iraq border war, which erupted in the winter of 1980, was partly provoked by Iran's conduct and appreciably contributed to its further isolation. For the first time, Arab political influence thus predominated in the Gulf. After the setback of the occupation of the mosque in Mecca in November 1979, Saudi Arabia had regained some of its old stature and established a delicate state of equilibrium with Iraq, which had itself been weakened as a result of its conflict with Iran.[50] The danger of an

50. As early as April 1979, President Saddam Hussein made the remarkable statement that Iraq would attempt to defend Saudi Arabia against any external aggressor and that even the Soviet Union, a friend of Iraq, could not be permitted to take possession of Saudi territory. Quoted in A. Dawisha, *Saudi Arabia's Search for Security*, London, winter 1979/80 (IISS Adelphi Paper no. 158), p. 34.

incursion into Oman by South Yemen seemed averted for the time being. In relations between Aden and Baghdad, an ideologically-based community of interests had given way to estrangement.

The Saudi monarchy and the Emirates in the northern and southern parts of the Gulf, including the Sultanate of Oman at the entrance to (and outside) the Gulf, raised their co-operation to a qualitatively new level at the beginning of 1981, with the creation of the 'Gulf Co-operation Council'. However, this striving after institutional consolidation and co-ordination occurred less from a sense of the advantages of unified action than because of strongly perceived threats to individual regimes. These were primarily due to the domestic effects of oil wealth which were difficult to calculate, such as social inequalities, the disintegration of loyalty ties, the potential for popular unrest caused by the presence of foreign workers (not least Palestinians) and rapid modernisation, along with the retention of traditional rules of behaviour. Given the Shia minorities in all the Emirates and in Saudi Arabia, there was the growing danger from the religious-cum-political fervour of Shia-dominated Iran. And there was the ever-increasing involvement of outside powers, which could hardly be controlled to suit local perceptions of the desirability or undesirability of their activities.

Thus the political and institutional community of interests of Arab oil-producers in the Gulf, which is taking shape in this way, initially revealed signs of weakness rather than of strength. It was focussed on defence and co-ordination, as ASEAN had been at the time of its establishment a decade earlier before it consolidated itself as a result of external pressure. Outside pressure on the Gulf region during the 1980s will however be much more intense than was that on ASEAN countries, and internal tensions will be at least as great.

The most important events influencing change between the situations outlined here at the beginning and the end of the 1970s were probably:
— the first energy crisis of 1973–4 and its far-reaching economic and political as well as strategic consequences;
— the 1975 agreement between Iraq and Iran, followed by a period in which policies were directed towards regional *rapprochement* and the expansion of influence outside the region — a trend in which Saudi Arabia was also involved;
— the repercussions on the Gulf region of events in the Horn of Africa and of other Soviet gains in 1978;
— since the beginning of 1979, the Iranian Revolution and the ensuing changes in the involvement of outside powers.

The disruption caused by OPEC, the epicentre of which was the Persian Gulf, had major repercussions on the world economy. There were price increases, production cuts and a boycott. These last two measures were fully applied only by oil producers from the Arab side of the Gulf (Saudi Arabia, Kuwait, Qatar and Abu Dhabi), whereas Iraq joined in the boycott only gradually and its production quickly returned to normal. Iran on the other hand was mainly responsible for the magnitude of the price increases. Japan and Western Europe were particularly affected, whereas in the United States oil imports at that time accounted for only one-sixth of total energy consumption.[51]

The boycott, the so-called 'oil weapon', was the political instrument used, together with economic measures, for the specific purpose of exerting on the West pressure that would have a decisive effect on the Arab-Israeli conflict. Saudi Arabia had previously come out strongly against using the oil weapon. In the autumn of 1973, however, it saw a good opportunity to exploit the economic dependence of the West as a way of consolidating Arab unity under its own leadership. So Saudi Arabia, whose support for the West had hitherto been considered unconditional, was now a champion of the anti-Western and more particularly anti-American cause. Leaving aside the price increases, the boycott as such was not a great political success and even the oil price increase threatened to slip out of Saudi Arabia's control. Riyadh, setting the pace once more, therefore brought the boycott to an end in March 1974.[52]

By far the most important outcome of the crisis was that the significance of the Gulf region rose by leaps and bounds and that from this time onward the area was a factor in all global political considerations. At the same time, however, counter-forces were emerging in the West. To some extent these were in keeping with the concerns of the oil-producers, especially in so far as the need to develop alternative sources of energy and to conserve oil was recognised. But there were other completely different repercussions. In the United States the first plans for a military occupation of oilfields were drawn up. The 'unreliability' of its European allies regarding supplies for Israel during the October war in 1973 led to an upgrading of routes through the Pacific to the Indian Ocean. This was also one of the main reasons put forward for the extension of Diego Garcia, and US rights to use foreign military bases in the Western part of the Indian Ocean region took on a new significance.

In March 1975, Iran and Iraq concluded an agreement in which

51. See D.A. Rustow and J.F. Mugno, *OPEC: Success and Prospects*, (New York, 1976), pp. 24 f.

52. See B. Shwadran, *Middle East Oil: Issues and Problems*, (Cambridge, Mass., 1977), pp. 77 f.

they settled their main points of discord, these being the boundary line in the Shatt al-Arab and Teheran's support for the Kurdish minority in Iraq. OPEC was one of the decisive factors on this occasion. The agreement introduced a period of reduced tension throughout the Gulf region (although it was to the detriment of the Kurds in Iraq).[53] Whereas previously countries outside the region had had to weigh up carefully the implications of their dealings with these two states, they were now free to cultivate close links with both Baghdad and Teheran at the same time. After the risk of confrontation between the two ideologically opposed Arab Gulf states, Iraq and Saudi Arabia, had been somewhat reduced in 1974, Iran feared that these two countries might come to an understanding with each other at its expense, but the agreement with Iraq seemed to avert this danger. Meanwhile Baghdad carefully began to dissociate itself from Moscow. Developments after the Iranian revolution later revealed how quickly Iran could indeed become isolated.

In spite of exaggerated aspirations towards hegemony and an overestimation of his country's potential, the Shah's regional policies have nonetheless also displayed a remarkable degree of realism. This can be shown even without reference to the contrasting period which followed his fall. Between 1974 and 1977, Iran pursued constructive plans for co-operation with its neighbours to the East — Afghanistan, Pakistan and India —, for these countries' needs and exports complemented those of Iran to a considerable extent.[54] Links to the Arabian peninsula were more difficult because of historical and cultural divisions no less than because of Iran's general claim to supremacy to enable it to protect the oil routes in and around the Gulf. Here from 1972 onwards the United States increasingly relied on Iran's military power, and Iran lived up to expectations, especially when, at the end of 1973, it became involved in putting down the Dhofar rebellion in Oman. Saudi Arabia did not welcome this intervention by Iran any more than Iran's enormous arms build-up, and it failed to take up Iranian plans for Gulf states to institutionalise co-operation in security matters. Even so, common interests, both in suppressing the Dhofar rebels and more generally in ensuring that the Gulf retained a pro-Western stance, continued to prevail. Saudi Arabia covered itself by keeping a safe distance from and yet cultivating relations with both sides — with

53. See U. Braun, *Veränderungen im politischen System der Golfregion*, Ebenhausen, Feb. 1976 (Stiftung Wissenschaft und Politik, SWP-AZ 2098).

54. See D. Braun, *Neue Konstellationen zwischen dem Indischen Subkontinent und Westasien*, Ebenhausen 1974 (Stiftung Wissenschaft und Politik, SWP).

its ideological opponent Iraq, as well as Iran, now heavily involved in power politics.

Between 1975 and 1977, Saudi Arabia also pursued a separate and increasingly distinctive regional policy, with heavy emphasis on the Islamic component. Apart from North Yemen, which it all too obviously included in its own sphere of influence, Saudi attention was chiefly focussed on the African Red Sea countries — Egypt, Sudan and Somalia (see below). Financial resources were channelled into these countries with the specific aim of countering Marxist tendencies and strengthening Islamic ones. It met with some success for example in promoting co-operation between countries on the Red Sea, in 'purchasing' Somalia's freedom from Soviet influence, and even in getting the Marxist-governed South Yemen involved, at least peripherally. However, the war between Ethiopia and Somalia quickly put an end to most of these schemes.

These events, on the other hand, explain why Saudi Arabia, which had meanwhile gained the respect of the United States both as a leading Arab and as an international financial power, reacted in an exceptionally critical way to the hesitant American response to events in the Horn of Africa at the beginning of 1978. It was at this point that Riyadh began to dissociate itself from Washington, a process which intensified both quickly and dramatically as Saudi Arabia perceived additional gains made by the Soviet Union in 1978 (pro-Moscow coups in Aden and Kabul) but especially because of the United States' handling of the Iranian crisis. In 1978–9, confidence between Saudi Arabia and the United States, which had been restored following the energy crisis of 1973–4, was once more being eroded, and this process was accelerated by American press reactions to the occupation of the mosque at Mecca.

As the most important country on the Arab side of the Gulf, Saudi Arabia estimated between 1978 and 1980 that the balance of power between the super-powers had shifted to the disadvantage of the United States. It considered that this was almost exclusively due to Soviet political and strategic advances beyond the Gulf region, in the Horn of Africa, South Yemen and Afghanistan — a development which Saudi Arabia perceived as a policy of encirclement.[55] Aside from its relative gains from the Iranian revolution, which however were offset by losses as well, the Soviet Union did not make any

55. See U. Braun, *Saudi-Arabien im Spannungsfeld zwischen Nahost, Golf und Rotem Meer, unter besonderer Berücksichtigung des saudi-arabisch-amerikanischen Verhältnisses* (Stiftung Wissenschaft und Politik, SWP-AZ 2248) and the same author's *Saudi-Arabiens veränderter Standort*.

substantial headway[56] within the sub-region. The conflict between Iran and Iraq gave the Soviet Union comparatively more opportunities for exerting influence over both parties, since the United States had no diplomatic representation either in Baghdad or in Teheran. Furthermore, its geographical proximity was a natural bonus. Yet the Soviet Union now once again found itself — as it had done before 1975 — in a position of having to weigh carefully each step taken to support one side in the light of the effect it would have on the other. There can be no doubt that a pro-Soviet Iran is a top priority for the Soviet Union, although to achieve this it will have to reckon with long-term developments which will certainly include setbacks. Iran's version of Islamic rule is particularly difficult for the Soviet Union to deal with for a number of reasons — not least, Iran's proximity to its own Asiatic provinces.[57] Yet even a victory for leftist forces in an internal power struggle would not necessarily bring Moscow the expected gains. In this strategically important Gulf state a coup from above, along the lines of the one in Afghanistan, might very well involve the risk for the Soviet Union of a clash with its opponent, the United States.

In the Gulf region the position of the United States, which despite all setbacks continued to be of prime importance at the beginning of the 1980s, is increasingly handicapped by the Palestinian problem in the Middle East. Except for Oman, all countries in the region have harshly condemned the 'Camp David process'; therefore, so long as Washington's position stands in the way of the over-riding aims of Arab states in their conflict with Israel, the Soviet Union continues to have an important political advantage which gives it potential access to the Gulf. Its support for these Arab aims makes it valuable as a possible ally. The communiqué of the Islamic Conference summit at Taif (Saudi Arabia) in January 1981 showed clearly where the emphasis lay with regard to the super-powers, for in spite of being handicapped by Afghanistan, the Soviet Union came off better than the United States. This has been accentuated by events in Lebanon in 1982.

Brezhnev's proposal, made in Delhi in December 1980, for an agreement between all the powers concerned to safeguard the Gulf (no foreign bases, no threats to use force, respect for the non-aligned

56. So far, the Soviet Union has diplomatic relations only with Kuwait (since 1963). Soviet deliveries of arms to Kuwait followed in the 1970s.

57. See Y.P. Hirschfeld, 'Moscow and Khomeini: Soviet-Iranian Relations in Historical Perspective', *Orbis*, vol. 2, no. 2 (Summer 1980), pp. 219–39. See also S. Chubin, *Soviet Policy towards Iran and the Gulf*, London 1980 (IISS Adelphi Paper no. 157).

status of Gulf countries as well as for their rights to their own natural resources and free passage for all shipping) met with no response in the region.[58] Precisely because of the Soviet Union's continued occupation of Afghanistan, this proposal was interpreted as a diplomatic countermove to the Carter Doctrine of January 1980 in which the Gulf had been declared a vital security area of the United States. In response to this the Soviet Union once more put forward its claim to be a party to regional developments, exactly as it had done in its comprehensive plan for the collective security of Asia.

The Brezhnev proposal brought into sharp relief the fact that the Gulf region had quickly developed into a dangerous grey area between the antagonistic power blocs. In alluding to the need for a code of conduct — however difficult it might appear to be to find one given the existing circumstances — the leader of the Eastern bloc was referring to a threat to world peace which had meanwhile become generally recognised. A potentially inflammable situation had developed; this could lead to a widespread conflict which could no longer be locally containable. This situation combined an escalating arms build-up in the Gulf itself with the geographical expansion of Gulf politics and strategy, as well as with a lack of preconditions for crisis management among the major powers.

Many politicians and commentators in the West, especially but not exclusively in the United States, are convinced that Soviet control over oil in the Gulf would be the decisive step on the way towards altering the 'correlation of forces' to the benefit of the socialist bloc; the geostrategic conditions for pre-emptive action by Moscow would be favourable, and the West would have few means of averting or rather deterring such a move.[59] There are controversial schools of thought on this basic thesis. The numerous unknowns of future developments in global politics are usually taken to support one's own hypothesis. A more important development would be if the West were to face the sober fact that the Soviet Union aspires for the time being to use the political means at its disposal to obtain more

58. Only Kuwait showed any interest in the proposal, though it has not since then taken any further action.

59. See R.W. Tucker, 'The Purposes of American Power', *Foreign Affairs*, vol. 59, no. 2 (Winter 1980/1), pp. 241–74. Tucker and other critics of Carter policy from the right of the political spectrum in the United States, e.g. James Schlesinger ('Third World Conflict and International Security in the 1980's' in *Survival*, vol. 22, no. 6, Nov./Dec. 1980, pp. 274–81) called for the 'restoration of American power' in important regions of the Third World, in other words for a credible military intervention capability, as the most suitable means of safeguarding Western interests against the expansion of Soviet power in chronically unstable areas.

of a say in Gulf matters. One of its most useful means remains its attitude towards the Arab-Israeli conflict.[60]

The Arab Gulf states themselves are realistic in that they primarily fear those threats to their security which are the most obvious: domestic unrest, sabotage, espionage, intra-regional conflicts, and so on. To counteract these threats they are attempting to develop closer co-operation in precisely those areas which affect their security.[61] On the other hand they are not really expecting a direct Soviet seizure of the oilwells. To guard against this possibility, as well as to stem Soviet expansion in neighbouring sub-regions, they are quite prepared to accept a Western presence on the periphery of the region — in other words, 'over the horizon' in the Indian Ocean. (Even post-revolutionary Iran is implicitly counting for its own protection on the ability of the super-powers to deter each other.) To counter any further military involvement by the Soviet Union, on the grounds that its national security would be endangered,[62] the Arab Gulf states — and again this primarily applies to Saudi Arabia — are concerned to keep any additional American presence out of the Gulf.[63] In this connection the Gulf states also made use of a Peace Zone formula (see p. 173), which implicitly rules out defence agreements with external powers. On the other hand, it became clear since the war between Iran and Iraq that because of the serious threat to the oil route through the Strait of Hormuz, Western countries were much more interested in the prompt military protection of their energy supplies than in other considerations, and indeed that the Arab oil-producers were themselves dependent on this passage remaining open, since it is their economic life-line too.[64]

The characteristic desire to remain completely independent and

60. This is firmly denied by Tucker, ibid.

61. See *Middle East Economic Survey*, vol. 24, no. 19, 23.2.1981, p. 6.

62. 'Those who are planning a further aggravation of tensions in the regions neighbouring the Soviet frontiers should clearly be aware that the Soviet Union cannot show indifference to such plans' (L. Medvedko, 'The Persian Gulf: a Revival of Gunboat Diplomacy', *International Affairs*, Moscow, Dec. 1980, no. 12, p. 29).

63. With a (small) number of naval units in Bahrain, the United States is present there on a limited scale. In addition in Saudi Arabia itself the United States is substantially represented by military advisers who are involved in the construction of military installations and the like. (In 1981 there were over 1,000 Americans there for that purpose.) See 'Security Dilemma in Gulf', *IHT*, 12.3.1981.

64. The four AWACS surveillance aircraft which, at Saudi Arabia's request, have been in constant use since the outbreak of the conflict have also to be viewed in this context.

non-aligned as well as to 'keep out all powers foreign to the area', which is common to the majority of the littoral states of the Indian Ocean, seems particularly unrealistic when it is applied to the Persian Gulf. A decade earlier, some states in this sub-region were taking their first steps towards national independence and towards becoming involved in international politics. But just because of the outstanding significance they have acquired in the world since then, the constituent parts of this sub-region have no choice but to remain strongly involved with outside interests. This state of affairs will only change to the extent that the oil ceases to flow, a situation which is already foreseeable for several Gulf states — though not for Saudi Arabia.

As the Gulf region is likely to remain highly unstable, chiefly because of internal political and social factors, it would be to its advantage if as few additional disruptive factors as possible were brought in by Western countries. Such factors would include:
— public discussion of the need for a Western military presence in the Gulf (see the remarks made by Britain's Prime Minister during her visit to Washington at the beginning of 1981);[65]
— loud speculation as to whether the oilfields would be occupied in the event of regional unrest;
— reports in the media on the instability of regimes in that region and the questioning of their legitimacy (this could become a self-fulfilling prophesy);
— the supplying of inappropriate amounts of highly sophisticated military equipment which then has to be balanced out by equivalent deliveries to Israel;
— irresponsible 're-cycling' of petrodollars in civilian economic sectors, as a result of which national development plans are inflated without sufficient absorptive capacity being available.

In the 1980s, the West's 'Gulf policy' should therefore be shaped predominantly by a sense of shared responsibility for a region which can no longer be a Western domain, but which substantially consolidates the foundations of its economics and of its security.

(e) *The Red Sea and the Horn of Africa: ideologies, nationalism and strategic significance*

This sub-region also underwent fundamental changes during the 1970s. As was demonstrated by the two most populous and most

---

65. See 'Die Golfstaaten gegen westliche Militärpräsenz', *NZZ*, 7.3.1981, p. 1.

important states — Egypt and Ethiopia —, alignments oscillated widely. The fact that all these countries, as distinct from the Gulf region, were in a strategic position at the intersection of two continents and on important sea routes, were the traditional reasons for the rapid growth in outside interest in internal and inter-state events there. This was connected, indirectly at least, with the flow of crude oil around the Cape of Good Hope and through the Suez Canal. Developments in Southern Africa following the dissolution of the Portuguese empire increased the strategic importance of an 'intermediate station' on the Horn of Africa.

At the beginning of the decade the route to the Mediterranean was closed;[66] Israel had reached the canal and was engaged in a war of attrition with Egypt. The use of giant tankers ensured oil supplies to Western Europe, and the route around the Cape of Good Hope (and therefore the Republic of South Africa) became more important as a result, whereas ports on the Red Sea and in the Gulf of Aden were placed at a disadvantage. The loss of the Canal was particularly inconvenient for the Soviet Union's merchant and naval fleet, especially as a great proportion of Soviet supplies for North Vietnam had to go around Africa.

Pro-Soviet governments, or those prepared to adopt socialist development models, were in power in Sudan, South Yemen and Somalia, as well as Egypt. Pro-Western Ethiopia, which also maintained close ties with Israel, was afforded little security by its contractual agreements with the United States in confronting the danger of isolation which faced it on two fronts. It risked a confrontation with the Arab and Islamic camp because of the liberation movement in Eritrea, and with 'progressive' countries in the region (notably Somalia and South Yemen), which had the support of the Soviet Union. Ethiopia's supplies and trade were mainly transported through the French colony of Djibouti, the political future of which seemed very uncertain. Of Ethiopia's two Red Sea ports, Massawa and Assab, the former was comparatively underdeveloped and the latter politically insecure. Ethiopia consequently availed itself in 1971 of the opportunity to develop better relations with China and at the same time tried to maintain its relations with the Soviet Union, which were in part based on tradition.

It was now evident that both Moscow and Peking had perceived the potential significance of the strategic area on the Horn and the Red Sea and were prepared to compete with one another for a

66. See J. F. Campbell, 'The Red Sea and Suez' in Burrell and Cottrell, (eds), op.cit. pp. 129–53, and A.A. Castagno, 'The Horn of Africa and the Competition for Power', ibid., pp. 155–79.

presence in countries of socialist leanings (South Yemen, Somalia, Sudan and, decreasingly, North Yemen) as well as in pro-Western, feudal Ethiopia. The United States attempted to ignore ideological obstacles, no doubt out of similar motives. However, by about 1970 its relations with Somalia had deteriorated so far that there remained hardly any opportunities for exerting influence. It had failed completely to gain a foothold in South Yemen.

This pattern was first disrupted by the expulsion of Soviet military advisers from Egypt in 1972, and a short time before this in 1971 there had been an unsuccessful communist coup in Sudan,[67] which caused the Soviet Union to lose much of its influence. But as a result of the October war in 1973, Moscow once more rose in the estimation of Arab countries, since its political and military support for the Arab cause was seen (with good reason) as having been a significant factor in the recovery of a part of Sinai. During this war, Arab (mainly Egyptian) warships blocked the Bab-el-Mandeb Strait to ships bound for Israel, and units of the Seventh US fleet on their way to the area had problems refuelling in Indian Ocean states. Both events were of some significance for subsequent US crisis planning, and it was at this juncture that Arab Gulf states imposed their selective oil boycott.

After the war, Egypt was very soon ready to resume normal relations with the United States, and during this period the Soviet Union sought to consolidate its position in Somalia. In July 1974 it concluded a friendship agreement with Somalia,[68] which granted Moscow extensive rights to use its military facilities, rights which, till 1977, exceeded those which the Soviet Union had been granted in South Yemen. A comparison of the number of port visits made by units of the Soviet navy in the Indian Ocean area reveals that between 1969 and 1976 Somalia was well in the lead with 283 calls. The number of visits doubled between 1972 and 1973 and again between 1973 and 1976. South Yemen, which was in second place, received less than half as many visits as Somalia. In fact visits to South Yemen declined by about 50 per cent between 1974 and 1976, evidence of the Soviet Union's uncertain position there at the time.[69]

The Soviet Union's activities in Somalia, along with the other

67. The bilateral friendship agreement was however only denounced by Egypt in 1976. Till then the Soviet Union retained limited rights to military facilities in Egypt, particularly for its navy. In Sudan too, Soviet military personnel were not expelled until 1977.

68. The agreement was only made public three months later.

69. See R. Remnek, *Soviet Policy in the Horn of Africa: The Decision to Intervene*, Annapolis, Jan. 1980 (Centre for Naval Analyses, Professional Paper no. 270).

strategic changes in the Western Indian Ocean, led France, even at the beginning of 1974, to strengthen its Indian Ocean fleet and give it a new command structure.[70] In Ethiopia at about the same time, a military junta began to unseat the Emperor and there was thus uncertainty over the country's future development and political alignment. The United States was no longer prepared to consider requests for increased military assistance, which Ethiopia said it needed because of the Soviet Union's support for Somalia. It decided forthwith to close down Kagnew station, its large signal centre at Asmara which was under threat from Eritrean rebels and in any case no longer played a useful technological role. This decision meant an appreciable decrease in the American military presence in Ethiopia. The Soviet enlargement of Berbera in Somalia was however used by the Pentagon in 1975 as an important reason for advocating the extension of Diego Garcia (see above).

The mid-1970s were thus already marked by several important shifts in the regional balance of power and in international interests. Egypt and Sudan carefully moved away from radical Arab positions and in so doing took themselves out of the Soviet sphere of influence. For the first time, Saudi Arabia emerged as a regional factor in the Red Sea and in the Horn of Africa. Islam thus demonstrated its political force, while at the same time revolutionary Marxist movements were asserting themselves or were strengthening their positions both in post-feudal Ethiopia and in South Yemen and Somalia, and among an important rebel group in Eritrea (the EPLF — the Eritrean People's Liberation Front). Djibouti's future was still unclear, but because of the events already outlined, France showed little inclination to comply with the prevailing trend and to withdraw from the danger zone. However the United States, in the wake of Angola and Vietnam — and its domestic (Watergate) crisis, was clearly uncertain about its future role in regional conflicts as well as about using military power in unstable Third World areas. Nonetheless, the growth of Soviet power in Africa following the dissolution of Portugal's colonial empire was clearly registered in Washington and, as already mentioned, it caused the United States to review its policy towards Africa.

A significant year for the entire sub-region was 1977. When it began, there was still considerable scope for a variety of possible developments; at its close, decisions had been taken with consequences for the 1980s. In mid-1977, bilateral negotiations on arms limitation in the Indian Ocean began between the super-powers (see above), and rapid progress was made. But by the end of the year

70. See *IHT*, 25.2.1974, p. 5, and *Le Monde*, 7.3.1974, p. 7.

these talks had all but broken down due to Soviet and Cuban activity in Ethiopia and following the Soviet Union's loss of its base at Berbera.

There was considerable support for a peace zone formula for the Red Sea, its main promoters being Saudi Arabia and Egypt. In March 1977 a conference of Red Sea states was held in Taiz, North Yemen, at which both South Yemen and Somalia were represented but from which Ethiopia was excluded. In the communiqué it was stated that no outside power would be entitled to exercise influence or to have bases in the Red Sea.[71] It was obvious that both Soviet and Israeli shipping would have been particularly affected had there been any development in the Red Sea towards arrangements dictated in this way by the Arabs.

At this juncture, however, South Yemen was once again on the way to becoming more firmly incorporated into the socialist bloc, and Saudi Arabia's efforts to woo it were therefore of no avail. After a new junta under Mengistu had come to power in Addis Ababa at the end of 1976, the outlook in the Horn of Africa improved for the 'socialist camp' (of which Cuba was an influential member in that region). The Soviet Union delivered arms to Ethiopia for the first time, whereas the new administration in Washington decided to discontinue its own support because of human rights violations there. As a result of this decision, American military liaison staff were expelled from Ethiopia in April 1977.[72]

It therefore seemed an opportune moment for the Soviet Union and Cuba to give ideologically-based support to the creation of a confederation of socialist states in the Horn and in Southern Arabia, in which the Marxist Eritrean EPLF could also be included. These plans undoubtedly also took into account Djibouti's forthcoming independence. In Aden, Fidel Castro personally tried his hand at bringing together opposing ethnic and nationalist factions by appealing to the basic socialist convictions which they all shared. At almost the same time, in March 1977, the Soviet President Podgorny visited Mogadishu to try to persuade Somalia, by referring to their friendship treaty, to cease using force in pursuit of its irredentist claim in the Ogaden on Ethiopian territory.[73]

71. R. Glagow, 'Das Rote Meer — eine neue Konfliktregion?' *Orient*, vol. 18, nos. 2 and 3 (June, Sept. 1977), pp. 16–50 and 25–68 respectively.
72. On this and subsequent events described below, see Remnek, op. cit.
73. See C. Kühlein, 'Die politisch-strategischen Veränderungen im Raum Horn von Afrika/Rotes Meer' in Stiftung Wissenschaft und Politik (ed.), *Polarität und Interdependenz. Beiträge zu Fragen der Internationalen Politik*, Baden-Baden 1978 (Internationale Politik und Sicherheit, vol. 1), pp. 373–90.

Thus two strong competing supra-regional political forces were simultaneously at work in this area: Islam and pan-Arab nationalism were opposing Marxism, which was appealing for international socialist solidarity. Yet ultimately two other motivating factors, only indirectly connected with the former, proved decisive. They were nationalism inspired by conflicts between individual countries (e.g. Somalia versus Ethiopia) and great power calculations based on strategic interests. The latter applied to the Soviet Union only, since at this juncture the United States had still not perceived the significance of the Horn of Africa.

During the whole of 1977, the outcome of these conflicts, which were operating at different levels, remained uncertain. The Soviet Union increasingly devoted itself to Ethiopia, at the same time trying to keep a hold on its strategically important ally Somalia; the United States, not least because of Mogadishu's aggressive pursuit of its claim to Kenyan as well as Ethiopian territory, showed restraint in the face of the opportunities which seemed to come its way in the area. When the Somali President Siad Barre decided to carry the war further into Ethiopia and finally in November 1977 to terminate the treaty with the Soviet Union, he had no more than vague American promises of military aid behind him. Saudi financial assistance also proved ineffective. At this point, the Soviet Union set an example. It demonstrated both its determination to help its new friend Ethiopia to defend itself against external aggression and its ability to achieve this aim in the shortest possible time by providing massive military assistance and by co-ordinating this assistance with the operations of Cuban troops. Perhaps it was not fortuitous that this undertaking was given shortly after President Sadat had made his spectacular announcement that he intended to visit Jerusalem and when the new opportunities for US policy which had emerged as a result meant that the Soviet Union now found itself excluded from the Middle East peace process. The Horn of Africa was to some degree a substitute for positions lost by the Soviet Union in the Middle East.

As referred to above, Saudi Arabia in particular was disappointed by the American refusal to give active support to Somalia against the Soviet Union (and Cuba) and it associated Washington's attitude with earlier (and in the period that followed with further) American 'signs of weakness'.[74] But the United States had only limited room for manoeuvre because it did not want to go against the OAU majority view. It also had to take account of Kenya, which was and still is allied with Ethiopia against Somali irredentism. Washington's

74. See U. Braun, 'Saudi Arabien im Spannungsfeld zwischen Nahost, Golf und Rotem Meer', op. cit., pp. 57–63.

reaction, which consisted of cancelling the arms limitation talks on the Indian Ocean then in progress with the Soviet Union (a version of 'linkage'), was an appropriate step and one which upset Moscow's plans in this wider setting. The United States could also count on Soviet activities both in Africa and in the Third World generally triggering mixed reactions in the longer term, for Moscow had once again demonstrated its ability and willingness to intervene, although in a conflict for which it was relatively easy to provide political and diplomatic support.

Although its internal stability increased in the period which followed, Ethiopia had continual problems with Eritrean rebels,[75] and Soviet and Cuban support has so far not substantially improved the situation. Cuba did not have very strong reasons for fighting these guerrillas, as it had itself previously supported some of them against the Emperor. The Soviet Union on the other hand may even attach importance to ensuring that this disruptive element does not completely cease to be a problem for Addis Ababa, as it would otherwise lose a considerable amount of influence over the revolutionary regime. Over the problem of Eritrea, it was important for Addis Ababa that the Sudan, whose southern border areas had for many years provided the rebels with sanctuary, had recently become increasingly interested in sound relations with Ethiopia because of its own problems of internal stability. This meant that it was therefore no longer giving overt support to the liberation movements. However, like many legacies from the colonial era, the Eritrean problem is likely to preoccupy the central government in Addis Ababa for a long time to come.

By 1978, the course to be taken within this sub-region in the 1980s was determined. The Soviet Union's friendship treaty with Ethiopia, like the bilateral agreement between South Yemen and Ethiopia which followed,[76] corresponded exactly to the 'collective security' model which had been tried out earlier in Asia and which, a short time later, was to be repeated in Indochina in the form of a friendship agreement between the Soviet Union and Vietnam and in the subsequent treaties between Vietnam and its communist neighbours.

75. After Eritrea was established as an autonomous territory under Ethiopian sovereignty in 1950 as a result of a United Nations resolution, in 1962 it was unilaterally incorporated into the empire. The Eritrean Liberation Front was formed as early as 1961, and the Marxist-inspired EPLF split off from it in 1968. In 1976 an additional small group, inspired by Islam, was set up.

76. The text of the People's Democratic Republic of Yemen — Ethiopian Treaty of Friendship and Co-operation is in *SWB*-ME (Middle East) 6289/A/2, 5.12.1979.

In this context, in March 1979 with the border war between North and South Yemen,[77] the next 'domino' appeared to be about to fall. Yet the situation there proved highly complex. Saudi Arabia was (and still is) involved in North Yemen, not always to the liking of the Sanaa government. In any event, sudden massive deliveries of American weapons to North Yemen (via Saudi Arabia) were not, as it turned out, an effective way of influencing events there.[78]

Confrontation between East and West had been on the increase since 1979, and was reflected in the countries of the Red Sea and the Horn. There were ever-increasing inter-state tensions, floods of refugees, and arms build-ups in the area, as well as involvement in the great power pattern of conflict. Libya too now emerged more clearly as an actor seeking to gain influence in the sub-region. Its occupation of parts of Chad in 1980–1 caused alarm in the Sudan's western provinces. Sudan was already well acquainted from earlier years with Libya's ability to make trouble. The 1977 defence pact between Sudan and Egypt gained in importance as a result. Because the new configuration in the Gulf was unfavourable to the United States, the significance of Egypt greatly increased. President Sadat's emphatic pro-Western policies and the strategic position of the country in relation to the Arabian peninsula were decisive factors in American crisis planning under the Carter Doctrine. Egypt granted the United States rights to use its military facilities, notably at Ras Banas on the Red Sea, but reserved to itself the right to exercise sovereign control as had meanwhile become customary.[79]

Thanks to its two client-states, South Yemen and Ethiopia, the Soviet Union had on the other hand acquired a dominant position on the Bab-el-Mandeb Straits at the southern outlet of the Red Sea. France, in Djibouti (see p. 102), is the only Western force counter-balancing the Soviet Union's strong presence in Aden (which meanwhile must have more than compensated for its loss of Berbera) and its military use of the South Yemen island of Socotra and of the Dahlak islands belonging to Ethiopia.[80] The use by the United States

77. The Soviet Union and South Yemen signed a bilateral treaty of friendship in 1979.

78. See U. Braun, ibid., pp. 40–51.

79. Ras Banas was still not very developed at the beginning of the 1980s. It has been estimated that it will cost at least US$250 million to make it suitable for American purposes. See *IHT*, 20.1.1981, p. 5.

80. Reports as to the level of potential and actual use of the latter are based on US satellite photos: two docks, a floating dry dock, housing for about 150 Russians etc. Those reports are vehemently denied by Ethiopian officials. *Washington Post*, 2.1.82, p. A8.

of Somali bases, which from purely military and strategic points of view were potentially of great significance for its entire disposition in the north-west Indian Ocean, met with considerable political problems because of Somalia's continual irredentist claims to neighbouring territories, claims which evoked a common reaction from the governments of Ethiopia and Kenya despite their ideological differences. Because Kenya is of great significance in the context of US policy towards Africa, this development placed the United States in a considerable dilemma.

In retrospect, both super-powers chalked up advantages as well as losses in this sub-region. At the beginning of the 1980s pro-Western governments predominated in the Red Sea area and pro-Soviet ones in the Horn and on the Gulf of Aden. Neither Moscow nor Washington will be able to count on the continuation of this state of affairs — of which the assassination of President Sadat was a warning signal. From Cairo to Addis Ababa, no government is so stable that changes involving new foreign policy alignments can be excluded. Antagonistic political forces — Islam and Pan-Arabism, Marxism and proletarian internationalism, nationalism and ethnically- or tribally-based separatist interests — interact with a potential for virulent social and economic conflict, which exists throughout the region; as a result, changes and upheavals are the rule, and stability, in the sense of the continuity of existing political structures, is the exception. This sub-region thus contains a singularly large number of factors of uncertainty. This is also why the influence of outside powers and especially rights to use strategically located facilities are generally based on weak foundations.

The People's Democratic Republic of Yemen (South Yemen) is perhaps the sole exception to the above. The Soviet Union's position there has been strengthened by Cuba and East Germany, and appears relatively secure. On the one hand, the government in Aden, the only Marxist one in an Arab country, has obviously been firmly in line with Moscow since the change of leadership in mid-1978 — this despite the fact that the hardline President Fatah Ismail was replaced in 1980 by the more flexible Ali Nasser Mohammed, who has tried to be on better terms with conservative Gulf states and with the Arab world at large. On the other hand, it is difficult to envisage how serious opposition forces could develop in a country which is sparsely populated outside Aden and which, because of its present structures, is relatively easy to control. Because of South Yemen's extremely important strategic location, the situation there should be particularly advantageous to Moscow in the context of its longer-term plans.

Continuing militancy in Aden would have implications for South Yemen's neighbours on the Arabian Peninsula, namely Oman, North Yemen and Saudi Arabia, all of which perceive this comparatively well-armed people's republic as a potential or even an acute threat, given the active support it is receiving from several countries in the socialist bloc. South Yemen's efforts at unification with the Yemen Arab Republic (North Yemen) actually met with some response there, even though the chances of it being achieved are slim in view of the fact that Aden could be expected to dominate any sort of union. It is worth noting here that the combined population of the two Yemens is larger than that of Saudi Arabia.

Increasingly close relations between South Yemen and Ethiopia — with financial backing from Libya — are also likely to confront Djibouti and Sudan with growing problems.[81] For the foreseeable future, in spite of all the other uncertainties in the Horn and the Red Sea, there are thus some indications that no progress will be made towards any version of a Zone of Peace.

(*f*) *Eastern and Southern Africa: the central conflict intensifies*

Whereas in the 1970s the political situation in the Persian Gulf, the Red Sea and in the Horn of Africa was subject to structural change, this was not so in Eastern and Southern Africa. The dissolution of Portugal's colonial empire and Zimbabwe's independence had a permanent effect on the balance of forces within the region as well as the potential for external influence. However at the beginning of the decade the predominant conflict — that between Black Africa and the Republic of South Africa — had long since been mapped out. At that time, the following developments had begun to emerge:

— The West was certainly willing to make rhetorical noises condemning apartheid and the internal system of the Republic of South Africa associated with it, but it continued to pursue its economic co-operation with South Africa, which in fact it extended.

— Black African states saw a direct connection between Western security interests in and around the Indian Ocean and the strengthening of South Africa which resulted from them.

— The South African government was making no serious effort to

81. At the beginning of 1981, the President of South Yemen visited Addis Ababa where a military mutual assistance pact is believed to have been concluded. See *Arab News* (Jeddah), 9.3.1981. In a joint communiqué, the two countries called for a conference of Red Sea countries to free the region from 'the presence of imperialists'. See *IHT*, 19.2.1981, p. 1.

introduce radical social changes in favour of its Black population.
— At the same time, because of its strong position as a trading partner of the West and its strategic position, South Africa was able to remain relatively unperturbed in the assurance that the West would not introduce boycott measures.
— Benefitting from this state of affairs, the Soviet Union was able to pursue a policy of gaining the kind of long-term influence in the Black states of the sub-region, which would not suffer substantial damage in the event of setbacks.

In 1970, the new Conservative government in London was convinced that protecting the route around the Cape for Western shipping went hand in hand with the need to co-operate militarily with South Africa. The Simonstown Agreement of 1955 provided the basis for this. The Commonwealth Heads of Government Meeting in Singapore at the beginning of 1971 was marked by a clash between Britain (still at that time supported by Australia) and most of the Third World member-states, which sharply condemned renewed British arms deliveries to South Africa for whatever reason.[82] In the first half of the 1970s, Britain continued its modified policy towards South Africa.[83] The change of government to Labour resulted in the unilateral termination of the Simonstown Agreement (1975) and this in turn led to an appreciable easing of London's strained relations with Black Africa.

In the 1960s, at a time when neither the United States nor Britain was supplying arms to South Africa, France had become Pretoria's main partner in this sphere. By 1973 it had supplied weapons (chiefly naval equipment) to the value of about US$200 million. Licences and co-production agreements gave South Africa the opportunity to acquire the most modern systems. (Until 1972 joint naval manoeuvres also involved Madagascar.) In the political sphere, Paris arranged South Africa's contacts with francophone states in Black Africa. However, 1975 also saw a substantial reduction in heavy French involvement in South Africa, at any rate where the arms business was concerned.[84] Pressure from Black Africa and the

82. The previous Labour government had suspended military co-operation from 1964. At that time, President Nyerere had suggested that Britain might wish to protect its security interests in the region by extending military installations on Mauritius.

83. The largest joint naval manoeuvres since the Second World War took place in July 1973, also with the aim of protecting the route around the Cape. See *NZZ*, 11.7.1973, p. 5.

84. See C.A. Crocker, 'The African Dimension of Indian Ocean Policy' in *Orbis*, vol. 20, no. 3 (Autumn 1976), pp. 647 f.

changed situation in the southern part of the continent had made themselves felt. But it was not until the autumn of 1977 that a formal embargo was imposed on arms exports.

South Africa for its part had constructed various scenarios of the potential threats facing it at the beginning of the 1970s, and these pointed towards incorporating the country into a major Western security system (cf. the proposal for a South Atlantic Treaty Organisation). Soviet expansion in Africa provided the main supporting reason, although in the early 1970s its development had hardly begun. This all changed once the final disintegration of Portugal's colonial empire began early in 1974. The line of argument adopted by Pretoria in 1970 still largely forms the basis of its policy at the beginning of the 1980s. In 1970 great play was made of the link between these arguments and strategic considerations that were quite general throughout the West.[85] The most important elements of South Africa's reasoning were:
— that in the confrontation between East and West, the strategic areas of conflict were shifting to the Southern hemisphere to the benefit of positions held by the East;
— that in Africa, the Soviet Union and China were quickly gaining ground both in rivalry against one another and also by their collaboration with radical Black African terrorist forces;
— that given instability in Black Africa, South Africa was the 'last bastion' protecting vital Western economic, political and strategic interests;
— and that in any case, with its developed industry, infrastructure, raw materials and commanding position on the Cape, South Africa represents the prime target of communist countries even though it may perhaps be their ultimate one.[86]

Seizing on the Nixon Doctrine as the broad outline of the new American policy towards the Third World, South Africa therefore put itself forward as the West's major partner in the region. But the offer was hardly taken up by Washington, which deliberately retreated behind past and present European colonial powers in Africa (associated with this was the expectation that Portugal would still be able to hold out for some time to come). The possibility of a conflict in Southern Africa was therefore given low priority. Only after the Soviet Union and Cuba crossed a danger threshold in

85. See *inter alia* L. Martin, 'The Cape Route', *Survival*, vol. 12, no. 10, (Oct. 1970), and T.B. Millar, *The Indian and Pacific Ocean: Some Strategic Considerations*, London May 1969 (IISS Adelphi Papers, no. 57).

86. See P. Smit, 'South Africa and the Indian Ocean: The South African Viewpoint', in Burrell and Cottrell (eds). op. cit., pp. 267–92.

Angola, and *inter alia* upset Secretary of State Kissinger's conceptions of global equilibrium, did the situation change substantially. The policy towards Southern Africa subsequently implemented by the Nixon administration introduced new trends and was chiefly directed against the system of rule in Rhodesia/Zimbabwe. However, in a speech in Lusaka in 1976, Kissinger acknowledged the legitimacy of white interests in South Africa when he said that the whites were 'historically an African people.'[87]

The Soviet Union's motives for becoming increasingly involved in the sub-region were outlined above. They chiefly consisted of rivalry — with Western powers and, particularly in the early 1970s, with China. But in addition they were also tied up with exporting Moscow's model of socialism, with its own economic interests (which included fishing in the Western Indian Ocean), and finally with its strategic interests in the context of expanding and consolidating its influence in important regions in the Southern hemisphere.

In Eastern and Southern Africa, racial conflicts provided the most suitable opportunity for the Soviet Union to show its solidarity and to win a say in issues involving the security of several Black African countries. After China's similar endeavours had been parried from 1975, Soviet policy was predominantly directed against the West and the latter's close links, which remained fundamentally unchanged, with South Africa. Assistance given with arms and training served to create dependence. Co-ordination with other countries in the socialist bloc, primarily Cuba and East Germany, permitted the establishment of a pattern for a division of labour whereby wide areas of the political and social development of those Black African states with analogous political leanings were drawn in. In the Indian Ocean region this particularly applied to Mozambique which concluded a friendship treaty with the Soviet Union in 1977 and which has since given valuable support to the 'anti-imperialist' positions adopted by the Soviet Union in international conflicts including those involving Afghanistan and Cambodia.

But Mozambique is an example which at the same time highlights the limits of Soviet influence. For one thing, despite its links with the Soviet Union, Maputo continues to have strong relations with China dating back to when China supported Frelimo in Tanzania. Secondly, the Soviet Union has so far not managed to reduce Mozambique's substantial economic dependence on South Africa; on the contrary, Maputo's problems with its socialist planned economy meant that this dependence increased still further. Finally,

87. See Crocker, op. cit., pp. 660 f.

Mozambique has not so far been willing to lessen its ties with Western countries especially those from which it derives economic benefits. On the other hand, this policy with its elements of independence continues to come up against its limits as a result of unchanged, indeed increasingly tense relations with South Africa. At the beginning of 1981, the situation escalated when South Africa carried out a commando operation against a base of the South African resistance movement, the African National Congress (ANC) in a suburb of Maputo. The Soviet Union took advantage of this occurrence, assured Mozambique as its treaty-partner of support, and took the occasion to strengthen its naval presence in Mozambique's ports.[88] Whereas the government in Maputo had not previously encouraged such demonstrative acts by the Soviet navy, this event provided the Soviet Union with an opportunity to show off its support as it had done in previous regional conflicts in the Indian Ocean. The strength of the Soviet military presence in Mozambique can be expected to increase to the extent that Mozambique's conflict with South Africa should intensify and subsequently the economic co-operation currently taking place should decrease.

A scenario which an Australian political scientist put forward as 'plausible' is of interest in this connection. It postulates South African resistance groups attacking targets inside South Africa and withdrawing to sanctuaries in Mozambique. South African forces then pursue them into Mozambique and destroy their bases. Guerrilla (or Mozambican) forces fire Soviet missiles at cities or at other targets in South Africa; South Africa then enters Mozambique and fights the army there which is backed by Cuba. The Soviet Union refers to its treaty obligations *vis-à-vis* Mozambique and embarks on a counter-invasion of South Africa. Western powers come to South Africa's assistance and a large-scale war breaks out.[89]

In the mid-1970s, South Africa was still hopeful that by the use of economic co-operation, a political agreement could be reached, initially with one or two countries but later with other Black African states, besides those few rather weak countries which were directly dependent on it.[90] This was to be South Africa's 'outward policy'. Such hopes dwindled away almost entirely on being confronted with the reality of developments in Angola, where South African troops became involved in an African conflict for the first time; also because of the continual unanimous condemnation of South

88. See *NZZ*, 24.2.1981, p. 1.
89. See D.J. Goldsworthy, 'South Africa' in M. Ayoob (ed.), *Conflict and Intervention in the Third World*, New York, 1980, p. 235.
90. Malawi, Botswana, Swaziland, Lesotho.

Africa's internal system by OAU member-states. To be sure, exports of South African goods to Black Africa — often disguised or sent via third countries — increased in volume. But this led to no qualitative improvement in Pretoria's political relations.

In the meantime the countries of Black Africa have gained importance in political and economic terms both individually (e.g. Nigeria) and collectively (the OAU). Their demands, which are addressed to the West and to Japan, call for effective boycott measures against South Africa and pose what is for the time being an insoluble dilemma. Because of the rapidly deteriorating world economic situation, the economic partnership of Western industrial countries and of Japan with South Africa has increased in significance. South Africa supplies important minerals (manganese, chrome, cobalt and platinum) for which other minerals could be substituted only in the long term, as well as minerals of particular value for military technology. It also imports a substantial quantity of Western industrial goods. A significant shrinkage of this market would accordingly have unfavourable consequences for employment in those countries which are South Africa's most important partners.[91]

In addition, South Africa is of strategic significance because of its very efficient ports on the Indian Ocean and its surveillance capacity on the Cape. About 20,000 trading vessels sail around the Cape each year, of which about one-third normally call at South African ports. In an international crisis, the south-western route into the Indian Ocean could only be controlled in collaboration with South Africa; bases in Western Australia and Diego Garcia could not do the job. In the event of a blockade, or particularly another obstruction of the Suez Canal or the entrance to the Red Sea, the Cape would immediately take on renewed significance for any operation embarked upon from the Atlantic.[92] Mozambique likewise has a well-developed maritime infrastructure. If, projecting the developments outlined above, the Soviet Union were to gain a stronger military foothold in Mozambique, the United States would no doubt have to reassess the situation and this would greatly affect its Western allies. When President Reagan's administration came to office, the first signs were that a policy containing new elements of

91. In 1980, France delivered goods worth 4,500 million francs to South Africa. The United States, West Germany and Britain each supplied over double that value. In addition the very high value of investments and credits of Western countries in particular should be noted. At the end of 1980 the former were estimated at about 150,000 million francs. See *Le Monde*, 5.3.1981, p. 3.

92. See 'Reduzierte Rolle für Südafrikas Flotte', *NZZ*, 20.12.1980, p. 5.

co-operation might be pursued towards South Africa.[93] After the Carter administration's approach, which responded altogether more positively to Black African expectations, the United States will have to reconcile the modified policy (Reagan) towards South Africa with its aims in Black Africa and the Third World at large. This is likely to be extraordinarily difficult. Nigeria, the most important country in Black Africa, is particularly uncompromising in its condemnation of the South African system of discrimination against the black majority. And Kenya, which puts its military facilities at the disposal of the Americans in connection with the strategic line of defence in the vicinity of the Gulf, may feel badly compromised by more pronounced American support for Pretoria. Soviet bloc propaganda would then have an easy time of it, and the Soviet Union would probably find more military and political openings in Eastern and Southern Africa.

This may be a high price to pay for improved co-operation with Pretoria. On the other hand, every attempt made by the West to compromise between Black African interests and those of South Africa has at best only gained time. The only solution to the problem would be if concessions were to be made to the Black majority by the government in Pretoria and by the White minority which sustains the government in power. If Black Africa is to be brought round, such concessions would have to go far beyond anything which has so far ever emerged in terms of willingness to compromise on the part of South Africa.[94] The hypothetical question which it is justifiable to ask is whether a substantially different policy on South Africa's part would not transform the character of the country, its economic structure and its foreign policy orientation so fundamentally that the result would be new power balances coming into being outside Southern Africa as well. It cannot be ruled out that with each future development in South Africa, with or without apartheid, the West may be on the losing side. That, by the same token, the Soviet Union would be the winner in every case is certainly conceivable, but not by any means inevitable.[95] The most disadvantageous combination from the point of view of Western interests would be a further

93. In March 1981, five high-ranking South African officers, among them a lieutenant-general, the head of military intelligence, visited Washington unofficially, but held official talks with American authorities. See *IHT*, 16.3.1981, p. 2.

94. 'Time is against compromises which are not the outcome of armed conflict.' (K. Freiherr von der Ropp, 'Globalteilung als Strategie friedlichen Wandels in Südafrika', Stiftung Wissenschaft und Politik, *Internationale Politik und Sicherheit*, vol. 1, pp. 411–31.

95. See on this Kühne, 'Die Politik der Sowjetunion', op, cit.

consolidation of relations between South Africa and Israel, on the lines along which these developed from the late 1970s out of a common feeling that they were being treated internationally as 'pariahs'. Such a development might bring the oil weapon back into use to compel the West to distance itself from South Africa. It could also result in the end of the United Nations as a global institution.

The unexpected circumstances surrounding Zimbabwe's independence have shown that developments against Western interests are not yet inevitable in Southern Africa. Whereas a victory for Mugabe had — before it happened — been labelled, by South Africa in particular, as the worst of all possible outcomes for the West, it has since then become apparent that the new situation was mainly disadvantageous to the Soviet Union, which had backed Mugabe's rival Nkomo. So far Mugabe has shown open-mindedness on the question of co-operation with the West, and with China. In comparison with the situation earlier, the new state represents an element of stability in the region despite all its potential dangers. (This is due in no small measure to the dogged and patient diplomacy of Western countries, especially Britain (see p. 96).

Developments in this sub-region cannot be dealt with in more detail here. It did however seem important to show what a profound influence events in this area could have on the whole configuration in the Indian Ocean. Even if for a time the situation does not culminate in a crisis, the antagonism between Black Africa and South Africa will in all probability remain a source of constant concern for the West, and will be bound up with pressures to reach continuing and often embarrassing compromises.

(g) *The islands in the western Indian Ocean: exposed to variable winds*

From South Africa's point of view, the political environment changed for the worse during the 1970s not only on the continent of Africa but also in the neighbouring islands of the Indian Ocean. Around 1970, Pretoria could still count on a considerable amount of sympathy from Madagascar and Mauritius: both those states kept their distance from Black Africa and abstained from voting when the OAU condemned Western arms deliveries to South Africa. At the time, the Malagasy Foreign Minister even spoke of the 'converging views' of his country and South Africa over developments in Southern Africa, and he alluded among other things to China's support for liberation movements.[96] At that time the Seychelles and

96. See P.M. Allen, 'New Round for the Western Islands', in Burrell and Cottrell (eds), op. cit., p. 314.

the Comoros were just about to become independent; all the islands were either still governed by Britain or France or else were politically aligned with them.

In 1965–6, Britain had moreover, for strategic reasons, succeeded in creating modified sovereign rights. Almost uninhabited islands and groups of islands — some in the western Indian Ocean, some further east in the central Indian Ocean area — which hitherto (under colonial administration) had belonged to Mauritius and to the Seychelles, were divided off and brought together into a new 'British Indian Ocean Territory' (BIOT). Among those islands was the atoll Diego Garcia in the Chagos Archipelago, to which Mauritius (independent in 1968) subsequently again laid claim — a claim it still maintains.

Mauritius was the first island to become involved in the international struggle for influence which quickly developed with the arrival in the Indian Ocean of a regular Indian Ocean contingent of the Soviet navy. In 1970 it entered into an agreement with the Soviet Union granting restricted use of Port Louis to Soviet fishing vessels. In return, Moscow promised to assist with the development of the local fishing industry. In this island-state an active and conflict-ridden domestic political scene nurtured by economic problems, youth unemployment and racial differences had already emerged before independence. India exercised a perceptible influence through the majority of the population being of Indian origin, their ancestors having been brought to work on the sugar plantations by the British in the nineteenth century. A radical left-wing party, the *Mouvement Militant Mauricien* (MMM), showed clear pro-Chinese leanings. Nevertheless the tendency to look towards both the British metropolis and the francophone cultural community, which had been (and so far remains) dictated primarily by pragmatic economic concerns, predominated. From the mid-1970s the MMM gained in importance as the opposition party. Whereas the Labour Party, prior to the national elections in June 1982, emphasised its links with the West, the MMM strongly played up the Diego Garcia issue.

After its landslide victory, however, it toned down some of its former radical demands in the field of foreign policy, naming both France and India as beacons for orientation. (Thus it was no longer feasible to uphold the former claim for independence of La Réunion.) On the occasion of Mrs Gandhi's state visit shortly afterwards, prominence was given to Diego Garcia by both sides, with India fully supporting Mauritian demands for a return of the island. It can be expected that the new government will emphasise the issue internationally to the fullest extent possible, and the Soviet Union thereby gained another useful instrument for attacking US positions in the Indian Ocean. Otherwise, the socialist government has clearly outlined a foreign policy in keeping with that of both Madagascar and the Seychelles, emphasising non-alignment and discouraging the taking up of military positions of outside powers in the area.

Madagascar, the world's fourth-largest island and by far the biggest and most populous island of the sub-region, began to change its political colours in 1972, initially as a result of nationalist but later also because of socialist influences. From 1973, France lost what had till then been a privileged position in every way and had to give up its naval base at Diego Suarez (since renamed Antsiranana). Under President Ratsiraka, the country's foreign policy changed direction from 1976 and became based on 'anti-imperialist, anti-capitalist' principles. It was, in other words, opposed on the whole to the United States and combined this with an attempt to maintain sound relations with both communist powers at the same time. Its relations with France were still ambivalent. After a period in which they cooled rapidly, there was an improvement from 1978 to the benefit of interests on both sides but without again developing into anything remotely like an exclusive relationship.

It was against this background that in the later 1970s Madagascar began to use its influence with the aim of bringing the left-wing governments or parties in Mauritius, the Seychelles and Réunion closer together, while also stressing the need for the islands to be culturally independent.[97] Strong emphasis was given to the joint demand for an Indian Ocean Peace Zone. Madagascar then set an example in rejecting the presence of naval vessels belonging to countries foreign to the region, and in 1977 undertook to close its ports to warships of all external great powers.[98] Thus, according to various reports, it gave a negative reply in the spring of 1980 to the Soviet Union, which is supposed to have inquired about using installations at Antsiranana.[99] The United States appreciated this attitude, and has since stepped up economic aid, which is of considerable importance to Madagascar.

If hitherto the Soviet Union had only been able to gain a very limited military foothold in the western Indian Ocean, it nevertheless succeeded in making considerable political gains under the

97. See Thompson, 'Madagascar' in *Africa South of the Sahara, 1980–1*, p. 599.

98. *Monitor Dienst* (MD), Africa, 20.12.1977, p. 6.

99. See, e.g., *Jeune Afrique*, vol. 20, no. 1009, 7.5.1980, p. 53. According to Pentagon estimates there were however about 300 Soviet military advisers on the island in 1981. See *Washington Post*, 22.3.1981, p. 22.

'anti-imperialist' banner with the aid of rhetorical support for the Peace Zone proposal and on the basis, among other things, of its condemnation of apartheid. In this respect the Seychelles have, since 1979, pushed their way into the front line next to Madagascar.

Following its independence in 1976,[100] the Seychelles initially steered a pro-Western course. A president who was too business-minded and extravagant made it relatively easy for his left-wing rival Albert René, with assistance from Tanzania, to stage a coup and take over power in 1977. A one-party state in the socialist mould came into being although it was attenuated by tropical *laissez-aller* and growing Western tourism. In 1979, Tanzania again provided support in the form of a contingent of troops when an attempted coup was put down.

In late 1981, the pattern was repeated when mercenaries from South Africa tried in an astonishingly amateurish coup to topple the René government. This incident caused serious damage to the already strained relationship between the Seychelles and South Africa; it also gave an opportunity for both Soviet and French warships to visit Victoria as a sign of support to the government.

The Seychelles' foreign policy increasingly followed Soviet guidelines, which were manifested for example in a vehement condemnation of the US base on Diego Garcia. In 1980 President René visited Vietnam where among other things he declared: 'Our two countries have chosen the socialist path for their development.'[101] In the UN vote on Afghanistan in November 1980, the Seychelles was one of the few Third World countries which supported the Soviet Union. It is difficult though to reconcile this with the fact that the Seychelles, like Madagascar, has so far maintained relations with China which have included diplomatic visits. However, the fact that it has close ties at the same time with Tanzania and with India indicates that it is attempting to pursue a foreign policy which, although friendly relations with the Soviet Union are undoubtedly valued, is also committed to Third World solidarity.

It is therefore very doubtful whether the Seychelles would be prepared to go beyond rhetorical support and — as was reported in the Western and South African press on several occasions around 1980 — to concede to the Soviet Union rights to use military facilities on the islands. It is more likely to take a course similar to that of Madagascar and, lately, of Mauritius. Moreover there has

100. On gaining independence, the Seychelles got back the islands it had lost in 1965, which, along with those formerly belonging to Mauritius, among them Diego Garcia, had been included in the BIOT.

101. *SWB* FE/6536/A5/12, 30.9.1980.

apparently not so far been any serious attempt to persuade the United States to give up its satellite tracking station on the main island of Mahé, which is quite obviously used for military purposes. It seems that negotiations hitherto have only been concerned with increasing the American payments relating to the station.[102]

The Comoros went the opposite way — from radical beginnings with Maoist tendencies to an Islamic republic. After it became independent in 1976, a 'democratic, secular, socialist republic' was proclaimed and ties with France were drastically reduced. However the government's revolutionary enthusiasm met with a weak response from the population,[103] and the economy did not take off. In 1978 a coup was carried out by European mercenaries re-installing a former president, who sought and quickly established links with the Arab League. Western aid was welcome once again and the OAU gave its blessing to this new course despite the dubious attendant circumstances. The new constitution declared the Comoros an 'Islamic republic'. Only mildly irredentist claims were made in respect of the 'fallen' island of Mayotte which France continued to use for military purposes. After a two-year interruption, France resumed its heavy involvement in developments on the Comoros.[104]

By contrast, France today influences Madagascar, Mauritius and the Seychelles only indirectly. This influence is predominantly economic and yet is more far-reaching when it comes to French language and culture, which still play an important role in the western Indian Ocean (in conjunction with Roman Catholic missionary activities). Réunion was the obvious geographical centre for this activity, and its radio and television broadcasts reach the entire sub-region; it has its own central educational and cultural institutions as well as numerous regional training and cultural programmes.[105]

After the more or less radical socialist tendencies on these islands which have caused an affinity with the 'socialist camp', and after the emphasis on non-aligned Third World solidarity of which Tanzania and India represent the beacons, the cultural and economic output of France is thus the third most powerful political element in the western Indian Ocean. Hitherto these external influences have offset

102. See *NZZ*, 29.5.1980, p. 5.

103. There were about 350,000 inhabitants, excluding those on the island of Mayotte, which decided in favour of remaining with France.

104. See R.J.H. Church, 'The Comoros' in *Africa South of the Sahara*, pp. 309 f.

105. See Gomane, 'France and the Indian Ocean' in Bowman and Clark (eds) op. cit., p. 195.

one another so that no single one has been able to become decisive. In future, a fourth factor may perhaps develop in the form of intra-regional cooperation, which has been strongly suggested by the three 'socialist' island republics. So far — because of the colonial legacy but also because of strong cultural religious and ethnic differences — this form of co-operation has not yet made much progress. Outside influences — socialism, Third World solidarity and francophone culture — are in any event working towards a situation in which, as communication among the island states develops further, their awareness of common interests will grow.

What is more, in the 1970s it became clear everywhere in the area just how strongly the sub-region was exposed to outside interests, chiefly strategic ones. This was a reference not just to distant great powers but also to the display of power among Indian Ocean countries. Such interests have made themselves clearly evident and have emanated from the African continent, formerly from South Africa and later from Tanzania and the OAU. In the mid-1970s, while engaged in ambitious maritime endeavours, imperial Iran attempted to gain a foothold in Mauritius. India's political, economic and (cautious) military sorties in this area of the Indian Ocean have likewise begun.[106] In future, Islamic countries may seek to gain a hold in a few individual areas (notably the Comoros Islamic Republic) while attempting to spread Islam to Southern Africa.

All the island-states are weak economically and have considerable domestic problems. It is all the more remarkable that they have hitherto largely preserved their new independence and that their strategic position has not driven them into new forms of dependence, as was often feared in the West around 1970. The coup in the Comoros and similar events in other small island-states (but not in Madagascar) showed how easy it is in that region for a regime to be overthrown from outside, for these countries have hardly any indigenous armed forces. On the Comoros this benefitted French strategic interests, but developments elsewhere could involve Moscow and its allies.

All appearances suggest that an adroit policy for an island is to diversify its foreign relations as far as possible and balance them in such a way that no single relationship becomes exclusive. Mauritius so far provides a good example of this policy. The attempts of other island-states to maintain relations with Peking as well as Moscow point in the same direction. Madagascar and the Seychelles have veered off a long way towards a 'natural alliance' with the socialist

106. See Braun, *Indien und die Dritte Welt*, esp. pp. 107–18.

bloc, but the position in which they have come to be is not yet irreversible. The very limited attraction of communist countries when it comes to economic aid may yet make itself felt.

The demand that the Indian Ocean be made a peace zone is of particular significance for the island-states, because of their hope that this would lessen pressure from outside. Madagascar especially has attempted since 1974 to create a distinctive image for itself in connection with this concept.[107] Yet which of the now numerous interpretations of it should they endorse? What new risks and forms of dependence might be created if outside powers were to withdraw militarily? What are the specific interests of the sub-region which ought to be pursued in conjunction with a zone of peace? We will now examine these questions more generally.

107. Most recently in 1980 when it proposed (in vain, as it turned out) a conference to be held in 1981 or 1982 in Tananarive of all great powers and littoral states with a view to reducing military forces in the Indian Ocean. For details of earlier Madagascan initiatives, see R. Gupta, *The Indian Ocean: a Political Geography*, New Delhi, 1979, pp. 26 f.

Part IV
REGIONAL AND MULTILATERAL SECURITY CONCEPTS AND INITIATIVES

Chapter 6
THE INDIAN OCEAN PEACE ZONE

(a) *'Peace Zones': a preliminary note*

As a concept, 'Peace Zone' is sufficiently imprecise and all-embracing to lend itself to the most varied political aims. 'Peace' is, moreover, so positively 'loaded' that no individual or country can come out against a plan or aim thus labelled without immediately incurring moral opprobrium. What kind of ideas have hitherto been associated with this term?

In the mid-1950s, Jawaharlal Nehru used the term to refer to the uncommitted states which cultivated similar relations with the power blocs of both East and West and, in so doing, contained the danger of war.[1] Soon afterwards, at the XX Congress of the Communist Party of the Soviet Union, Khrushchev called for the creation of a 'Peace Zone' by means of an association between the socialist bloc and countries in Asia and Africa which had gained their independence. Sri Lanka (then Ceylon), which had been the first to propagate the idea of an Indian Ocean Peace Zone (IOPZ), initially focussed on a 'demilitarisation principle' whereby the littoral states, as well as outside powers, would be called upon to limit their military capability and related activities.[2]

During the 1970s, the demand for a peace zone proliferated in the Indian Ocean region in direct proportion to the growing perception of threats from individual countries or from groups of countries with similar political alignments:

— In 1971, the ASEAN countries declared their intention to seek

---

1. See his speech in Parliament on 25.2.1955, in J. Nehru, *India's Foreign Policy — Selected Speeches*, New Delhi 1961, p. 67.

2. See P. Towle, *Naval Power in the Indian Ocean — Threats, Bluffs and Fantasies*, Canberra, 1979, pp. 56 f.

neutrality for their sub-region (see p. 124 above). In 1978 Vietnam put forward its own peace zone proposal for South-East Asia as an alternative to the ASEAN proposal. Given the growing polarisation in the area, the aims of these two concepts turned out to be mutually contradictory.[3]

— Nepal demanded international recognition of its national territory as a peace zone, a demand which has always been almost exclusively directed against India's claims to supremacy.[4]

— From 1980 the Arab Gulf states adopted this useful term in connection with their initiative to institutionalise their co-operation (see p. 148).

— On the Red Sea littoral there arose a situation similar to that in South-East Asia (see p. 153). The peace zone concept was used in 1977 by the Arab coastal states in conformity with their interests at the time. Later, in 1981, it was adopted by South Yemen and Ethiopia in the context of the Soviet Union's regional policy.

Underlying these proposals in each case was the desire to ward off unwelcome external attempts to exert influence and to gain recognition of the proposer's own political system and ideological guidelines. In some cases it was implied that a certain political approach should be adopted by the prospective peace zone partner, with the result that 'peace' became synonymous with the complete acceptance of a particular political system. In 1980 the Deputy Prime Minister of Singapore, Mr Rajaratnam, had this in mind when he said that the Vietnamese wanted to spread socialism throughout the whole of South-East Asia: 'According to their idea of a peace zone, you have to accept this fundamental thesis. If you don't accept it, then it is no longer a peace zone. . . .'[5] The Foreign Minister of Vietnam, Mr Thach, retorted that so long as ASEAN countries permitted the military presence of the United States and other Western countries, they had no right to speak of a peace zone.[6]

Such examples show the paradox of ideas which underlie demands for a peace zone. The ASEAN countries are afraid of Vietnam, which has a vast military superiority to them, and they are therefore seeking outside protection or credible security guarantees. Vietnam, on the other hand, is afraid of China and wants a guarantee of protection against it from the Soviet Union. Similarly, external powers are being drawn into regional conflicts all around the Indian

3. See Leifer, op. cit., pp. 33 f.

4. It was first formulated in 1973 and was incorporated into the constitution (Directive Principles) in 1980.

5. SWB FE/6509/A3/1, 29.8.1980.

6. *Far Eastern Economic Review*, 6.2.1981, pp. 8 f.

Ocean. The tangible threats to the security of Indian Ocean littoral states are, as a rule, of a regional nature. In other words, weaker countries are afraid of their neighbours and look for outside protection against them. This type of conflict mostly outweighs fears of direct interventions from outside. (This latter involves the classic 'gunboat diplomacy' type of intervention but not the crossing of territorial frontiers such as those between China and India, China and Vietnam, and the Soviet Union and Afghanistan — which should be assessed according to other criteria.) Besides, in the face of indirect methods of exerting influence used by great powers — military assistance including guarantees or refusals to supply certain weapon systems, political support for opposition groups, etc. —, peace zones as defined hitherto cannot achieve anything.

During the 1970s, while negotiations on peace zones in the Indian Ocean were going on, the Cold War increasingly penetrated the region — much more than in earlier decades. Regional conflicts drew in foreign powers, which would hardly have obtained or even sought opportunities for exerting such decisive influence had these negative conditions not existed. A community of solidarity in the Indian Ocean region might otherwise have become a strong element in the international system. Of this potential only those few attempts which have begun to exert an effect at sub-regional level (ASEAN, the Arab Gulf states) still remain. Conversely, the aggravation of the East-West and Sino-Soviet conflicts, by introducing new factors, meant that regional conflicts were made more intractable. It is therefore less likely that regional attempts to resolve disputes will be successful.

(b) *The 1971 United Nations initiative*

Awareness among the Indian Ocean littoral states of the increased military and strategic activities of both super-powers in the second half of the 1960s underlay the Indian Ocean Peace Zone initiative. The Soviet Union's regular, if limited, naval presence from 1968 onwards followed the Anglo-American agreement on Diego Garcia. For countries which for centuries had been ruled by external powers with naval access to the region, this led to a strong reaction which in turn gave rise to the idea of a peace zone and has subsequently kept this idea alive. Naval power seemed synonymous with rule from outside. On the basis of collective determination, external powers were therefore to be denied the right to appeal to the freedom of the high seas; rather, this right was to be curtailed in such a way that the region would be protected from the East-West conflict and from other exogenous conflicts.

The basic elements of the Indian Ocean Peace Zone were formulated for the first time at the Non-Aligned summit at Lusaka in 1970, and subsequently activities shifted to promoting the proposal within the United Nations. Sri Lanka thus made itself both spokesman and co-ordinator, and it was perhaps not irrelevant that Mr Amerasinghe, Sri Lanka's permanent representative at the United Nations, was at the same time taking a leading role in looking after Third World interests in the negotiations on a new international law of the sea, since the Indian Ocean Peace Zone was directly related to this larger issue. The following were its most important elements:

— The region should not offer the pre-requisites for involvement in a military confrontation between the super-powers. It should therefore be free from military bases, from the regular presence of navies, and from nuclear weapons.

— The littoral states should not enter into any military commitments with the super-powers (especially military pacts) which were obviously conceived in the context of global super-power rivalry.

— The littoral states want to reserve for themselves, by means of a special regime and in keeping with the concept of collective self-determination, the decision to limit rights of free passage and of sojourn, as well as rights to fly over the region and other military uses of the ocean by external powers.

Sri Lanka's Prime Minister, Mrs Bandaranaike, introduced these tenets in a speech to the United Nations General Assembly in October 1971. The vote on the corresponding resolution followed two months later.[7] The key sentence read: 'The General Assembly . . . solemnly declares that the Indian Ocean, within limits to be determined, together with the air space above and the ocean floor subjacent thereto, is hereby designated for all time as a zone of peace.' The great powers were urged to enter into immediate consultations with Indian Ocean coastal states, one of the aims being to 'eliminate' from the region all 'military installations', while ships and aircraft were to be prohibited from using the Indian Ocean 'for any threat or use of force against . . . any littoral or hinterland state'.

Sixty-one countries supported the resolution. There were no votes against it (probably because of the symbolic content of the 'peace' concept); however, fifty-five countries abstained. Among these were the NATO and Warsaw Pact countries, but they also included several Indian Ocean littoral states, namely Australia, South Africa, Madagascar, South Yemen, Thailand and Singapore. Of the littoral

7. For the text see Appendix F, pp. 214–15.

states voting in favour of the resolution, it could be assumed that their support for its content was unqualified in a few cases only. There were no active supporters of the resolution apart from Sri Lanka, India and Tanzania, and other countries either voted without comment or else expressed misgivings over the operational parts of the resolution (particularly Iran, Malaysia and Indonesia.) Altogether about half the Indian Ocean littoral states shared such misgivings.[8]

The United States and the Soviet Union respectively issued similar statements which made clear their respective strong reservations about a proposal which would curtail the freedom of the high seas and which moreover would summon them to appear before a tribunal of developing countries which were weak, albeit numerically strong in votes, and which would force arms control provisions upon them. Amerasinghe illustrated this point of view when he commented to the General Assembly that 'for the first time the General Assembly conceived the idea that athletes run backward'.[9]

(c) *The attempt at institutionalisation in the 1970s*

At the twenty-seventh regular session of the United Nations in 1972, there was another vote on this resolution, or rather on its implementation, and this has since been repeated every year. In 1972 the result was appreciably more clear-cut than in 1971. There were now ninety-five votes in favour of the resolution and thirty-three abstentions. At the same time an Ad Hoc Committee of fifteen countries — twelve littoral states and one hinterland state,[10] together with China and Japan — was nominated. This committee was supposed to co-ordinate the appropriate practical measures which would lead to the setting up of a peace zone. Australia was also on the committee, notwithstanding that it was a member of a Western security alliance, as were Iran and Pakistan.

The first of these measures involved commissioning a study on the military presence of outside powers in and around the Indian Ocean. The study was carried out by three independent experts appointed by the Secretary General, and was published in May 1974 under the quaint title 'A factual statement of the great powers' military presence in all of its aspects, in the Indian Ocean, with special reference to their naval deployment, conceived in the context of great

8. See Misra, op. cit., pp. 70 f.
9. ibid., p. 91.
10. The aggregate figure of both was given as forty on this occasion, and during the 1970s it increased to forty-six.

power rivalry'.[11] The report consisted of twenty-two pages, with a fifteen-page appendix including a map showing the 'bases' and other military installations belonging to the great powers.

The ensuing history of this statement revealed in a nutshell the confusions, disappointments and self-deceptions that remain connected with the peace zone project to this very day. Immediately after its publication, the representatives of the four great powers with a naval presence in the region, as well as Madagascar, North Yemen, Ethiopia, Somalia and Tanzania among the littoral states, protested, some of them in vituperative terms. These latter countries denied absolutely that they had granted any military rights whatsoever to one of the great powers, as had been alleged in the statement. The Secretary General was compelled to withdraw the report immediately and to designate it as invalid. An expurgated thirteen-page version with a two-page appendix and without a map was then produced. This appeared in July 1974, bearing the same document number with 'Rev. 1' added, but it was now an uncontroversial summary of data, most of which had already been published elsewhere and were well-known. Many details and judgements included in the first version had been removed; yet even this version was rejected by several countries, notably the Soviet Union and several of the littoral states, some of them again in highly critical terms. The incident showed that it was quite impossible to establish a consensus among the countries concerned, even on the basis of this smallest of common denominators. The united front of signatories to the peace zone appeal immediately broke apart when it came to a factual presentation of the prevailing situation in which the interrelation of the interests of outside powers with those of the littoral states became obvious. For the Soviet Union the term 'great power rivalry' was already a reason for taking umbrage. It had hitherto always rejected it, while China did its utmost to ensure that it was preserved.

From the outset, differences among the littoral states were reflected in varying definitions of the peace zone, and these differences intensified in the course of the 1970s. Thus Pakistan consistently emphasised the need for security arrangements in the regional sphere (i.e. *vis-à-vis* India) as a pre-requisite for a withdrawal by outside powers. To this Sri Lanka added the demand that all littoral countries should undertake that they would not themselves strive to possess nuclear weapons — this was before India exploded a nuclear

11. A/AC.159/1; 3.5.1974. See on this D. Braun, 'Der Indische Ozean und die Vereinten Nationen', in *Vereinte Nationen*, vol. 23, no. 4 (Aug. 1975), pp. 107 f.

device in May 1974.[12] In 1975 Mr Amerasinghe declared in the First Committee of the United Nations:

We do not want any great Powers there. By the same token, we do not intend that we should drive out Satan by Beelzebub and allow some other Powers within the group of littoral and hinterland States to take the place of the super-Powers.[13]

Despite such differences, the littoral states succeeded not only in keeping the zone of peace on the UN agenda but also in obtaining increasing support, especially in the context of North-South debates. The Non-Aligned movement, from which the idea originated, made this theme a permanent feature of its programme, and in so doing generally maintained a degree of balance between the super-powers, using their 'rivalry' as the *leitmotiv*.

This was despite the fact that since 1973 the Soviet Union has tried to defuse the issue by putting rhetorical emphasis on interests of its own which run parallel with those of the Third World Indian Ocean countries; it has even gone so far, using diplomatic instruments, as to link it directly with its own pet schemes (such as 'collective security for Asia'). The results were limited, yet Moscow at this stage showed a much greater flexibility and willingness to find answers to Third World problems than did the West. The United States, like the majority of Western countries, showed little interest in the issue and adopted a negative line. In fact the Soviet Union was never prepared to give way on the substantive issue, i.e. the critical question of limiting sovereignty over the use of the high seas, but it packaged its refusal much more skilfully. Also, before 1977, it did not accept the littoral states' main demand for a large conference, to be held under United Nations auspices, at which all external countries which were maritime users of the Indian Ocean would be required to grapple with the peace zone proposals.

The events of 1977 changed this situation of stalemate. The United States and the Soviet Union met for bilateral limitation talks, and the littoral countries had meanwhile come to realise that their pressure alone could not suffice to attenuate the other side's negative attitude.[14] The super-powers' bilateral reduction talks were therefore hailed as a step in the right direction, and the United Nations

12. See D. Braun, in Amirie, op. cit., (chapter C, footnote 35).

13. A/C/PV. 2098, November 1975, p. 36.

14. See the clear-sighted analysis published as early as 1975 by an Indian scholar particularly concerned with this topic: K.P. Misra, 'International Politics in the Indian Ocean', in *Orbis*, vol. 18, no. 4 (Winter 1975), pp. 1088–1108.

resolution on the peace zone at the end of 1977 gave expression to this view. For the first time the Eastern bloc countries also endorsed the proposal, whereas the United States, along with the EEC members, Canada and Norway, still abstained from voting. The ratio of votes had now shifted drastically. There were 123 votes in favour and thirteen abstentions.

The date of the vote (December 1977) also represented the turning-point after which bilateral relations between the super-powers greatly deteriorated once more (see above). If the negotiations between them had opened up for the first time the possibility of putting the demand for a peace zone into effect, even in a substantially modified form, it was immediately apparent that the end of a willingness to talk at this level also meant the interruption of the whole process. Henceforth the peace zone diplomacy of the littoral states once again met with responses from both super-powers that were intended as propaganda. The Soviet Union tried to derive advantage from its formal endorsement. After losing Berbera, it attacked the extension of Diego Garcia by the United States all the more vehemently, using the argument that the build-up was aimed against the peace zone concept. In the summer of 1979, when Brezhnev and Carter met in Vienna, the United States was still giving assurances to the Soviet Union — and thus to the littoral countries too — of its willingness to continue bilateral limitation talks; but it had already decided at this point to consolidate its military position in the Indian Ocean, partly because of the Soviet Union's improved position in the Horn of Africa and in South Yemen, but particularly in the light of the Iranian revolution.

Against this background, forty-four Indian Ocean littoral and hinterland states consulted together within the framework of the United Nations in July 1979 and called, more vigorously than in earlier years, for the removal of all military installations belonging to the super-powers. This caused difficulties for one member of the Ad Hoc Committee, namely Australia, since it alone still permitted US bases on its soil (in contrast to other countries which stressed the limited nature of their respective 'facilities'). Canberra, therefore, pointing out the prevailing differences between littoral states, maintained that it would be wrong to hold 'super-power rivalry' solely responsible for instability in the Indian Ocean region and that all littoral states should begin by signing the Non-Proliferation Treaty on nuclear weapons (a demand which Australia never tires of repeating). Iraq, which was already assuming the role of a leader of the Non-Aligned at this time, rejected Australia's proposals. The Soviet Union, an observer at this conference, vigorously supported all the radical demands.[15] The signpost for the forthcoming summit conference of the Non-Aligned in Havana had already been put up. At the same time it was decided to hold the large conference of all littoral states and of the most important maritime users of the Indian Ocean in 1981 in Colombo (this conference having been called for as early as 1971). The meeting also made an appeal to all countries in the region not to acquire any nuclear weapons, as such a move might entail a threat to world peace.[16]

In the autumn of 1979, the Ad Hoc Committee called on the permanent members of the Security Council not to stand aside any longer and to join the committee as full members (China, as already mentioned, had been represented from the outset). At the beginning of 1980, the Soviet Union, the United States, France and Great Britain acquiesced. Coming eight years after the first peace zone resolution, their endorsement thus represented an important procedural breakthrough as the great powers now seemed prepared to co-operate. But meanwhile the Soviet Union had invaded Afghanistan, and this event once again effectively jeopardised the diplomatic efforts of the Indian Ocean countries.

(d) Recent Peace Zone diplomacy: East-West divide in a North-South context

In 1980 a paradoxical situation thus emerged once again. With the permanent members of the Security Council, the co-option of an additional eleven countries on to the Ad Hoc Committee, and the addition of six major maritime users, including West Germany, the United Nations body could count on the co-operation of forty-four countries. At the same time, however, the chances of a successful outcome to the endeavours of Indian Ocean countries was pushed still further into the background because meanwhile there had been a dramatic increase in conflicts in and around the Indian Ocean. In the summer of 1980, the first sitting of the committee in its expanded and upgraded form adjourned without results. The main conflict was between the Soviet Union and the United States. While the Soviet Union's main demand was that the United States should vacate Diego Garcia, the United States countered with Afghanistan, to the effect that as long as Soviet troops were stationed in a

15. See Towle, 'The United Nations Ad-hoc Committee', in Bowman and Clark, op. cit. (chapter B, footnote 71), pp. 211 f.

16. See UN General Assembly, *Report of the Littoral and Hinterland States of the Indian Ocean*: Official Records, 34th Session, supplement no. 45 (A/34/45), New York 1979.

hinterland state of the Indian Ocean it was pointless talking about a peace zone. A group of nine countries was appointed to expedite preparations for the conference scheduled for July 1981. The composition of the group largely reflected the spectrum of opinion: Bulgaria and East Germany alongside Canada and Australia, Pakistan and Somalia alongside India and Ethiopia, with Sri Lanka as chairman. The number of committee members increased to forty-five and the level of dissension rose as well.

A key word in these debates was 'trust'. Thus the French delegate to the Ad Hoc Committee declared that security was dependent on trust, but that recently in the Indian Ocean region this trust had been damaged; like détente, trust was indivisible, and countries with global responsibilities (a typically French way of seeing things) were called upon to restore the trust that had been lost. The Pakistani delegate took up this catchword and said that trust was indeed an important element of security and that it was therefore crucial for the creation of a peace zone that countries in the region should not acquire means of power with which to intimidate their neighbours.[17]

In the early 1980s there can be no doubt that a lack of trust between the super-powers, between East and West, between the Soviet Union and China, but not least between individual states in the Indian Ocean region, has deeply eroded the peace zone idea. Confidence-building measures between countries and sub-regions of the Indian Ocean could be initiated, even in the face of prolonged tension between the power blocs in East and West, and thus the preconditions at least for a peace zone could be created.[18] A British scholar made various suggestions which included hot lines between potential adversaries so as to avoid miscalculations, the exchange of military delegations, notification of troop movements, regional courts of arbitration for maritime disputes and for the apportioning of resources, and exchange of information on armaments and on arms imports.[19]

Measures such as these, however impractical they may appear at the moment, could certainly indicate an effective way forward to the creation of a peace zone (rather than sterile concentration on 'super-power rivalry'). The American representative on the Ad Hoc

17. See Indian Ocean Committee, 109th Meeting, 30.7.1980, UN Department of Public Information, Press Section, New York, pp. 2 f.

18. For years West Germany had made this a *leitmotiv* both inside and outside the United Nations, not least in view of conflicts in the Indian Ocean region.

19. See Towle, op. cit., pp. 218 f.

Committee, J. Kahan, observed in July 1980: 'We cannot refute the excellent logic of the distinguished permanent representative of Madagascar who pointed out that such rivalry exists. Although we too deplore it, it is clear how much simpler life would be for the Soviet Union if it had no 'rivals' in the Indian Ocean area.'[20]

During the United Nations debate on the Indian Ocean Peace Zone in December 1980, the EEC spokesman (from Luxembourg) made a joint statement, the essence of which was that the UN charter had been violated in 1980 by serious events connected with the Soviet intervention in Afghanistan; trust, the basis of all security policy, had been severely undermined. The Indian Ocean Peace Zone idea took different forms, and the EEC member-states therefore considered that the following *principles* should apply:

— The United Nations charter gave every country the right to individual and collective self-defence. This right should not be curtailed by an Indian Ocean Peace Zone.

—- The security of the Indian Ocean region depended just as much on the countries in the region as on outside powers, and therefore the former should first sort out among themselves their regional security relations.

— There should be no restrictions on the freedom of the high seas.

On the basis of the above principles, the EEC member-states adopted the following *position*:

— The immediate, total and unconditional withdrawal of foreign troops from Afghanistan must be a precondition for an Indian Ocean Peace Zone.

— The threat to stability in the Indian Ocean does not derive principally from any naval presence but rather from numerous conflicts producing tension within the region.

— The Ad Hoc Committee should define the geographical limits of an Indian Ocean Peace Zone, should draw up criteria for defining military presence, and should examine the problem of verification.

— For all these reasons, it was premature to hold a large conference in 1981. The European members of the Committee would, however, continue to co-operate in these matters and seek to clarify the unresolved questions mentioned above.[21]

As the result of a truly herculean debating effort, it was at last decided that the conference should be held not later than in the first half of 1983. By now, a three-tier pattern had established itself, with the Soviet Union and its allies at one end of the spectrum and the

20. *USWB*, 5.8.1980, p. 14.
21. See A/35/PV. 94, 15.12.1980.

United States and Western countries at the other, and the bulk of the littoral and non-aligned states in the middle. (Whereas there are hardly any nuances of difference recognisable among statements emanating from the first, Soviet-led group, such differences are very apparent with the others.) The three-tier formation was in evidence in mid-1981 when West Germany introduced a draft resolution on behalf of 'like-minded delegations' (postpone a conference) while Sri Lanka offered another one on behalf of the Non-Aligned (convene a conference), to which the Soviet bloc acceded, albeit with its own line of arguments.

In fact, the Soviets — following the tenor of Leonid Brezhnev's address to the XXVI CPSU Congress — presented their point of view during 1981 in a series of publications, thereby stressing the importance they accorded to the subject.[22] The United States, on the other hand, did not conceal the fact that to them, since 1979, the whole strategic set-up in the Indian Ocean had changed so greatly that old precepts, and in particular a 1971-vintage peace zone resolution and the following mandate to the United Nations, simply no longer corresponded with reality. The Soviet Union as a land power with a vast military — including airlift — potential had come into full view through its occupation of Afghanistan, a hinterland state of the Indian Ocean, and thus it was an absolute necessity for the United States not only to maintain its relatively limited military presence in and around the Indian Ocean but to augment and improve it for cases of acute crisis. This view has been basically shared by other Western nations, but there are different national interests as well as different attitudes towards procedural matters.

The peace zone debate has developed once more — i.e. after the early 1970s — into one across an East-West divide, with the Soviet Union now trying very hard to keep close to the non-aligned littoral states. This group is also much divided, although it has usually managed to speak with one voice at major events where a Southern stance *vis-à-vis* the North has been called for. There are 'moderates' and 'radicals', pro-West and pro-Soviet countries, those which fear their non-aligned neighbour much more than any outsiders or those which hope to step in where external powers may step out. During 1981, Malaysia and Pakistan, among others, tried to mediate

22. See A. Alexeyev/A. Fialkovsky, 'For a Peaceful Indian Ocean', *International Affairs* (Moscow), February 1981; S. Vladimirov, For a Zone of Peace, *New Times*, no. 8/1981; S. Vladimirov, 'An Important Conference', *New Times*, no. 22/1981; A. Ladoshsky, 'The USSR's efforts to turn the Indian Ocean into a Zone of Peace', *International Affairs* (Moscow), August 1981.

between East and West. The Malaysian delegate at the Ad Hoc Committee called both Diego Garcia and the occupation of Afghanistan destabilising, so a peace zone should come about after three steps had been agreed: the withdrawal of all foreign forces from the area, settlement of regional disputes by peaceful means only, and no use of force on the part of big powers against regional states.[23] Pakistan advocated a step-by-step approach towards implementation of a peace zone, without too many expectations for the beginning, i.e. for the first comprehensive conference. Both the great powers and the regional states would be under the obligation to adhere to the principles of a peace zone.[24]

India, one of the most ardent advocates of the peace zone concept, went much further by lauding the Soviet Union for its positive attitude and chiding the United States for its negative stance. In April 1982, there was a mammoth conference in New Delhi, sponsored jointly by the World Peace Council, the Afro-Asian Peace and Solidarity Organisation and several other notorious pro-Soviet groupings, with 150 foreign and about 1,000 Indian participants; both Mrs Gandhi and Leonid Brezhnev sent messages.[25] The tenor of the conference was fully in line with Soviet policy, condemning the United States for threatening the national independence of Indian Ocean countries, for trying to control their natural resources, and so on.

The Reagan administration's frankness regarding its military and strategic aims in the Indian Ocean region (as elsewhere) has indeed invited a Soviet diplomatic offensive which, at least partly, can count on sympathy from regional countries. As mentioned before, the geostrategic advantage of the Soviet Union, i.e. its proximity to South-West Asia and particularly to the Persian Gulf, is being accepted as a fact of life while the cumbersome US build-up of facilities in littoral countries and of a Rapid Deployment Force will continue to draw local criticism. The reasons are many; one of them is the Arab/Islamic perception of the US-backed state of Israel as the number one enemy, with the Soviet Union ranking more or less far behind. Constant Soviet repetition of its own readiness for a new round of bilateral military reduction talks with the United States, covering the Indian Ocean area, meets with the approval of most of the regional states. Against this, the position of the United States has, until very recently, appeared rigid, with its pronouncements at times having a tone of haughtiness. This may be understandable

23. *Far Eastern Economic Review*, 3.7.1981, pp. 26 f.
24. *Dawn* (Karachi), 7.3.1981, p. 7.
25. *Times of India*, 26.4.1982; *Link* (New Delhi), 2.5.1982.

vis-à-vis the prospect for Washington to see Diego Garcia or the Rapid Deployment Force being debated in a huge conference, dominated by the Soviet Union and none-too-friendly non-aligned states. But it is not very helpful in the given context.

There has, very recently, been a change of attitude on the part of the US delegation in the Ad Hoc Committee. There is now more flexibility in the American attitude to co-operation; but at the same time Washington insists that the 1971 mandate of the Indian Ocean Peace Zone must be changed: its main emphasis should no longer be on the elimination of foreign navies and military installations, but rather a much more comprehensive concept should lead to a strengthening of elements of peace in the area. What is required, according to the American position — which seems to be supported by other Western delegations —, is a code of conduct to which all the regional and the relevant external countries would adhere. Military and security issues would remain in the centre of a new peace zone mandate, supported, however, by political and economic issues. The latter, in particular, by raising expectations regarding more North-South co-operation for technological, industrial and scientific development, could be an interesting new element for Indian Ocean littoral countries, provided that the promises that are made can be substantiated. The Reagan administration's attitude to Third World aid in general has not hitherto favoured such an approach. On the other hand, a number of 'moderate' Indian Ocean states might be inclined towards such new proposals, not least because for some of them it would be important to see a stronger neighbour under the obligation to adhere to principles of regional security.

It can be expected that the Soviets will strongly oppose any such change of the original peace zone mandate as this would also shift the focus away from their prime target, the American military activities in the area. Moscow's position is, as indicated above, clearly outlined and is being supported, in different degrees, by a fair number of littoral states. It seems, therefore, that any Western attempt to alter the previous UN mandate substantially could result in a new closing of ranks between the Soviet Union and the Non-Aligned. Progress towards a modified mandate, which appears to be a basically sound proposition, could only be achieved gradually. There is thus no exit so far from the impasse of the East-West-South entanglement over a peace zone, but a direction has been indicated in which it might lie.

The Indian Ocean Peace Zone idea — in so far as it is not a utopian scheme for 'driving out' major powers from an ocean which, after all, does not belong to the littoral states — will make some progress only if and when the present confrontation between the United States and the Soviet Union is reduced. Only then would both be willing to give a lower priority to their military presence in or near the area. One important step in this direction would be mutually acceptable surveillance and verification procedures, mainly by the use of satellites. However, the Indian Ocean will never become an idyllic lake of peace; it never was one in the past — something which is conveniently forgotten by people who think only in simplistic terms of foreign devils responsible for all their ills. Even the two super-powers can not wield control over the Indian Ocean region; neither a *pax sovietica* nor a *pax americana* stands the least chance of being imposed there. The very idea of either of these outside powers having an exclusive influence is absurd in view of the multi-faceted, problem-ridden, colourful realities of an area where nearly one-third of humanity lives.

Chapter 7
NUCLEAR-WEAPON-FREE ZONES: THE CASE OF SOUTH ASIA

The Tlatelolco Treaty, signed in Mexico at the end of the 1960s and declaring Latin America a nuclear-weapon-free zone (NWFZ),[1] had repercussions in several other regions of the world where in the 1970s similar initiatives were being either revived (Europe, Africa) or newly adopted (the Middle East and South Asia). The United Nations Committee for the Conference on Disarmament (CCD) in 1975 put forward a 'comprehensive study of the question of nuclear-weapon-free zones in all their aspects'.[2] The aims of the concept were described as follows:

The concept of nuclear-weapon-free zones has stemmed from the realisation that a number of States in various regions of the world have or could have the capacity to develop a nuclear weapon capability within a relatively short period. [. . .] Should this occur it could present new threats to the security of States in areas at present free from nuclear weapons; [this] could precipitate a ruinously expensive and perilous nuclear arms race in those areas . . .

There can be no doubt that discussion of this topic was given considerable impetus following India's nuclear explosion in May 1974, which also inspired initiatives on the part of countries supplying nuclear technology (the Suppliers' Club) to impose limitations on themselves and to improve international control mechanisms, etc. We have mentioned that already before this event and in connection with defining the Indian Ocean Peace Zone, Sri Lanka had indirectly tried to clip India's wings by urging that all littoral states should undertake not to seek to acquire atomic weapons. India refused and continued to argue that a ban on all nuclear weapons in the Indian Ocean region would apply to outside powers, especially the United States with its strategic submarines.

Following India's demonstration of its nuclear capability, Pakistan prepared various diplomatic initiatives, primarily in the United Nations. There in 1974 India also found itself on the receiving end of a draft resolution in the First Committee, expressing the 'deep concern' of the overwhelming majority of members over the possible transition from civil to militarily relevant nuclear

1. Brazil, Argentina and Chile, the most important countries in this context, have not acceded to the treaty. Nor has Cuba so far ratified it.

2. This is the sub-title of the report on the question, CCD/476, 28.8.1975, III, p. 1.

explosions, and calling for international verification in accordance with the Non-Proliferation Treaty (NPT).[3] On this occasion India sided with China against the Eastern bloc.

Taking advantage of the fact that the United Nations was about to deal with several regional anti-nuclear-weapon initiatives, Pakistan introduced a proposal at the 29th regular session in the autumn of 1974 to declare South Asia a nuclear-weapon-free zone. There was a temporal as well as a geographical connection between this proposal and analogous ones for the Middle East (jointly introduced by Egypt and Iran) and the larger Indian Ocean area (IOPZ). The UN Secretary General, Kurt Waldheim, gave his backing to the Pakistani project, calling it not only useful but necessary in connection with universal disarmament efforts.[4] India firmly defended itself against any attempt to involve it in multilateral agreements in this sphere, but in so doing found itself in danger of isolation. India argued quite plausibly that this kind of scheme would first of all require the establishment of a consensus among the countries concerned, and moreover that as a sub-region South Asia was hardly a suitable area for such a zone since it bordered on China which was a nuclear weapon state, and included countries which had military pacts with other nuclear weapon states.[5]

In opposition to Pakistan's draft, which included the provision that all countries in South Asia should relinquish the *testing, use, manufacture, production, acquisition or storage of any nuclear weapons or nuclear launching devices*, India put up its own resolution urging countries in South Asia to take their own initiatives towards a nuclear-weapon-free zone, in other words without bringing in the United Nations. Nor did the Indian proposal contain any provisions which could be made operational. Both resolutions were voted on at the end of 1974 in the General Assembly. India obtained a few more votes than Pakistan (104 as against 96); China sided with Pakistan and the Eastern bloc with India, and Western nuclear weapon countries abstained in both cases. Nepal and Sri Lanka voted for both resolutions, while Bangladesh and Bhutan voted only for India's. Furthermore, India and its satellite Bhutan were the only countries to vote against the Pakistani proposal, while Pakistan abstained on the Indian one.

3. See UN Draft Resolution A/C.1/L.690, 10.11.1974.

4. Quoted in S. Ahmed, 'Pakistan's Proposal for a Nuclear-Weapon-Free Zone in South Asia', *Pakistan Horizon* (Karachi), vol. 31, no. 4 (1979)., pp. 92–130.

5. For details of India's line of argument see A. Kapur, *India's Nuclear Option — Atomic Diplomacy and Decision Making*, New York 1976, especially pp. 238–44.

This process was repeated with monotonous regularity in every subsequent year and soon became a kind of ritual. It nevertheless represented a constant source of irritation for India, since Pakistan was continually reminding the world that the development of India's nuclear science and technology was subject to no external control. Its proposals also regularly obtained a majority which included the votes of most of India's neighbours (including, from 1975, Bangladesh). India and Bhutan were alone in their continual opposition to the Pakistani resolution.

All this changed in 1976 when Pakistan announced its intention to purchase a plutonium reprocessing plant from France. Because Pakistan was as uncommitted to the Non-Proliferation Treaty as India, this decision brought the United States and Canada on to the scene (Canada had built Pakistan's only nuclear power station near Karachi). Pressure was brought to bear not only on Islamabad but also on Paris, and at the end of 1976 this bore fruit since France hesitated over the deal and Canada suspended its nuclear co-operation with Pakistan.

In the United Nations vote in 1977, the United States (and Britain) backed the Pakistani proposal for the first time, presumably as a supporting measure to prevent proliferation on the Indian sub-continent (i.e. to prevent development of a nuclear capability by Pakistan too) as well as the Indian counter-measures which would be bound to follow. The Carter administration and the United States Congress had (as mentioned above) given non-proliferation policy a high priority, with the result that this issue soon pushed other problems in US relations with India and Pakistan into the background. In the spring of 1979, Washington considered putting forward its own version of a nuclear-weapon-free zone for South Asia, for which it sought but did not obtain Moscow's endorsement. The aim was to involve India and Pakistan with a view to getting them both to allow international supervision of their nuclear installations. India, however, insisted that China should be included in any such arms control plans and at the same time stressed the link between horizontal and vertical proliferation.[6]

In view of the growing certainty that Pakistan was pursuing a secret nuclear research and development programme with a specific aim in view,[7] its persistent campaign in the United Nations for a

6. See A.G. Noorani, 'US Proposal on N-free Zone', *Indian Express*, 7.6.1979.

7. From 1979 onwards, there was a series of indications that Pakistan had purchased, or had tried to purchase in various Western countries (such as Canada, West Germany, Switzerland and Britain) components and instru-

nuclear-weapon-free zone lost some of its credibility. The United States 'punished' Pakistan in April 1979 when it discontinued economic and military aid in accordance with the guidelines on non-proliferation laid down by Congress. In August 1979 India stated that if Pakistan persisted in its efforts to develop a nuclear weapon capability, Delhi would be compelled to re-assess its own nuclear policy. Were this to happen, India would certainly find itself in a difficult position. Even if Pakistan were to explode a nuclear device, it would only have drawn level with India, and to prove that the decisive further step towards developing weapons had been taken would be just as difficult for Pakistan as it would for India.[8] Pakistan would continue to stress the peaceful nature of its nuclear programme and India would have to violate its own principles if it wished to condemn a developing country's pursuit of a national nuclear programme without permitting international controls. After all, its own nuclear policy had been based on this principle from the start.

In any case, there is now a strong likelihood that Pakistan will soon have its own nuclear weapon capability. The most probable consequence would be steps by India which would lead to escalation, since Pakistan would again follow suit.[9] In the context of the present analysis, this is all that can be said. The complex issue of proliferation requires separate treatment and a different framework to that used in this study. In any event, if developments in the nuclear sphere were to evolve along these lines, this would substantially enlarge the potential for conflict in the Indian Ocean region. The peace zone would then finally have been laid to rest.

ments essential for setting up a plutonium processing plant, as well as a uranium enrichment plant.

8. For the Pakistani line of argument on this matter, see 'Denuclearisation of South Asia', *Dawn*, 15.12.1980. p. 7.

9. For a recent appraisal by an Indian writer of the possible consequences of a nuclear explosion by Pakistan, see Onkar Marwah, 'India and Pakistan: Nuclear Rivals in South Asia', in *International Organization*, vol. 35, no. 1 (Winter 1981), pp. 165–79.

Part V

SIGNIFICANT DEVELOPMENTS SINCE 1970:

Chapter 8
A PERSPECTIVE VIEW

It was not until the 1970s that the Indian Ocean acquired the attributes which subsequently identified it as a separate region attracting international interest and as a source of major international conflict. This large area had not previously been looked upon by any party as politically or strategically coherent, let alone united, least of all by the littoral and hinterland countries, most of which belonged to the Third World. Instead, the states of this region — and even the ocean itself — were divided up into a large number of individual areas which in turn were regarded as parts of greater geopolitical units, without reference to the Indian Ocean. Thus the East African coastal states were viewed in the context of Africa, the littoral states of the Red Sea and the Persian Gulf in that of the Middle East, South-East Asia in that of the Pacific and of China, and so on. There did not even appear to be any strategic connection. Also, the numerous regional conflicts in the 1950s and '60s were always treated as isolated events by the outside powers involved in them.

All this changed when the area was first drawn into the strategic, and later also into the overall political plans of the great powers. The United States took the first steps in this direction when, in the mid-1960s jointly with Britain, it decided to exploit for military purposes the centrally located atoll of Diego Garcia in the Northern Indian Ocean. From 1968 this development was followed by the small but regular Soviet naval presence in the ocean. Even before the end of the Vietnam war, the United States navy also increased its level of activity there. At the beginning of the 1970s, the Soviet Union concluded its first long-term bilateral friendship and mutual assistance treaties with Egypt, India and Iraq, and advocated 'collective security for Asia', an indication of its desire for an increasing say in the affairs of the region — in its capacity, among other things, as an Asiatic power.

Numerous Indian Ocean littoral states, which at that time also comprised the clear majority of Non-Aligned countries, thought that they recognised a reincarnation of colonial methods in the activities of the great powers, namely a threat to their political independence resulting from the military, strategic, political and economic calculations of outside powers. The 'Indian Ocean Peace Zone' strategy developed, on the initiative of Ceylon (Sri Lanka), India and Tanzania, out of the Non-Aligned summit at Lusaka in 1970. In the United Nations at the end of 1971, the proposal obtained a majority which included China's vote, in spite of abstention by all the outside maritime states with an interest in the Indian Ocean. The concept involved a curtailment of the freedom of the high seas, in keeping with the view of a majority of the Indian Ocean littoral states which still had to be determined. This would have created a precedent, in view of the ambitions of the countries of the South for a new international law of the sea and a New International Economic Order.

For their part, Western countries with interests in this region thought they perceived a threat to their free access and to their traditional transport and trading links, which was made all the more ominous by what they saw as the possibility of an alliance between Non-Alignment and world communism. Both Moscow and Peking were clearly expanding in that area around 1970, albeit in competition with one another. However the Non-Aligned countries — while exercising great caution towards 'new imperialisms' — were receptive towards these ideologically-contending powers in so far as they promised an alternative to the international *status quo* under which Western powers still claimed many prerogatives; there was an inherent anti-Western climate in post-colonial Asia and in Africa with its offshore islands, where colonial rule still persisted in some countries.

Accordingly, both Moscow and Peking had high expectations of revolutionary changes in this area at the beginning of the 1970s. They both lent support to most of the efforts towards emancipation made by Indian Ocean littoral states, the difference between them being that the Soviet Union, as an ambitious super-power, simultaneously strove to extend its own influence along traditional lines and to consolidate its strategic positions, whereas China with its much more limited potential, especially after the upheavals of the Cultural Revolution, confined itself to giving selective support to liberation movements and communist parties. Alongside programmes based on ideology, however, the two leading powers of revolutionary world socialism also increasingly cultivated co-operation with established regimes when strategic reasons — protecting their frontier regions (in particular the southern flank of the Soviet Union, South-East Asia and Pakistan, where China was concerned) —, as well as economic interests, seemed to require it. Such co-operation took place according to classical rules governing the acquisition of influence. In the Indian Ocean region, the Sino-Soviet conflict itself developed in the 1970s into a decisive factor — a 'second Cold War', as it was dubbed in the region.

On the other hand, the policy of détente between East and West moderated the rising level of conflict, in spite of a substantial growth of varying interests in the region on the part of both super-powers. For the United States and the West as a whole, the Persian Gulf sub-region moved into first place from 1973. The Soviet Union likewise extended its positions in the north-western quadrant of the Indian Ocean, with the result that strategic lines intersected there and the policy of securing influence was more vigorously pursued by both countries. In this process, the United States, in keeping with the Nixon Doctrine, relied especially on Iran as a potential regional leading power, whereas the Soviet Union was only able to gain a foothold on the periphery of the actual Gulf region in Iraq, South Yemen and the Horn of Africa. From the mid-1970s, however, Moscow reaped great advantage from the collapse of Portugal's African empire. It was not only the West that lost out in Angola and Mozambique; just as important for the Soviet Union were the losses that hit China, which could not hold its own when it came to projections of military power.

In contrast to the escalating conflicts in Africa, there were signs in the northern and eastern areas of the Indian Ocean region of willingness to settle inter-state conflicts and even to engage in intra-regional co-operation. The conciliation between Iran and Iraq added to this, just as much as did the Shah's policy towards his eastern neighbours, Afghanistan, Pakistan and India, which aimed to strengthen economic co-operation. The countries of the Indian sub-continent also won the opportunity to put to good use their human resources and partial technological lead over the Arab oil-exporting countries. In South-East Asia, attempts at *rapprochement* started between ASEAN and Indochina soon after the fall of Saigon, with the aim of defining and, if possible, balancing interests. The fact that there was limited tension between the super-powers had the effect of encouraging all these initiatives. In 1977 the super-powers even held a dialogue on arms limitation in the Indian Ocean area, which was hailed by the majority of littoral states as a step towards the establishment of a peace zone.

In the Indian Ocean, the political atmosphere changed greatly in the early part of 1978, due to regional and indeed also to extra-regional and global developments. The super-powers henceforth offset their grievances one against the other, and in so doing each followed its own line of reasoning. Trust was quickly replaced by mistrust, as of old. In consequence, détente was discredited in the 'grey areas' of the Third World before the 'central areas' in East and West were affected. From the point of view of the United States, the appearance of its opponent in force in the Horn of Africa, supported by Cuba, was a reason for reacting with a moderate policy of 'linkage': the negotiations on arms limitation in the Indian Ocean were cancelled. During 1978, the Soviet Union used treaties to strengthen its relations with Ethiopia, Afghanistan and Vietnam, and in South Yemen there was a pro-Soviet coup. The United States, for its part, derived benefits from the agreement reached between Japan and China and from the new guarded attitude of the ASEAN countries towards Vietnam.

The decisive change of direction came in 1979. Instead of efforts to reach understanding that transcended the boundaries between ideologies and systems, polarisation now intensified across a deep East-West divide. Although the overthrow of the Shah's regime placed Iran in a position that was, in formal terms, equidistant from both world powers, in reality Iran's portrayal of the United States as the main enemy was greatly to the Soviet Union's advantage. The Vietnamese occupation of Cambodia during the same period created a distinct division in South-East Asia, in the course of which states along the Pacific — Japan, China, ASEAN and Australia — formed a common front against Moscow-backed Hanoi. The United States once more proved to be a protecting power in that region, and to this the decision to cancel the withdrawal of its troops from South Korea contributed. A pattern thus emerged with the Soviet Union gaining advantageous positions in the north-western Indian Ocean and in the Horn of Africa, while pro-Western elements, including China for that matter, consolidated their position in the eastern region where the Indian Ocean meets the Pacific. This pattern will probably remain basically unchanged in the 1980s.

A strong catalyst for the Indian Ocean area was the Soviet invasion of Afghanistan at the end of 1979 — although this applied less to the African littoral states and the islands of the western Indian Ocean, where pro-Soviet neutrality was prevalent. The majority of Islamic countries took up a position against Moscow. Pakistan considered itself under a new kind of threat, and India's neighbours condemned the Soviet action as did the ASEAN countries. India was the only country which met the Soviet Union more than half way, thus isolating itself accordingly. Its recognition of the new regime in Phnom Penh a short time afterwards further widened the area of dissension between itself and the rest of Asia, together with the majority of Non-Aligned countries.

The US President formulated the 'Carter Doctrine', defining the

Gulf as an area vital to American interests, as a direct consequence of the Soviet occupation of Afghanistan. Washington's ensuing policy involved improving its military and strategic positions in the vicinity of the Gulf, and strengthening its naval presence in the Indian Ocean, as well as setting up a rapid deployment force (RDF) — which had been planned earlier — to make up for the Soviet Union's geostrategic advantage. The Soviets took counter-measures, in particular in the southern Red Sea and in the Gulf of Aden. All these measures were steps in a process of escalation which rapidly led to a more unyielding confrontation between the super-powers, the contours of which became sharper still after the Reagan administration took office. On both sides, diplomacy was made to serve the new confrontationist attitude. In this process the Soviet Union was and continues to be able to make good use of some advantageous positions in relation to the Indian Ocean littoral states. Thus its military potential, which puts the north-western Indian Ocean area within striking distance from Soviet territory, is scarcely vulnerable to attack on political grounds and — in contrast to its presence in Afghanistan — is hardly visible. The United States, on the other hand, requires the approval of countries in the region in order to establish and maintain a limited counter-presence (an exception being Diego Garcia but even here its presence remains controversial). Some of these countries are rather unstable, and in general it is difficult for them to reconcile the granting of military rights to a super-power with the principles of non-alignment.

The motives of the governments concerned can almost certainly be interpreted in terms of their hopes that the development by the United States of military installations remaining under local sovereign control, together with the concomitant strengthening of their armed forces, will improve their position *vis-à-vis* potentially hostile neighbours. These activities make the United States vulner-able to some extent to the repercussions of regional instabilities. However, the Soviet Union is in a similar position wherever it claims the right to use military facilities; a change of political direction by one country in the region could jeopardise strategic positions built up over many years, as happened in Egypt and Somalia. The Soviet Union seeks to insure against this eventuality mainly by continually strengthening its political and ideological links with important Third World partners, by training cadres, by contacts on a party level and by the supervision of internal security etc. The Soviet Union's allies, particularly East Germany and Cuba, take part in these activities. In the longer term the limited ability of the Soviet-led bloc to give substantial amounts of economic aid could lessen the effect expected from these endeavours.

From the American point of view, the use of Diego Garcia is a considerable asset in the strategic equation. Since restraint was abandoned, and since the inception of the Carter Doctrine, efforts to extend the small atoll to the maximum degree possible were stepped up, and its communications, provisioning, maintenance and stationing facilities were increased. Because Diego Garcia is a British possession (although its status as such is challenged by Mauritius), and American activities on the island require British approval, friction could result from a change in the political situation — e.g. if a generally pacifist Labour government were to take power in London.

The same applies to other US allies, notably to Australia and Western countries with interests in the Indian Ocean. In this connection France has a special role to play; its military presence in Djibouti and in the western Indian Ocean has hitherto been an important factor for Western interests taken as a whole. But here too the situation could change if Paris should decide to change its foreign policy priorities. Hitherto, French policy towards the Indian Ocean has remained fairly consistent, and has been considerably more predictable than British or, in particular, United States policy.

The frequently reiterated request of the Indian Ocean littoral states in the United Nations for a peace zone was not helped by the new climate of confrontation. A paradoxical situation arose in 1980 when the super-powers and all outside countries with interests in the region for the first time declared their willingness to co-operate in a special committee on the Indian Ocean. Yet differences separating East and West were now so marked that no progress towards a zone of peace was possible; on the contrary, it quickly became clear that in view of changed premises the very concept was open to question and to conflicting interpretations. This was not only true of countries outside the area, but profound disagreements were also revealed within the region.

At this level enough evidence of conflict had been accumulated towards the end of the 1970s to refute the thesis that 'super-power rivalry' was the real reason for discord in the Indian Ocean. Historically- and ideologically-based conflicts between countries, fears of destabilisation on the part of weak regimes, problems concerning minorities, etc. resulted in a dramatic increase in the level of the arms build-up in some parts of the region. Attempts to counteract this and restore confidence were only undertaken in a piecemeal fashion. The border war between Iran and Iraq revealed a new type of conflict — from which hitherto the great powers have cautiously kept their distance.

On top of this, a tendency to acquire nuclear weapons is emerging in the Indian Ocean; for the moment it is Israel, South Africa, India and Pakistan, but Iraq, Egypt and other countries are likely to follow. If this trend were to develop — and there are many signs that it will — regional conflicts would be given a new dimension in which, however, the mutually deterrent effect of nuclear weapons would also become an important factor. It is a fact that nuclear weapons still endow their owners with considerable prestige. As long as the five states possessing nuclear weapons make up the permanent membership of the UN Security Council, this status will continue to be held in high esteem in the international system.

Under circumstances such as these, where there is increasing polarisation in the region, close institutionalised co-operation can only develop between countries with a similar political orientation which no longer threaten one another. ASEAN provides an example of this: its main achievement so far has been to resolve serious intra-regional conflicts, yet when it was established in 1967 there was no assurance that it could perform this role. The institutionalisation of links among the Arab Gulf states (excluding Iraq) in the form of the 'Gulf Co-operation Council', which took place early in 1981, may develop along lines similar to ASEAN, enabling internal threats to be dealt with by mutual agreement and those from outside the region to be perceived and handled in a similar way. However, there is an important difference between South-East Asia and the Gulf, namely that it would probably be extremely difficult in the Gulf to give impetus to the demand that 'all powers foreign to the area should be kept out'. More so than any other sub-region in the Southern Hemisphere, the Gulf will continue to be exposed to the contrasting interests of global politics.

In comparison with these two arrangements, the most recent attempt to develop understanding at the regional level, initiated this time by Bangladesh and concerned with 'co-operation in South Asia', has less chance of success because India is isolated from its neighbours not only on account of the rift created by its superior size and attributes of power, but also because its approach to a number of foreign policy issues is different. Given this situation, narrow limits are imposed on institutionalised co-operation. An example of an unsuccessful initiative of this kind under socialist auspices was the attempt made by the Soviet Union and Cuba in 1977 to set up a federation in the Horn of Africa with Ethiopia (including Eritrea) and Somalia, as well as South Yemen, in which ideological solidarity was supposed to offset ethnic and other divisive elements. Somali nationalism caused the project to collapse before it had even got started. On the other hand, in Indochina (i.e. outside the Indian Ocean) there is an association of pro-Soviet socialist countries currently in existence. It is an expression of Vietnam's claim to supremacy in Indochina, and it is perceived in ASEAN countries as a potential threat — albeit in different ways — in view of the possibility that it may seek to expand further.

A comparison of the West's political positions, prospects and handicaps with those of the Soviet-led bloc suggests that in the 1980s developments may be along the following lines. The Soviet Union will carry on deriving benefit — perhaps on an increased scale — from the fact that *vis-à-vis* both the Arab-Israeli and Southern African conflicts it is always on the side of the majority, i.e. of the Third World and the Non-Aligned. The West is likely to retain its ties with Israel as well as with South Africa, as much for reasons of *realpolitik* as from more fundamental motives connected with the recognition of the right of both states to exist as full members of the community of nations. Influential circles in the United States have long refused to acknowledge the close connection between the political situation in the Gulf and the problem of the Palestinians — an attitude which was once more evident when the Reagan administration took office. This connection should however be obvious. It stems not least from the Saudi monarchy's need to legitimise itself in Islamic terms and the consequent necessity for Riyadh to continue to be a protagonist for the main political demands of the Islamic world. As far as South Africa is concerned, there are no signs that Pretoria seriously intends to make any meaningful modification in its internal policies. The Reagan administration will have to reconcile any policy of strengthening official US relations with South Africa with the country's interests in Black Africa.

Afghanistan will probably remain the heaviest burden with which the Soviet Union has saddled itself. All the advantages, including the strategic ones, which Moscow may have worked out in connection with the occupation have probably turned out to be either questionable or the opposite of what was anticipated. Recognition of the Soviet-backed Afghan regime by the neighbouring states, Iran and Pakistan, could considerably improve the Soviet Union's position, which has come under heavy criticism internationally, and Moscow is therefore intensifying its efforts to gain this objective. But a successful outcome is hardly likely unless there is a change of basic attitude in both Teheran and Islamabad. Such changes are definitely among the Soviet leadership's expectations, at least in the medium term, and Moscow is therefore pursuing them as actively as is feasible. The occupation of Afghanistan is for the time being also obstructing Moscow's efforts to secure for itself, via diplomatic initiatives, a political say in the Persian Gulf along the lines of the proposals made by President Brezhnev both in Delhi in December 1980 and at the XXVI Congress of the Communist Party of the Soviet Union in February 1981. On both these occasions the Indian Ocean Peace Zone was once more adapted to suit Soviet diplomatic objectives (i.e. chiefly as an instrument to be used against the United States).

The future of the littoral, hinterland and island states of the Indian Ocean, which is a typical Third World region, will on the other hand be only partly determined by the involvement of these countries in international politics. More important determinants are the contributions made by individual countries and sub-regions to their own economic and social development. This, to an appreciable extent, calls for local initiatives on the basis of domestic decisions on priorities. Thus one of the main problems — rapid population growth — can be influenced from outside the countries concerned only with difficulty. This also applies to supporting measures in education and public health and, not least, to improved opportunities for women. National policies are required to halt the rural exodus and the trend towards the growth of cities. Throughout the region, agriculture needs to become considerably more productive if dependence on food imports is not to become still greater. Energy supplies are an important prerequisite both in this sector and for industrialisation. In this context, rising oil prices are having a particularly damaging effect. The development of alternative energy sources, for example the use of rivers flowing down from the Himalayas, should be tackled without further delay and as a matter of priority — where necessary, in an international or multilateral context. Undiluted nationalism is an obstacle to development.

To safeguard the basis of existence for what is structurally the poorest extended region in the world, the recycling of capital from the oil-exporting countries in the Indian Ocean area, combined with the application of technology from the industrialised countries of Europe and from the United States and Japan, ought to be the consequence of any long-term planning and of any rational appreciation. Yet in view of the situation it is easy to be sceptical and difficult to be optimistic. Data on the development of the Indian Ocean region do, however, reveal many positive elements. Life expectancy is increasing, progress is being made in various agricultural sectors, economic and technological co-operation is growing at the regional level (South-South relations), broader sections of the population are participating in the political process, and so on. The future remains uncertain. The year 2000, a prominent milestone in the history of mankind, is burdened with much expectation — and with much apprehension. It is not far away.

APPENDIX A

STATISTICAL DATA ON THE INDIAN OCEAN REGION COUNTRIES

	Area (km²)	Capital	Form of government	Population (m.)	GNP (US$m.)	Defence expenditure (US $m.)
1. THE SOUTH-EAST						
Australia	7,687,000	Canberra	parl. democracy, monarchy	14.42	117,700 (1979)	3,900 (1980/1)
Burma	677,000	Rangoon	republic	32.91	4,700 (1978)	164 (1977/8)
Indonesia	1,904,000	Jakarta	republic	148.47	43,100 (1979)	2,070 (1980)
Malaysia	330,000	Kuala Lumpur	elected monarchy	13.30	14,900 (1978)	1,470 (1980)
Singapore	581	Singapore	republic	2.36	8,100 (1978)	574 (1980)
Thailand	514,000	Bangkok	kingdom	46.14	21,900 (1978)	1,090 (1980)
2. SOUTH ASIA						
Afghanistan	647,000	Kabul	republic	15.49	2,900 (1979)	61.0 (1977/8)
Bangladesh	144,000	Dhaka	republic	86.64	9,500 (1979)	115.4 (1979)
Bhutan	47,000	Thimbu	kingdom	1.27	120 (1978)	*n.a.*
India	3,288,000	New Delhi	republic	684.00 (1981)	96,000 (1979)	4,400 (1980/1)

Maldives	298	Male	republic	0.15	25 (1980)	
Nepal	141,000	Kathmandu	kingdom	13.71	1,760 (1979)	19 (1980)
Pakistan	892,000	Islamabad	republic	84.00	18,500 (1978)	1,180 (1979)
Sri Lanka	66,000	Colombo	republic	14.74	2,800 (1978)	26.5 (1979)

3. THE PERSIAN GULF

Bahrain	622	Manama	sheikhdom	0.29	17,000 (1977)	98.0 (1979)
Iran	1,684,000	Teheran	republic	36.94	76,100 (1978)	4,200 (1980)
Iraq	435,000	Baghdad	republic	12.77	21,400 (1979)	2,670 (1979)
Qatar	11,000	Doha	sheikhdom	0.21	1,000 (1977)	61 (1978)
Kuwait	18,000	Kuwait	sheikhdom	1.20	11,900 (1977)	979 (1979)
Oman	212,000	Muscat	sultanate	0.86	2,550 (1977)	879 (1980)
Saudi Arabia	2,150,000	Riyadh	kingdom	8.11	94,600 (1979)	20,700 (1980/1)
United Arab Emirates	84,000	Abu Dhabi	federation of sheikhdoms	0.75	12,000 (1978)	750 (1979)

	Area (km²)	Capital	Form of government	Population (m.)	GNP (US$m.)	Defence expenditure (US $m.)
4. THE HORN OF AFRICA AND THE RED SEA						
Egypt	1,000,000	Cairo	republic	40.98	16,500 (1979)	2,170 (1979/80)
Ethiopia	1,222,000	Addis Ababa	republic	30.42	3,000 (1979)	385 (1980)
Djibouti	22,000	Djibouti	republic	0.11	335 (1976)	*n.a.*
Israel	21,000	Jerusalem	republic	3.78	16,400 (1979)	5,200 (1980/1)
Jordan	98,000	Amman	kingdom	3.09	2,690 (1979)	381 (1979)
Somalia	638,000	Mogadishu	republic	3.54	425 (1978)	95 (1979)
Sudan	2,506,000	Khartoum	republic	17.89	6,150 (1977)	242.6 (1977/8)
North Yemen	195,000	Sanaa	republic	5.79	1,500 (1977)	79 (1979)
South Yemen	333.000	Aden	republic	1.84	500 (1978)	56 (1978/9)
5. EASTERN AND SOUTHERN AFRICA						
Botswana	600,000	Gaberone	republic	0.79	401 (1978)	*n.a.*
Kenya	583,000	Nairobi	republic	15.32	6,300 (1979)	168.0 (1977)
Lesotho	30,000	Maseru	kingdom	1.31	360 (1978)	*n.a.*
Malawi	118,000	Lilongwe	republic	5.82	1,266 (1979)	61.7 (1979)
Mozambique	783,000	Maputo	republic	10.20	16,000 (1978)	177.0 (1978)

Zambia	753,000	Lusaka	republic	5.65	2,540 (1978)	387.9 (1979)
Swaziland	17,000	Mbabane	kingdom	0.54	310 (1978)	*n.a.*
Zimbabwe	391,000	Harare	republic	7.14	3,300 (1978)	444 (1980/1)
South Africa	1,221,000	Pretoria	republic	28.48	54,300 (1979)	2,560 (1980)
Uganda	236,000	Kampala	republic	13.22	8,360 (1978)	*n.a.*

6. ISLAND STATES IN THE WESTERN INDIAN OCEAN

Comoros	2,171	Moroni	republic	0.33	700 (1978)	*n.a.*
Madagascar	587,000	Tananarive	republic	8.51	2,320 (1978)	101.9 (1979)
Mauritius	2,045	Port Louis	republic	0.91	760 (1978)	*n.a.*
Seychelles	278	Victoria	republic	0.06	70 (1978)	*n.a.*

Sources: I.I.S.S., *The Military Balance 1980/81*, London 1980; *Vereinte Nationen*, vol. 29, no. 1 (Feb. 1981), pp. 39 f (population figures and areas); Ferenc A. Váli, *Politics of the Indian Ocean Region*, New York 1976; W. Draguhn, R. Hofmeier, and M. Schönborn (eds.), *Politisches Lexikon Asien und Südpazifik*, Munich 1980; Angelika Pathak, *Der Indische Ozean*, Institut für Asienkunde, Hamburg 1976; *Der Fischer Welt-Almanach* 1981, Frankfurt a.M. 1980 (Fischer); *Asia 1981 Yearbook*, Hong Kong (Far Eastern Economic Review Ltd.) 1981; *Dawn* (Karachi), 5.5.1971, p. 1.

APPENDIX B

PROPOSED GEOGRAPHICAL DEFINITION OF THE INDIAN OCEAN

1. The dividing line between the Atlantic and Indian Oceans is the meridian of Cape Agulhas (20° O' E).

2. The dividing line between the Pacific and Indian Oceans is the meridian of the south-east cape of Tasmania (147° O' E), the western exit of the Bass Strait and the median line between the north-west of Australia and the Malay peninsula (Cape Talbot through Timor, Sumba, Flores and the Sunda Islands, up to Sumatra).

3. The dividing line between the Antarctic Ocean and the Indian Ocean is the 60° O' S.

4. The northern limits of the Indian Ocean are clearly defined.

Source: UN Document A/AC.159/1, July 1974.

APPENDIX C

MAPS

Sources: 1. Based on Larry W. Bowman and Ian Clark (eds.), *The Indian Ocean in Global Politics*, Boulder, Colo. 1981, p. iv;   2. Sergei G. Gorshkov, *Seemacht Sowjetunion*, Hamburg 1978, p. 22; 3 and 4. R.K. Ramazani, *The Persian Gulf and the Strait of Hormuz*, Alphen aan den Rijn 1979, pp. 3 and 6; 5. US Senate, Committee on Foreign Relations, 'US Security Interests and Policies in Southwest Asia; Hearings before the Senate Committee on Foreign Relations', 96th Congress, 2nd Session, Washington DC 1980, p. 366; 6. *Frankfurter Allgemeine Zeitung*, 20.5.1980, p. 10.

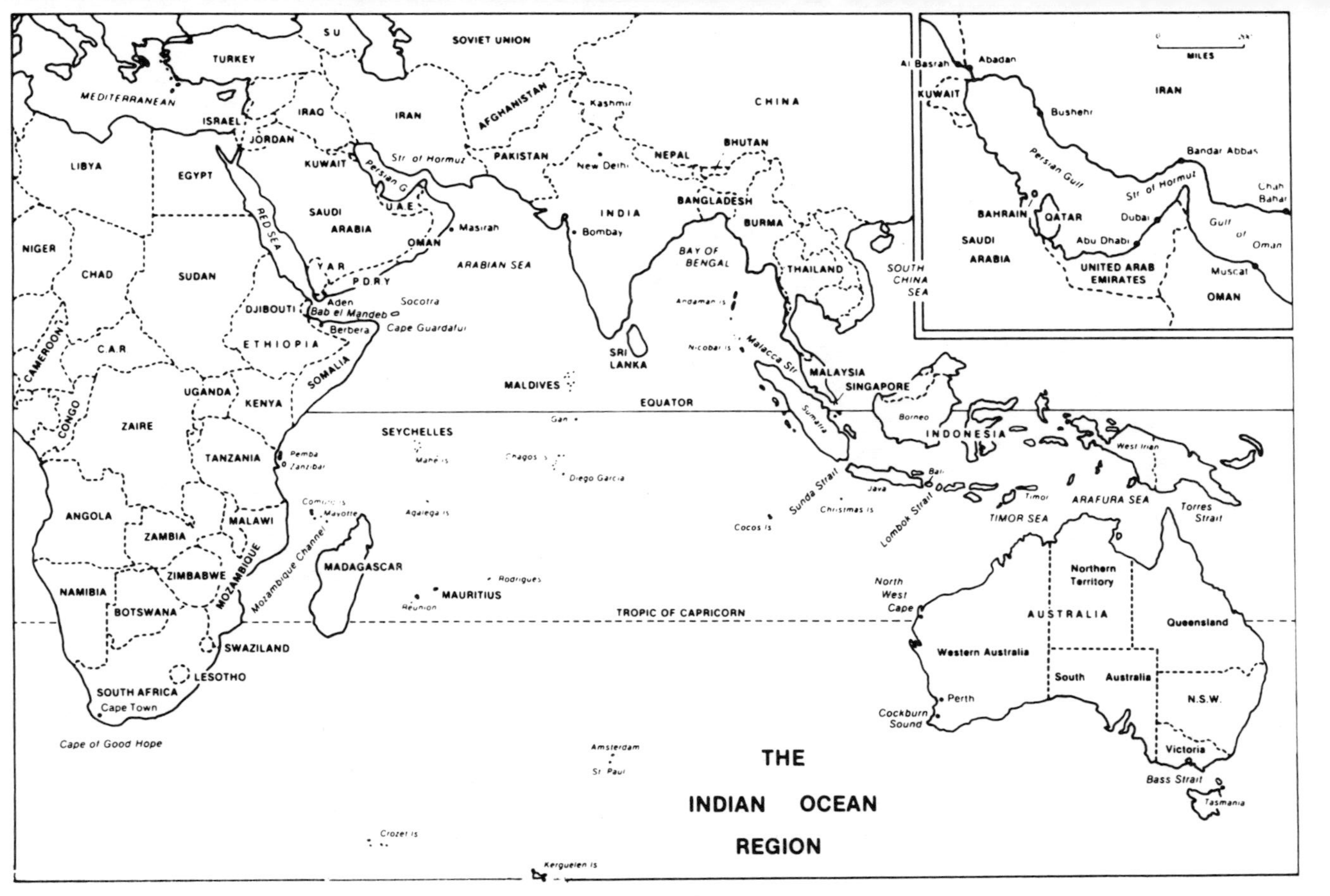

THE
INDIAN OCEAN
REGION
MEDITERRANEAN
TURKEY
SU
SOVIET UNION
ISRAEL
JORDAN
IRAQ
IRAN
AFGHANISTAN
Kashmir
CHINA
LIBYA
EGYPT
KUWAIT
Persian G.
Str. of Hormuz
PAKISTAN
New Delhi
NEPAL
BHUTAN
SAUDI ARABIA
U.A.E.
OMAN
Masirah
INDIA
Bombay
BANGLADESH
BURMA
NIGER
CHAD
SUDAN
RED SEA
Y.A.R.
P.D.R.Y.
ARABIAN SEA
BAY OF BENGAL
THAILAND
SOUTH CHINA SEA
CAMEROON
C.A.R.
ETHIOPIA
DJIBOUTI
Aden
Bab el Mandeb
Berbera
Socotra
Cape Guardafui
SOMALIA
SRI LANKA
Andaman Is.
Nicobar Is.
Malacca Str.
MALAYSIA
SINGAPORE
CONGO
ZAIRE
UGANDA
KENYA
MALDIVES
SEYCHELLES
EQUATOR
Gan
Sumatra
Borneo
INDONESIA
West Irian
TANZANIA
Pemba
Zanzibar
Mahe Is.
Chagos Is.
Diego Garcia
Sunda Strait
Java
Bali
Timor
ARAFURA SEA
Torres Strait
ANGOLA
ZAMBIA
MALAWI
Comoros
Mayotte
Aqalega Is.
Christmas Is.
Lombok Strait
TIMOR SEA
Cocos Is.
ZIMBABWE
MOZAMBIQUE
Mozambique Channel
MADAGASCAR
Rodrigues
MAURITIUS
Réunion
NAMIBIA
BOTSWANA
TROPIC OF CAPRICORN
North West Cape
AUSTRALIA
Northern Territory
Queensland
Western Australia
SWAZILAND
LESOTHO
SOUTH AFRICA
Cape Town
Cape of Good Hope
Amsterdam
St. Paul
Crozet Is.
Kerguelen Is.
South Australia
Perth
Cockburn Sound
N.S.W.
Victoria
Bass Strait
Tasmania
MILES
Al Basrah
Abadan
KUWAIT
IRAN
Bushehr
Persian Gulf
Bandar Abbas
Str. of Hormuz
Chah Bahar
BAHRAIN
QATAR
Dubai
Abu Dhabi
Gulf of Oman
Muscat
SAUDI ARABIA
UNITED ARAB EMIRATES
OMAN

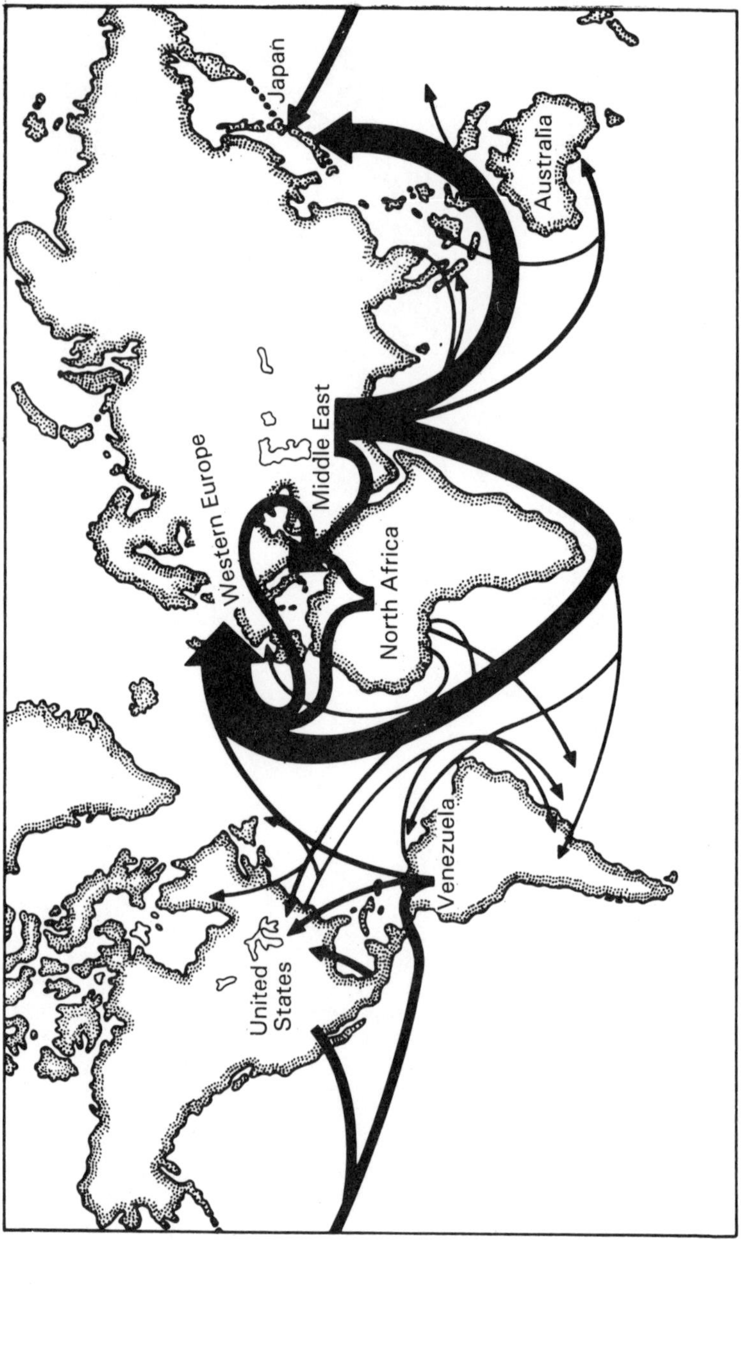

Sketch map of the oil routes.

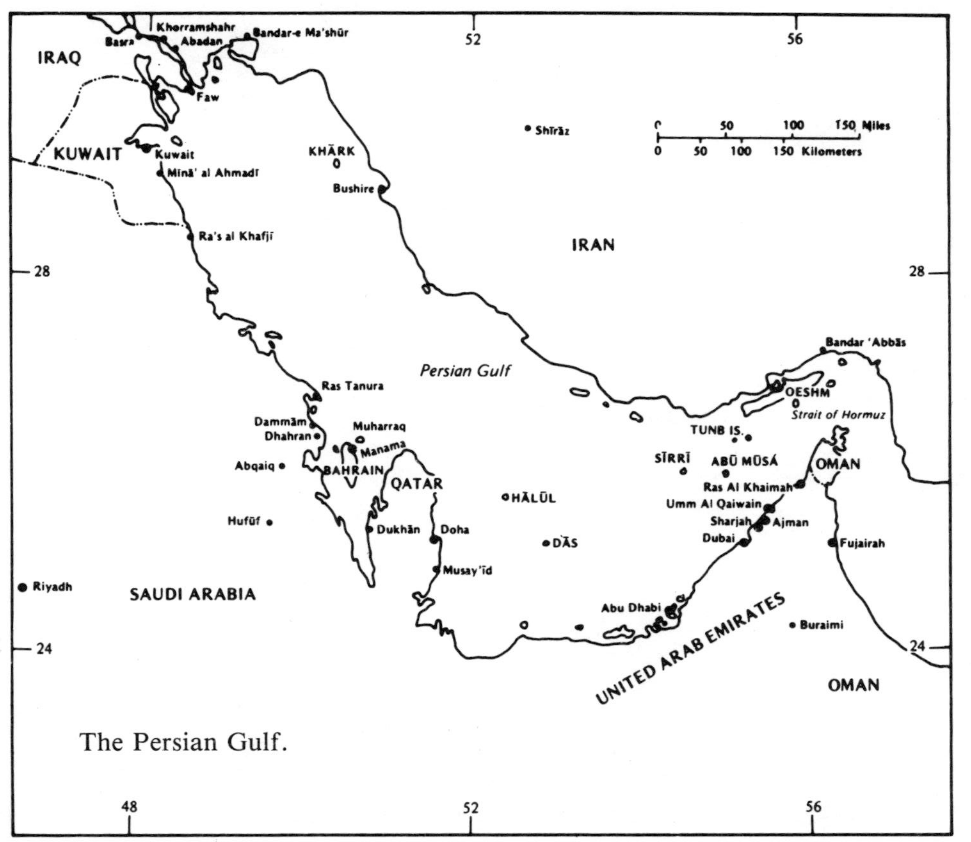

IRAQ
Basra
Khorramshahr
Abadan
Bandar-e Ma'shūr
Faw
KUWAIT
Kuwait
Minā' al Ahmadī
Ra's al Khafjī
KHĀRK
Bushire
Shīrāz
IRAN
50 100 150 Miles
50 100 150 Kilometers
Persian Gulf
Bandar 'Abbās
QESHM
Strait of Hormuz
TUNB IS.
SĪRRĪ
ABŪ MŪSĀ
OMAN
Ras Al Khaimah
Umm Al Qaiwain
Sharjah
Ajman
Dubai
Fujairah
Buraimi
Ras Tanura
Dammām
Dhahran
Muharraq
Manama
Abqaiq
BAHRAIN
QATAR
HĀLŪL
Hufūf
Dukhān
Doha
DĀS
Musay'id
Abu Dhabi
UNITED ARAB EMIRATES
Riyadh
SAUDI ARABIA
OMAN
The Persian Gulf.

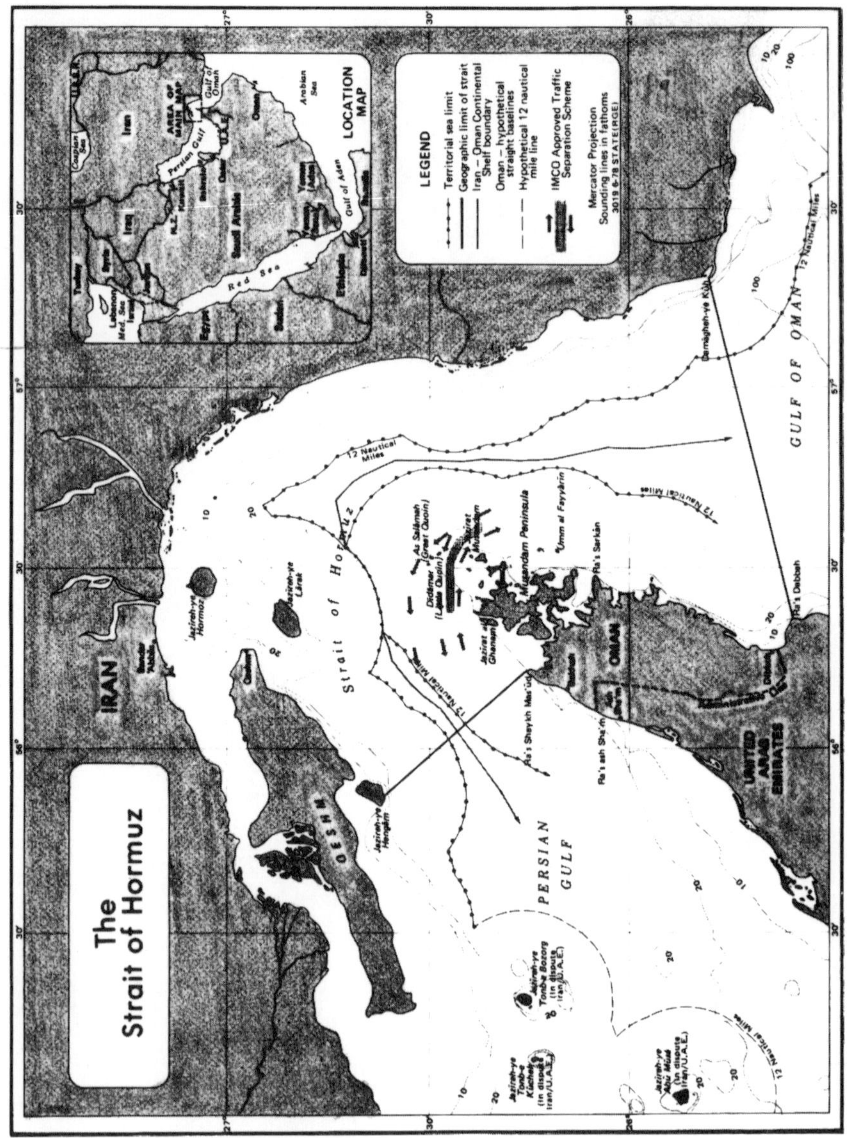

The Strait of Hormuz
LOCATION MAP
AREA OF MAIN MAP
LEGEND
Territorial sea limit
Geographic limit of strait
Iran – Oman Continental Shelf boundary
Oman – hypothetical straight baselines
Hypothetical 12 nautical mile line
IMCO Approved Traffic Separation Scheme
Mercator Projection
Sounding lines in fathoms
3019.6-78 STATE(RGE)
U.S.S.R.
Caspian Sea
Iran
Turkey
Syria
Iraq
Lebanon
Med. Sea
Israel
Egypt
Sudan
Saudi Arabia
Red Sea
Ethiopia
N.Z. Persian Gulf
Persian Gulf
Bahrain
Qatar
U.A.E.
Gulf of Oman
Oman
Arabian Sea
Yemen
Aden
Gulf of Aden
Djibouti
IRAN
Bandar Abbas
Jazireh-ye Hormoz
Jazireh-ye Larak
QESHM
Jazireh-ye Hengam
Strait of Hormuz
12 Nautical Miles
12 Nautical Miles
12 Nautical Miles
12 Nautical Miles
Damagheh-ye Kuh
GULF OF OMAN
Ra's Debah
OMAN
UNITED ARAB EMIRATES
PERSIAN GULF
Al Salamah (Great Quoin)
Didamar (Little Quoin)
Musandam Peninsula
Musandam
Jazirat Ghanam
Umm al Fayyarin
Ra's Sarkan
Ra's Sheykh Mas'ud
Ra'ah Sha'm
Jazireh-ye Tonb-e Bozorg (in dispute Iran/U.A.E.)
Jazireh-ye Tonb-e Kuchek (in dispute Iran/U.A.E.)
Jazireh-ye Abu Musa (in dispute Iran/U.A.E.)

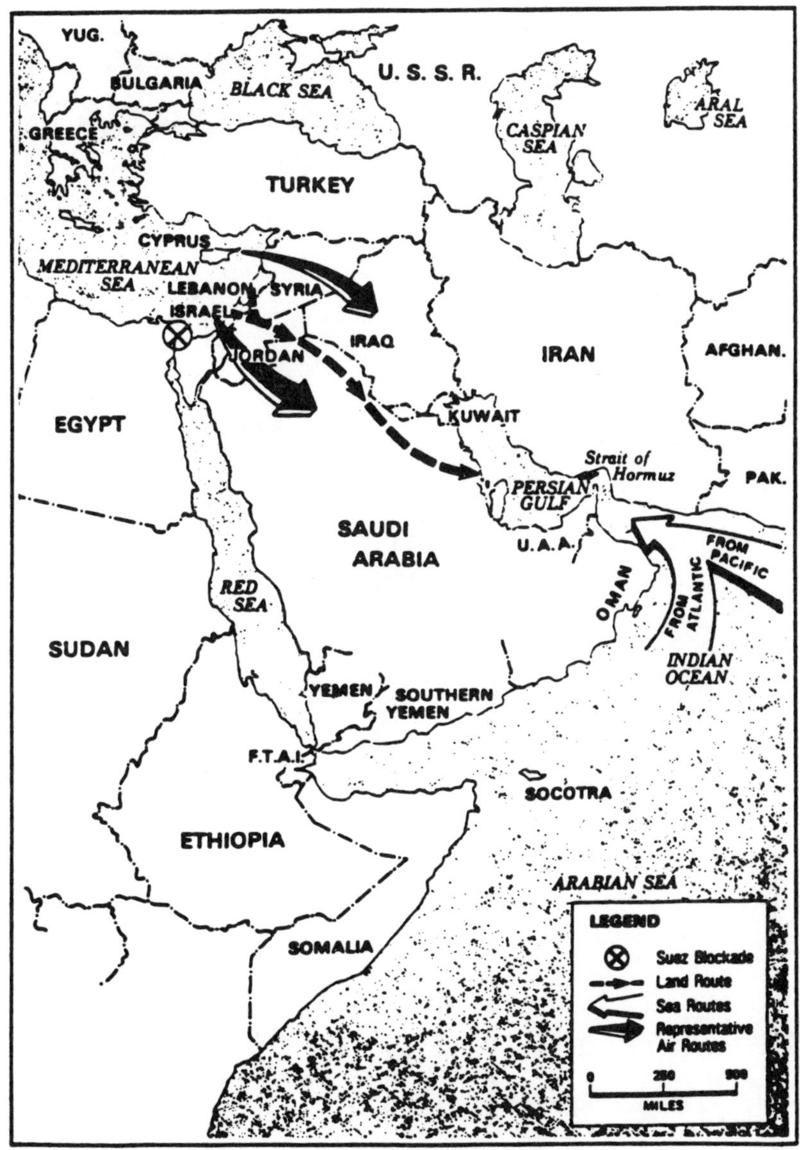

US routes into the Persian Gulf.

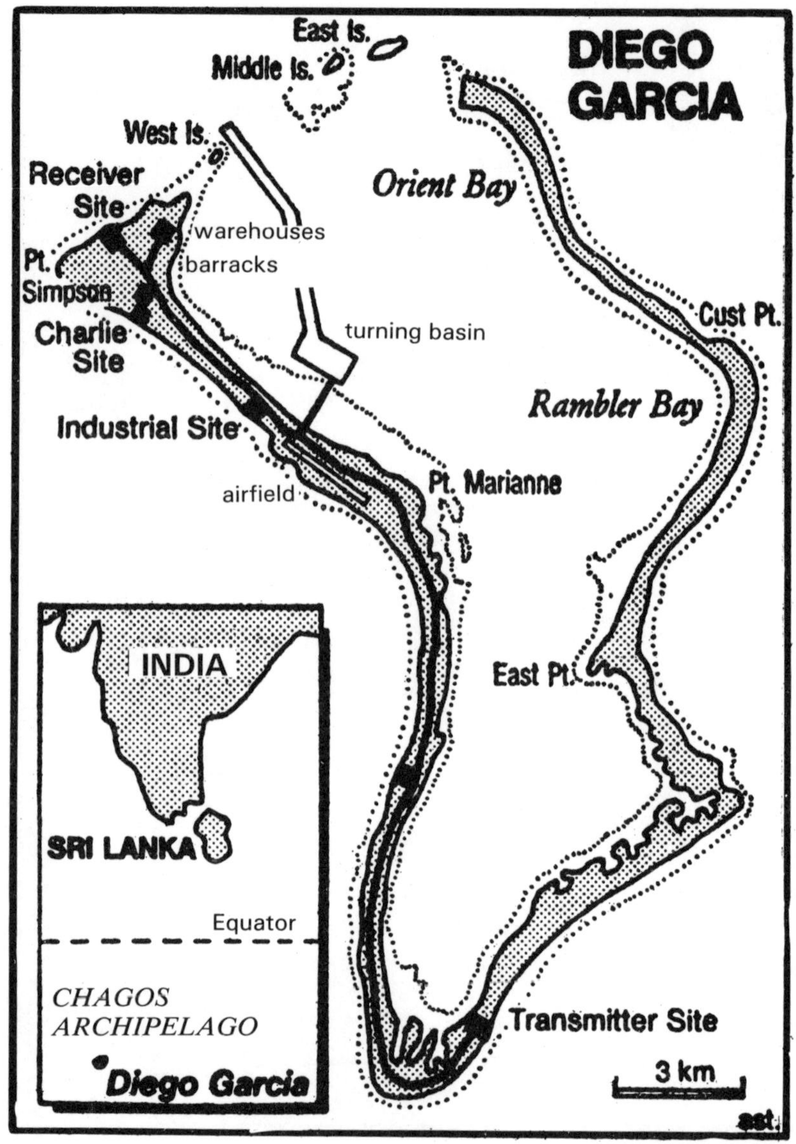
DIEGO GARCIA
East Is.
Middle Is.
West Is.
Receiver Site
Pt. Simpson
Charlie Site
warehouses
barracks
turning basin
Orient Bay
Cust Pt.
Rambler Bay
Industrial Site
airfield
Pt. Marianne
East Pt.
INDIA
SRI LANKA
Equator
CHAGOS ARCHIPELAGO
Diego Garcia
Transmitter Site
3 km

APPENDIX D

ON THE 'POST-AFGHANISTAN' STRATEGIC SITUATION IN THE NORTH WESTERN AREA OF THE INDIAN OCEAN

The Soviet military intervention in Afghanistan has been variously interpreted, ranging from the view that Afghanistan was but one more step in a process of inexorable Soviet expansion and the quest for global hegemony to a more circumscribed opinion that this intervention was dictated by regional, even local Soviet security interests and armed intrusion precipitated by the collapse (or the ineptitude) of a Soviet-sponsored regime, or yet again that Amin's political waywardness might have transformed him ultimately into an 'Asian Tito'. While the notion of Afghanistan as one more step in a master-plan for world domination is less than credible (and even if it were, then some encouragement can be derived from the fact that the Soviet Union cannot 'master' Afghanistan, much less the world), there is clearly more to the whole situation than a local entanglement on the south-eastern border of the USSR. There can be no doubt about overall Soviet 'theatre superiority' in this region, including Iran and the Persian Gulf. General Soviet deployment — taking in the Trans-Caucasus MD, North Caucasus MD and Turkestan MD — gives a total of some 26 divisions, of which 23/24 are motor-rifle divisions and two airborne (11 divisions Trans-Caucasus, 9 divisions Turkestan and 6 divisions North Caucasus), in all about 230,000 men with strong air support including 193 long-range bombers and almost 100 tactical fighters (with Su-24s) as well as bombers drawn from the naval air force (just over 100 aircraft). The Trans-Caucasus MD has always maintained strong forces — no less than 2,180 main battle tanks — and powerful air contingents (34th Air Army), while elements of its airbone component (104th Guards) were used in Afghanistan. The Trans-Caucasus also maintains three army HQs, illustrating the diversity of operational tasks assigned to this military organisation (a 'counter-NATO' role, defence of the Soviet Border and operations beyond the Soviet perimeter).

While this regional force is impressive, the US-Soviet 'balance' in the Iran/Persian Gulf area depends more on what forces can be introduced and maintained and at what pace: in theory, Soviet mobile/mechanised units could probably cross Iran and penetrate to the Gulf in something under a week, with an airborne division dropped to select objectives in less than 12 hours. By the same slide-rule calculations Soviet military airlift has the capacity to deliver ten airborne/motor divisional elements within the two-week period required for the United States to deliver a full mechanised infantry division. On the other hand, a Soviet airborne operation from the Trans-Caucasus MD involves a flight of some 1,000 miles to the head of the Gulf, an operation very vulnerable to air interdiction, while the ground movement into northern Iran faces some difficult terrain. A 'pincer attack' from the Trans-Caucasus and the eastern frontier of Iran (with two Soviet divisions deployed along the Iran-Afghan border and four Soviet air squadrons with MiG-21s, MiG-23s and Su-20s, with a flying time of 100 minutes to the Straits of Hormuz) might be possible, but that would mean a 'clean break' in the north and the assumption of no interdiction (an unlikely eventuality, even allowing for the gradual degeneration of the Iranian armed forces). Limited though the American response might be, with *adequate warning time* its effectiveness could be much enhanced.

Nor is the naval interdiction picture that much brighter for the Soviet side, for over the period of a month the ASW balance would swing against the Soviet Navy, which — using a submarine/bomber combination — could sink 30 per cent of the tanker traffic using the Gulf traffic lanes. Soviet naval deployment in the Indian Ocean depends on long-range reinforcement which consumes both time and resources, particularly for submarine deployment. Indeed, it has been hinted that a global naval exercise planned for the late spring of this year has been postponed due to "over-stretch" of Soviet naval forces due to the Iran/Afghanistan crises. As for naval capabilities against US carrier task forces in the Indian Ocean, the Soviet Navy could commit at most some 10 submarines and about 100 naval bombers as a current effort. The transit of the *Ivan Rogov* amphibious assault ship with its Naval Infantry battalion (400 men) hardly tips the balance in any disastrous sense. Nor are signs that the Soviet Union is developing a major capability on the American style: if anything, Soviet naval developments appear to be designed to frustrate the preferred American mode (naval intervention) rather than to compete with it.

Source: Statement made by the British military anaylst and Soviet expert, John Erickson of the University of Edinburgh in House of Commons, Foreign Affairs Committee, 5th Report, *Afghanistan: The Soviet invasion and its Consequences for British Policy*, London, July 1980, pp. 253f.

SHIP DAYS SPENT BY SOVIET NAVAL UNITS IN THE INDIAN OCEAN, 1979 AND 1980

The estimated number of days spent by individual Soviet warships in or near the Indian Ocean during 1979 and 1980. (Each reference to a class of ship represents a separate visit made by a ship of that class).

Class of Ship	1979	1980	Class of Ship	1979	1980
Carriers			**Minesweepers**		
Kiev	63	–	T-58	–	238
			T-58	–	88
Cruisers			*Natya*	6	92
Kresta	213	202	*Natya*	6	249
Kresta	164	58	*Natya*	164	–
Kresta	–	247	*Natya*	213	–
Kynda	39	150			
Kara	120	–	**Landing Ships**		
Kara	63	–	*Rogov*	63	182
Sverdlov	–	20	*Alligator*	6	142
			Alligator	124	268
Destroyers			*Alligator*	–	99
Kashin	–	70	*Alligator*	–	60
Kashin	–	88	*Polnocny*	–	56
Kotlin	213	83	*Ropucha*	120	102
Kotlin	39	213	*Ropucha*	234	–
			Ropucha	164	–
Frigates					
Krivak	27	69	**Submarines**		
Krivak	80	270	*Foxtrot*	115	182
Krivak	56	190	*Foxtrot*	44	194
Krivak	57	11	*Foxtrot*	143	178
Krivak	140	4	*Foxtrot*	28	–
Krivak	–	218	*Echo II*	103	182
Krivak	–	22	*Echo II*	25	190
Krivak	–	139	*Echo II*	–	113
Petya	6	66	*Echo II*	–	23
Petya	169	–	*Echo II*	–	2
Petya	166	–	*Total*	3,367	4,980
Petya	169	–			
Riga	25	138			
Riga	–	82			

Source: Department of Foreign Affairs Backgrounder (Canberra), no. 285, 27 May 1981, p. VIII. The table was part of a reply made by the Australian Defence Minister to Parliamentary Question no. 1656, 9 April 1981.

UN RESOLUTION ON A ZONE OF PEACE, DECEMBER 1971

General Assembly — subject: Declaration of the Indian Ocean as a Zone of Peace. Resolution 2832 (XXVI), 16 December 1971.

The General Assembly,
Conscious of the determination of the peoples of the littoral and hinterland States of the Indian Ocean to preserve their independence, sovereignty and territorial integrity, and to resolve their political, economic and social problems under conditions of peace and tranquillity,
Recalling the Declaration of the Third Conference of Heads of State or Government of Non-Aligned Countries, held at Lusaka in September 1970, calling upon all States to consider and respect the Indian Ocean as a zone of peace from which great Power rivalries and competition as well as bases conceived in the context of such rivalries and competition should be excluded, and declaring that the area should also be free of nuclear weapons,
Convinced of the desirability of ensuring the maintenance of such conditions in the area by means other than military alliances, as such alliances entail financial and other obligations that call for the diversion of the limited resources of these States from the more compelling and productive task of economic and social reconstruction and could further involve them in the rivalries of power blocs in a manner prejudicial to their independence and freedom of action, thereby increasing international tensions,
Concerned at recent developments that portend the extension of the arms race into the Indian Ocean area, thereby posing a serious threat to the maintenance of such conditions in the area,
Convinced that the establishment of a zone of peace in the Indian Ocean would contribute towards arresting such developments, relaxing international tensions and strengthening international peace and security,
Convinced further that the establishment of a zone of peace in an extensive geographical area in one region could have a beneficial influence on the establishment of permanent universal peace based on equal rights and justice for all, in accordance with the purposes and principles of the Charter of the United Nations,
1. *Solemnly declares* that the Indian Ocean, within limits to be determined, together with the air space above and the ocean floor subjacent thereto, is hereby designated for all time as a zone of peace;
2. *Calls upon* the great Powers, in conformity with this Declaration, to enter into immediate consultations with the littoral States of the Indian Ocean with a view to:
(*a*) Halting the further escalation and expansion of their military presence in the Indian Ocean;
(*b*) Eliminating from the Indian Ocean all bases, military installations, logistical supply facilities, the disposition of nuclear weapons and weapons

of mass destruction and any manifestation of great Power military presence in the Indian Ocean conceived in the context of great Power rivalry;

3. *Calls upon* the littoral and hinterland States of the Indian Ocean, the permanent members of the Security Council and other major maritime users of the Indian Ocean, in pursuit of the objective of establishing a system of universal collective security without military alliances and strengthening international security through regional and other co-operation, to enter into consultations with a view to the implementation of this Declaration and such action as may be necessary to ensure that:

(*a*) Warships and military aircraft may not use the Indian Ocean for any threat or use of force against the sovereignty, territorial integrity or independence of any littoral or hinterland State of the Indian Ocean in contravention of the purposes and principles of the Charter of the United Nations;

(*b*) Subject to the foregoing and to the norms and principles of international law, the right to free and unimpeded use of the zone by the vessels of all nations is unaffected;

(*c*) Appropriate arrangements are made to give effect to any international agreement that may ultimately be reached for the maintenance of the Indian Ocean as a zone of peace;

4. *Requests* the Secretary-General to report to the General Assembly at its twenty-seventh session on the progress that has been made with regard to the implementation of this Declaration;

5. *Decides* to include the item entitled "Declaration of the Indian Ocean as a zone of peace" in the provisional agenda of its twenty-seventh session.

RECORDED VOTE:

In favour: Afghanistan, Algeria, Bhutan, Burma, Burundi, Cameroon, Ceylon, Chad, China, Colombia, Congo, Costa Rica, Cyprus, Egypt, El Salvador, Equatorial Guinea, Ethiopia, Ghana, Guinea, Guyana, Iceland, India, Indonesia, Iran, Japan, Jordan, Kenya, Khmer Republic, Kuwait, Laos, Lebanon, Liberia, Libya, Malaysia, Mali, Malta, Mauritania, Mexico, Morocco, Nepal, *Nicaragua, Nigeria, Pakistan, Panama, Qatar, Romania, Saudi Arabia, Somalia, Sudan, Swaziland, Sweden, Syria, Togo, Trinidad and Tobago, Tunisia, Uganda, United Republic of Tanzania, Uruguay, Yemen, Yugoslavia, Zambia.

Against: None.

Abstaining: Argentina, Australia, Austria, Belgium, Bolivia, Brazil, Bulgaria, Byelorussia, Canada, Central African Republic, Chile, Cuba, Czechoslovakia, Dahomey, Denmark, Dominican Republic, Fiji, Finland, France, Greece, Guatemala, Haiti, Honduras, Hungary, Ireland, Israel, Italy, Ivory Coast, Jamaica, Lesotho, Luxembourg, Madagascar, Mongolia, Netherlands, New Zealand, Norway, People's Democratic Republic of Yemen, Peru, Philippines, Poland, Portugal, Rwanda, Senegal, Singapore, South Africa, Spain, Thailand, Turkey, Ukraine, USSR, United Kingdom, United States, Upper Volta, Venezuela, Zaire.

Absent: Albania, Bahrain, Barbados, Botswana, Ecuador, Gabon, Gambia,**Iraq, Malawi, Maldives, Mauritius, Niger, Oman, Paraguay, Sierra Leone, United Arab Emirates.

*Later advised the Secretariat it had intended to abstain.
**Later advised the Secretariat it had intended to vote in favour.

BIBLIOGRAPHY

Documents and other reference material

Australian Government Publishing Service, 'Indian Ocean', *Hemisphere*, vol. 23, no. 3 (May/June 1979).

Australia-Japan Relations, *Australian Foreign Affairs Record*, Canberra, April 1980.

Central Intelligence Agency, *Indian Ocean Atlas*, Washington DC 1976.

Committee of Armed Services, US House of Representatives, *Report of the Delegation to the Indian Ocean Area*, Washington DC 1980.

Congressional Research Service, Library of Congress, *Soviet Policy and United States Response to the Third World*, US Government Printing Office, Washington DC 1981.

Council on Environmental Quality and the US Department of State, *Global 2000, Report to the President*, Washington DC, July 1980.

House of Commons, Foreign Affairs Committee, 5th Report, *Afghanistan: the Soviet Invasion and its Consequences for British Policy*, London, July 1980.

Institute of International Strategic Studies, *Strategic Survey*, London 1979.

National Library of Australia, *The Indian Ocean: a Select Bibliography of Resources for Study*, Canberra 1979.

Nehru, J., *India's Foreign Policy — Selected Speeches*, New Delhi 1961.

Spiers, R., 'US National Security Policy and the Indian Ocean Area', *Department of State Bulletin*, vol. 64, no. 1678 (August 1971).

'State of the Union — Botschaft Präsident Carters', *Europa-Archiv*, vol. 35, no. 5 (March 1980).

The Senate Standing Committee on Foreign Affairs and Defence, *Australia and the Indian Ocean Region*, Canberra 1980.

UN, General Report of the Meeting of the Littoral and Hinterland States of the Indian Ocean, General Assembly, Official Records, 34th Session, Supplement no. 45 (A/34/45). New York 1979.

Books and articles

Adomeit, Hannes, *Das Vorgehen der Sowjetunion in internationalen Krisen und Konflikten*, Ebenhausen, March 1980 (Stiftung Wissenschaft und Politik, SWP-AP 2250).

Ahmed, Samina, 'Pakistan's Proposal for a Nuclear-Weapon-Free Zone in South Asia', *Pakistan Horizon*, vol. 31, no. 4 (1979), pp. 92–130.

Albinsky, Henry S., 'Australia and the Indian Ocean', in Larry W. Bowman and Ian Clark (eds), *The Indian Ocean in Global Politics*, Boulder, Colo. 1981, pp. 59–86.

Allen, Philip M., 'New Round for the Western Islands', in Alvin I. Cottrell and R.M. Burrell (eds), *The Indian Ocean: Its Political, Economic and Military Importance*, New York 1972, pp. 307–29.

Aspaturian, Vernon V., 'Soviet Global Power and the Correlation of

Forces', *Problems of Communism*, vol. 29, no. 3 (May/June, 1980), pp. 1–18.

Ball, Desmond, 'American Bases: Implications for Australia's Security', *Current Affairs Bulletin*, vol. 55, no. 5 (Oct. 1978), pp. 4–14.

Baumann, Herbert, 'Die Politischen Systeme in den afro-asiatischen Ländern', *Asien, Afrika, Lateinamerika*, vol. 8, no. 1 (1980), pp. 87–98.

Beazley, Kim C. and Ian Clark, *Politics of Intrusion — The Super Powers and the Indian Ocean*, Sydney 1979.

Best, Richard R., 'Indian Ocean Arms Control', *US Naval Institute Proceedings*, vol. 106, no. 924 (Feb. 1980), pp. 42–8.

Bezboruah, Monoranjan, *US Strategy in the Indian Ocean*, New York 1977.

Bräker, Hans, 'Die Aufnahme Vietnams in den RGW und die Politik der Sowjetunion und der VR China in Südostasien', *Berichte des Bundesinstituts für ostwissenschaftliche und internationale Studien*, no. 7, Köln, 1979.

Braun Dieter, 'Changes in South Asian Intraregional and External Relationships', *The World Today*, vol. 34, no. 10 (Oct. 1978), pp. 390–400.

——, 'The Indian Subcontinent and the Indian Ocean: the Soviet Union as an Asian Power', in Lawrence L. Whetten, (ed.), *The Political Implications of Soviet Military Power*, New York 1977, pp. 99–118.

——, 'Der Indische Ozean in der sicherheitspolitischen Diskussion', *Europa-Archiv*, vol. 26, no. 18 (Sept. 1971), pp. 645–58.

——, 'Der Indische Ozean und die Vereinten Nationen', *Vereinte Nationen*, vol. 23, no. 4 (Aug. 1975), pp. 104–8.

——, 'Die Staatsgründung von Bangladesch', *Die Internationale Politik 1970–1972*, München 1976, pp. 413–28

——, 'Großmachtinteressen und Regionalpolitik am Indischen Ozean*, Ebenhausen, April 1978 (Stiftung Wissenschaft und Politik, SWP-S 263).

——, 'Implications of India's Nuclear Policy for the Region', in Abbas Amirie (ed), *The Persian Gulf and Indian Ocean in International Politics*, Teheran 1975, pp. 197–214.

——, *Indien und die Dritte Welt*, Ebenhausen, July 1979 (Stiftung Wissenschaft und Politik, SWP-S 272).

——, ' "Krisenbogen" am Indischen Ozean. Regionale Einflußsicherung und die Rolle der Ideologien', *Europa-Archiv*, vol. 34, no. 17 (September 1979), pp. 513–22.

——, *Neue Konstellationen zwischen dem Indischen Subkontinent und Westasien*, Ebenhausen, May 1974 (Stiftung Wissenschaft und Politik, SWP-S 226).

——, *Patterns of Soviet Policies towards the Third World*, Ebenhausen, May 1977 (Stiftung Wissenschaft und Politik, SWP-AZ 2135).

Braun, Dieter and Joachim Glaubitz, 'Kollektive Sicherheit als Konzept sowjetischer Asienpolitik', *Europa-Archiv*, vol. 29, no. 1 (Jan. 1974), pp. 22–32.

Braun, Ursula, *Veränderungen im politischen System der Golfregion*, Ebenhausen, Feb. 1976 (Stiftung Wissenschaft und Politik, SWP-AZ 2098).

——, *Saudi-Arabien im Spannungsfeld zwischen Nahost, Golf und Rotem Meer unter besonderer Berücksichtigung des saudi-arabisch-amerikanischen Verhältnisses*, April 1980 (Stiftung Wissenschaft und Politik, SWP-AZ 2248).

——, 'Saudi-Arabiens veränderter Standort; Auswirkungen für den Westen', *Europa-Archiv*, vol. 35, no. 17 (Sept. 1980), pp. 539–46.

Buchan, Alastair, *The End of the Postwar Era*, London 1975.

Bull, Hedley, 'Von der Verantwortung der Weltmächte', *Europa-Archiv*, vol. 35, no. 18 (Sept. 1980), pp. 547–56.

Burke, S.M., *Pakistan's Foreign Policy: an Historical Analysis*, London 1973.

Caldwell, J.C., 'Population and Development in the Indian Ocean Region', in A. Kerr (ed.), *The Indian Ocean Region: Resources and Development*, University of Western Australia Press, 1981, pp. 1–17.

Campbell, John, F., 'The Red Sea and Suez', in Alvin I. Cottrell and R.M. Burrell (eds), *The Indian Ocean: Its Political, Economic, and Military Importance*, New York 1972, pp. 129–53.

Castagno, A.H. 'The Horn of Africa and the Competition for Power' in Alvin I. Cottrell and R.M. Burrell (eds), *The Indian Ocean: Its Political, Economic, and Military Importance*, New York 1972, pp. 155–79.

Chubin, Shahram, *Soviet Policy towards Iran and the Gulf*, London, 1980 (IISS, Adelphi Papers, no. 157).

Church, R.I. Harrison, 'The Comoros', in *Africa South of the Sahara 1980–81*, London 1980, pp. 307–15.

Clark, Ian, 'Soviet Arms Supplies and Indian Ocean Diplomacy', in Larry W. Bowman and Ian Clark (eds), *The Indian Ocean in Global Politics*, Boulder, Colo., 1981, pp. 149–71.

Collins, John M., *US-Soviet Military Balance, Concepts and Capabilities 1960–1980*, New York 1980.

Crocker, Chester A., 'The African Dimension of Indian Ocean Policy', *Orbis*, vol. 20. no. 3 (Autumn 1976), pp. 637–67.

Dawisha, Adeed I., *Saudi Arabia's Search for Security*, London, Winter 1979/80 (IISS Adelphi Papers, no. 158).

Dmitryev, Sergei, 'Facing a Choice', *The Current Digest of the Soviet Press*, vol. 31, no. 34 (Sept. 1979), p. 10.

Feigl, Hubert, 'Satellitenaufklärung als Mittel der Rüstungskontrolle', *Europa-Archiv*, vol. 34, no. 18 (Sept. 1979), pp. 555–70.

Fuller, Jack, 'Dateline Diego Garcia: Paved-Over Paradise', *Foreign Policy*, no. 281, Autumn 1977, pp. 175–86.

Glagow, Rainer, 'Das Rote Meer — Eine neue Konfliktregion?' *Orient*, vol. 18, no. 2 (June 1977); no. 3 (Sept. 1977).

Glaubitz, Joachim, 'Schwerpunkte der Außenpolitik Japans', in Manfred Pohl (ed.), *Japan 1978/79, Politik und Wirtschaft*, Hamburg 1979.

Goldsworthy, David I., 'South Africa', in Mohammed Ayoob (ed.), *Conflict and Intervention in the Third World*, New York 1980, pp. 205–38.

Gomane, Jean Pierre, 'France and the Indian Ocean', Larry W. Bowman and Ian Clark (eds), *The Indian Ocean in Global Politics*, Boulder, Colo., 1981, pp. 189–203.

Gorshkov, Sergei G., *Seemacht Sowjetunion*, Hamburg 1978.

Gupta, Ranjan, *The Indian Ocean: A Political Geography*, New Delhi 1979.

Haass, Richard, 'Naval Arms Limitation in the Indian Ocean', *Survival*, vol. 20, no. 2 (March/April 1978) pp. 50–7.

Harris, Lillian C., 'China's Response to perceived Soviet gains in the Middle East', *Asian Survey*, vol. 20, no. 4 (April 1980), pp. 362–72.

Harrison, Selig S., 'Nightmare in Baluchistan', *Foreign Policy*, no. 32, Autumn 1978, pp. 136–60.

Hauner, Milan, 'The Significance of Afghanistan: Lessons from the Past', *The Round Table*, vol. 70, no. 279 (July 1980), pp. 240–4.

Hickman, William F., 'Soviet Naval Policy in the Indian Ocean', *Proceedings*, vol. 105, no. 918 (Aug. 1979), pp. 43–52.

Hirschfeld, Yair P., 'Moscow and Khomeini: Soviet-Iranian Relations in Historical Perpective', *Orbis*, vol. 2, no. 2 (Summer 1980), pp. 219–39.

Hollen, Christopher Van, 'The Tilt Policy Revisited: Nixon-Kissinger Geopolitics and South Asia', *Asian Survey*, vol. 20, no. 4 (1980), pp. 339–61.

Jones, Rodney W., 'Ballistic Missile Submarines and Arms Control in the Indian Ocean', *Asian Survey*, vol. 20, no. 3 (March 1980), pp. 269–79.

Joshi, Nirmala, 'Soviet Intervention in Afghanistan', Foreign Affairs Report, Indian Council of World Affairs, vol. 29, no. 7 (July 1980).

Kapur, Ashok, *India's Nuclear Option — Atomic Diplomacy and Decision Making*, New York 1976.

Kissinger, Henry, 'Bismarck: The White Revolution', *Daedalus*, vol 97, no. 3 (Summer 1968), pp. 888–924.

——, *The White House Years*, London 1979.

Khrushchev, Nikita, *Khrushchev Remembers*, vol. 2, London 1977.

Kühlein, Conrad, 'Die politisch-strategischen Veränderungen im Raum Horn von Afrika/Rotes Meer', in Stiftung Wissenschaft und Politik, *Internationale Politik und Sicherheit*, vol. 1: 'Polarität und Interdependenz, Beiträge zu Fragen der Internationalen Politik', Baden-Baden 1978, pp. 373–90.

Kühne, Winrich, 'Schwarzafrika und die Sowjetunion. Die Bedeutung der Rüstungs- und Militärhilfe als Instrument der militärstrategischen, ökonomischen und ideologischen Einflußsicherung', *Europa-Archiv*, vol. 35, no. 10 (May 1980), pp. 325–34.

Larus, Joel, 'The End of Naval Détente in the Indian Ocean', *The World Today*, vol. 36, no. 4 (April 1980), pp. 126–32.

Leifer, Michael, *Conflict and Regional Order in Southeast Asia*, London, 1980 (IISS Adelphi Papers, no. 162).

Lipton, Michael and Firn, John, *The Erosion of a Relationship — India and Britain since 1960*, London 1975.

Loewenthal, Richard, 'Soviet "Counterimperialism" ', *Problems of Communism*, vol. 25, no. 6 (Nov./Dec. 1976), pp. 52–63.

Mahncke, Dieter and Hans-Peter Schwarz (eds), *Seemacht und Außenpolitik*, Frankfurt/M. 1974.

Martin, Laurence W., 'The Cape Route,' *Survival*, vol. 12, no. 10 (Oct. 1970), pp. 347–51.

——, 'British Policy in the Indian Ocean', in Alvin I. Cottrell and R.M. Burrell (eds), *The Indian Ocean: Its Political, Economic and Military Importance*, New York 1972, pp. 407–18.

——, 'Britische Verteidigungspolitik heute und morgen — Militarische Anstrengungen unter wirtschaftlichem Druck', *Europa-Archiv*, vol. 35, no. 21 (Nov. 1980), pp. 645–54.

Marwah, Onkar, 'India and Pakistan: Nuclear Rivals in South Asia', *International Organization*, vol. 35, no. 1 (Winter 1981), pp. 165–79.

McGwire, M. and J. McDonnell (eds), *Soviet Naval Influence — Domestic and Foreign Dimensions*, New York 1977.

Medvedko, Leonid, 'The Persian Gulf: a Revival of Gunboat Diplomacy', *International Affairs*, vol. 56, no. 12 (Dec. 1980), pp. 23–9.

Meissner, Boris, 'Sowjetische Aussenpolitik und Afghanistan', *Aussenpolitik*, vol. 31, no. 3. pp. 260–83.

Millar, T.B., *The Indian and Pacific Ocean: Some Strategic Considerations*, London, 1969 (IISS Adelphi Papers, no. 57).

Misra, K.P., 'International Politics in the Indian Ocean', *Orbis*, vol. 18, no. 4 (Winter 1975), pp. 1088–1108.

——, *Quest for an International Order in the Indian Ocean*, New Delhi 1977.

Momoi, Makoto, 'Japan and the Persian Gulf and the Indian Ocean', in Abbas Amirie (ed.), *The Persian Gulf and Indian Ocean in International Politics*, Teheran 1975, pp. 163–77.

Newell, Richard S., *The Politics of Afghanistan*, New York 1972.

Noorani, A.G., *Brezhnev Plan for Asian Security*, Bombay 1975.

Pauker, Guy I., 'Indonesian Perspectives of the Indian Ocean', in Alvin I. Cottrell and R.M. Burrell (eds), *The Indian Ocean: Its Political, Economic and Military Importance*, New York 1972, pp. 219–34.

Rees, David, 'Afghanistan's Role in Soviet Strategy', *Conflict Studies*, no. 118, Institute for the Study of Conflict, London, May 1980.

Reiss, Winfried, 'Deutscher Flottenverband im Indischen Ozean', *Marineforum*, no.1/2 1981, pp. 4–10.

Remnek, Richard B., *Soviet Policy in the Horn of Africa: The Decision to Intervene*, Center for Naval Analyses, Annapolis (Jan. 1980) Professional Paper 27.

Rondot, Philippe, 'Irak gegen Iran: Krieg ohne Entscheidung?', *Europa-Archiv*, vol. 36, no. 3 (Feb. 1981), pp. 67–76.

Ropp, Klaus Frhr v.d., 'Globalteilung als Strategie friedlichen Wandels in Südafrika', in Stiftung Wissenschaft und Politik, *Internationale Politik und Sicherheit*, vol. 1: 'Polarität und Interdependenz. Beiträge zu Fragen der Internationalen Politik', Baden-Baden 1978, pp. 411–31.

Rustow, Dankwart A. and John F. Mugno, *OPEC: Success and Prospects*, New York 1976.

Sagar, Imroze, 'Indo-Soviet Naval Interests and Collaboration', *Strategic Studies* (Islamabad), vol. 2, no. 4 (Summer 1979), pp. 79–89.

Sawhny, Ratny, 'Die strategische Lage im Indischen Ozean mit indischen Augen gesehen', *Marine-Rundschau*, vol. 68, no. 11 (Nov. 1971), pp. 645–55.

Schlesinger, James, 'Third World Conflict and International Security in the

1980s', *Survival*, vol. 22, no. 6 (Nov./Dec. 1980), pp. 274–81.

Schütze, Walter, 'Neuorientierung in der Außenpolitik Frankreichs', *Europa-Archiv*, vol. 35, no. 23 (Dec. 1980), pp. 701–10.

Sen Gupta, Bhabani, *Soviet-Asian Relations in the 1970s and Beyond*, New York 1976.

Sen Gupta, Bhabani, T.T. Poulose, Hemlata Bhatia, *The Malacca Straits and the Indian Ocean*, New Delhi 1974.

Sen Gupta, Bhabani, and D. Bobb, 'In Danger of Isolation', *India Today*, Dec. 1980, pp. 48–58.

Shwadran, Benjamin, *Middle East Oil: Issues and Problems*, Cambridge 1977.

Singh, K.R., *The Indian Ocean: Big Power Presence and Local Response*, New Delhi 1978.

Smit, P., 'South Africa and the Indian Ocean: The South African Viewpoint', in Alvin I. Cottrell and R.M. Burrell (eds.), *The Indian Ocean: Its Political, Economic and Military Importance*, New York 1972, pp. 267–92.

Subrahmanyam, K., 'The Afghan Situation and India's National Interest', *Foreign Affairs Reports* (Delhi), vol. 29, no. 8 (Aug. 1980).

Tahir-Kheli, Shirin, 'Proxies and Allies: the Case of Iran and Pakistan', *Orbis*, vol. 24, no. 2 (Summer 1980), pp. 339–52.

Thompson, Virginia, 'Madagascar', in *Africa South of the Sahara 1980–81*, London 1980, pp. 593–617.

Toussaint, Auguste, 'Shifting Power Balances in the Indian Ocean', in Alvin I. Cottrell, and R.M. Burrell (eds.), *The Indian Ocean: Its Political Economic and Military Importance*, New York 1972, pp. 3–13.

Towle, Philip, *Naval Power in the Indian Ocean — Threats, Bluffs and Fantasies*, Canberra 1979.

——, 'The United Nations Ad Hoc Committee on the Indian Ocean: Blind Alley or Zone of Peace?', in Larry W. Bowman and Ian Clark (eds), *The Indian Ocean in Global Politics*, Boulder, Colo. 1981, pp. 207–21.

Tucker, Robert, W., 'The Purposes of American Power', *Foreign Affairs*, vol. 59, no. 2 (Winter 1980/81), pp. 241–74.

Váli, Ferenc A., *Politics in the Indian Ocean Region — The Balances of Power*, New York 1976.

Wanandi, Jusuf A., *Security Dimensions of the Asia-Pacific Region in the 1980s*, Jakarta 1979.

Weggel, Oskar, 'Zwei Schritte vor, einen zurück. China wünscht nach 18 Jahren Feindschaft ein besseres Verhältnis zu Indien', *China Aktuell*, vol. 9, no. 7 (June 1980), pp. 569–78.

Willrich, Mason and John B. Rhinelander (eds), *SALT — The Moscow Agreements and Beyond*, New York 1974.

Writer, Rashna, 'Strategische Dimensionen des Indischen Ozeans', *Europa-Archiv*, vol. 37, no. 11 (June 1982), pp. 345–52.

INDEX OF NAMES

INDEX OF SUBJECTS